S0-ACP-198

THE REFORMATION OF
MACHISMO

Evangelical Conversion
and Gender in Colombia

By Elizabeth E. Brusco

University of Texas Press
Austin

Copyright © 1995 by Elizabeth E. Brusco
All rights reserved
Printed in the United States of America
First edition, 1995

Requests for permission to reproduce material from this work should
be sent to Permissions, University of Texas Press, Box 7819,
Austin, TX 78713-7819.

∞ The paper used in this publication meets the minimum requirements
of American National Standard for Information Sciences—Permanence
of Paper for Printed Library Materials, ANSI Z39.48-1984.

Library of Congress Cataloging-in-Publication Data

Brusco, Elizabeth E. (Elizabeth Ellen), date
The reformation of machismo : evangelical conversion and gender in Colombia /
by Elizabeth E. Brusco.—1st ed.
p.   cm.
Includes bibliographical references and index.
ISBN 0-292-70820-3 (alk. paper).—
ISBN 0-292-70821-1 (pbk.)
1. Evangelicalism—Colombia—Case studies. 2. Sex role—Columbia—Religious
aspects—Case studies. 3. Machismo—Colombia—Case studies. 4. Colombia—
Church history—20th century—Case studies. 5. Converts, Protestant—Colombia—
Case studies. 6. Family—Religious life—Colombia—Case studies.
I. Title
BR685.B78   1995
269′.2′09861—dc20   94-21340

For My Mother,
Helen Anna Kiendzior Brusco

Contents

Acknowledgments

I would like to thank David Stoll for his encouragement and advice, which made publication of this book possible. David's work has set new ground rules for the study of Latin American Protestantism. For decades, this field has largely been dominated by a few powerful axioms, which often stifled new insight into why people in Latin American convert. David's meticulous polemic-busting in *Is Latin America Turning Protestant?* opened up space for new understandings of a movement that has altered the religious landscape in Latin America.

The most important theoretical influence on the development of this study came from seminars conducted by Joan Kelly at the Graduate Center–CUNY during 1979–1980. I first learned about "the Doubled Vision of Feminist Theory" from Joan, and I am deeply grateful that I had the opportunity to benefit from her extraordinary vision and generosity.

At the Graduate Center of the City University of New York, May Ebihara, Eric Wolf, and Jane Schneider provided many useful comments and criticism. May's guidance and support have been a constant and essential resource for me, and I am profoundly grateful to her. At a crucial point in the writing, Lita Osmundsen provided an opportunity for me to read a wide range of anthropological literature I might otherwise have overlooked. I appreciate her kindness and support.

The National Science Foundation, the Wenner-Gren Foundation, and the Institute for Intercultural Studies supported the fieldwork in Colombia on which this book is based, and I am grateful to these organizations for their help. A Pacific Lutheran University Regency Advancement Award enabled me to return to Colombia in 1989.

My colleagues in the Department of Anthropology at Pacific Lutheran University, Laura Klein, Greg Guldin, and Dave Huelsbeck, have sustained and motivated me in many ways and I thank them for the supportive climate they have created.

Many other colleagues and friends have encouraged and soothed me at critical junctures as this project unfolded. I am especially grateful to Colleen Hacker, Dana Anderson, Kevin Troy, Claire Riley, Margo Matwychuk, Liz Sheehan, Gerald Creed, and Pam Wright. My heartfelt thanks to Glenys Lobban for help on many levels. Deb Gilchrist and Susan Dwyer-Shick enhanced this work with bibliographic suggestions and I thank them for keeping my research in mind. Three of my former students, Shana MacLeod, Jennifer Blecha, and Allison Sullivan, also provided valuable help.

Two friends deserve special recognition for their help and encouragement. I received immeasurable support from Donna Kerner in the formation of the ideas represented here. Mary Murphy shared her knowledge and insights about Colombia with me and facilitated my fieldwork in a myriad of ways. I thank both of them from the bottom of my heart for their help and friendship.

Timothy Wrye, Kathy Blessing, Linda Rumble, and Karen Fleischman have assisted in the preparation of this manuscript, and I appreciate their technical help.

The Colombian Institute of Anthropology (ICAN) kindly granted me permission to conduct the field research, and I would like to thank it for this courtesy. I am grateful to Dr. Roberto Pineda, director of ICAN at the time of the research, Dr. Horacio Calle, dean of research, and Dr. Virginia Gutiérrez de Pineda for their advice and help.

I am very thankful for the generosity, love, and support of the families in Colombia who let me share their lives for a time. I can never adequately thank the wonderful women who took me under their wings and cared for me as one of their own. My special thanks to all the individuals whose names have been changed in this book, but whose words (translated into English) have been here faithfully recorded. For their kindness, acceptance, and help, I thank the members of the evangelical churches who made this research possible. *Ojalá que perdonen todo lo malo que aquí se encuentren.*

Theresa May at the University of Texas Press maintained interest in this manuscript over the several years of its development. I thank her for her patience.

The sustenance without which this work would never have been realized comes ultimately from my family. I am grateful to my father and mother, Richard and Helen Brusco, and to my brother, David Brusco, for their interest, concern, and care, and for the background that enabled me to comprehend. This book is dedicated, with love, to my mother.

THE REFORMATION OF MACHISMO

On market day in El Cocuy, a young evangelical toasts the photographer
with a bottle of Colombiana soda pop.

The pastoral couple, Iglesia Pentecostal Unida, El Cocuy

Exhibition of agricultural produce, annual fiestas, El Cocuy

Decorated arches for the fiesta of Corpus Christi, El Cocuy

The Catholic priest in procession, El Cocuy

The mayor of El Cocuy, with a man drinking a *copa* of *aguardiente*

Women preparing food for a fiesta in a rural neighborhood of El Cocuy

A midweek women's meeting at a Pentecostal church in the south of Bogotá

Members of the Iglesia Cuadrangular (Four-Square Gospel church) parade through the streets of Barrancabermeja as part of their national convention.

A sign at an evangelical demonstration motivated by the murder of an Assemblies of God pastor reads "Enough! Enough already, of paying back evil for good!"

Evangelicals protest the murder of a pastor.

On market day in El Cocuy, men prepare for a game of *tejo*.

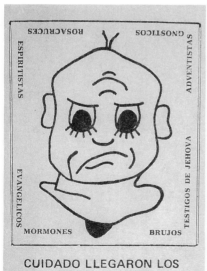

An illustration in a book called *Watch Out: The Protestants Have Arrived* lumps together Mormons, evangelicals, Spiritualists, Rosicrucians, Gnostics, Adventists, Jehovah's Witnesses, and Witches.

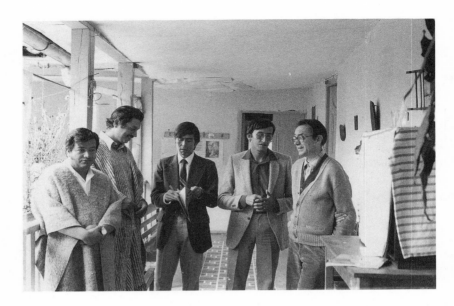

Lutheran pastors-in-training meet with a U.S. missionary during a retreat.

6-A · EL TIEMPO · MIERCOLES 8 DE JUNIO DE 1983

Buscan a sus padres (looking for their parents)

Los niños Simón Díaz, de 7 años; Edwin Ferney Vivas, año y medio; María Marcela Sánchez, año y medio; María del Pilar Camargo, 8 años, y Blanca Andrea Camargo, dos años y medio, se encuentran en el Hogar de Paso de la calle 10 sur No. 2-13, barrio La María, del Departamento Administrativo de Bienestar Social del Distrito. Se ruega a sus padres acercarse a reclamarlos o de lo contrario se iniciarán los respectivos trámites para entregarlos en adopción.

"Looking for their parents." Photos of children who have lost their parents appear with frequency in the Bogotá newspapers.

✤ 1 ✤
Introduction

Society is not a cohesive whole, but is constituted of categories of individuals who experience their culture in different ways. The essential contradictions within populations are often thrown into relief around issues of basic subsistence and reproduction, and may be expressed as competition, the disarticulation of role sets, and crises in the individual life cycle. Religious movements operate within this conflicted field, and it is in speaking to these contradictions that they may experience success.

Colombian evangelicalism is a new religious form specifically tailored to Colombian reality. As I will show in the analysis that follows, the arena of conflict that is most salient to an understanding of the development of evangelicalism in Colombia is that of gender, specifically, the roles of men and women in the family.

As a feminist anthropologist working on the topic of Latin American evangelicalism, my initial goal was to explore the role of women in this exploding religious movement. As my research and thinking about the subject progressed, my focus broadened to include all of the ways in which the gendered experiences of converts, both male and female, have shaped and are shaped by this form of Christianity.

During 1982 and 1983 I conducted fieldwork in rural and urban Colombia on the evangelical movement. I set myself the task of developing explanations for the tremendous success of Colombian Pentecostalism that would do justice to the numerical preponderance of women in these churches, as well as to their significant roles as leaders within the movement. I was motivated by the critique of male bias in anthropology, which had rendered women and their cultural contributions invisible. Although descriptions abounded of the significant part women played in the evangelical movement, they tended to be ignored when it came time to formulate a theoretical explanation for conversion. A major goal for me, then, was to keep women *in*, to keep them visible, beyond the level of pure description.

✛

CONTRADICTIONS IN A FEMINIST VIEW
OF EVANGELICAL WOMEN

Carrying out the field research and subsequently formulating the explanatory models for conversion were processes charged with contradictions. Some of these were grounded in a discordance between my own commitment to a feminist perspective, which identified certain social forms as connected to women's subordination, and my anthropological training, which compelled me to take a culturally relativistic view.

First, as a feminist, I was aware that religious ideology has been a powerful tool of patriarchy in the past, reinforcing women's subordination and mystifying it. Yet, as an anthropologist, I was committed to valuing "native explanation" as an important key to the connection between meaning and action.

Next, how was I to view Colombian women's domestic roles and the high degree to which their identities revolved around their roles as wives, mothers, and grandmothers? In Colombia, the male and female spheres—the domestic realm of the home and the family and the public realm of the street—are separated by entrenched cultural attitudes and values. The "public-private dichotomy," which I had learned was often a projection of Western bias onto other cultures, was undeniably a major parameter within which Colombian women and men operated.

Finally, how could I keep women visible when pushing to a "higher" level of analysis, one beyond the household? It was all too clear to me that other analysts of Latin American evangelicalism had lost the women who had figured so prominently in their descriptions of the churches as soon as they introduced concepts such as "the penetration of capital." How could I keep women's reality important beyond the level of the household? Or was the household, in fact, the proper focus for explanation?

My first step in resolving these contradictions was to take all of these categories as culturally specific. This led to a new set of questions. Specifically, I realized that asking how Pentecostalism empowered women to take on new roles in society was not as valid a question within the Colombian setting as exploring how women in their traditional roles are agents of change. I now argue that Colombian Pentecostalism can be seen as a form of female collective action. Unlike Western feminism, it is not attempting to gain access for women to the male world; rather, it elevates domesticity, for both men and women, from the devalued position it occupies as the result of the process of proletarianization. It does serve to transform gender roles, primarily by reattaching males to the family. And, like some forms of feminism in the West, it glorifies and supports what is female.

The interplay between feminist thought and the anthropological approach is by no means a simple one, and tough contradictions emerge in the attempt to unify these viewpoints. What is clear is that for Third World women the family cannot be discounted. If we are going to exclude women from feminism because they value the roles of mother and wife and because they see the family as their source of strength, if we accuse them of false consciousness, we are committing a grave error. Feminists continue to struggle with this issue in our own society.

✛

MORE CONTRADICTIONS: COLOMBIAN EVANGELICALISM AND THE ANTHROPOLOGY OF RELIGION

As anthropologists, our analytical models for understanding religious phenomena have not figured among our discipline's major contribution to scholarship. This is true despite a long-standing fascination with the rites and rituals, the myths and beliefs of the people we study. When we turn our attention to religious *change*, we are hampered by a similar paucity of adequate theory for grasping the complex scene before us. Specifically in terms of Christian missionization, our choices have included viewing the process as one of forced acculturation or, perhaps, syncretic blending wherein the "traditional" religion hides in the guise of the new one. At best, the population "resists" Christian aggression in the only way it can, by running away to the hills, where the old ways can be nourished remote from the forces of change (see, for example, Silverblatt 1987:197).

A proselytizing religion such as Christianity fares particularly badly in the eyes of anthropologists, in practical terms because it erodes or destroys our very subject matter, and more philosophically because it violates our fundamental belief in cultural relativism. On the basis of my graduate training, heavily influenced by Marxist approaches, it is easy for me to see the linkages between Christianity and cultural destruction in Latin America, beginning with the Conquest, when conversion was accomplished at the point of a sword, and continuing through present-day "ideological imperialism," when conversion to Pentecostalism creates "good workers" for U.S. economic interests and defuses revolutionary impulses (Lalive d'Epinay 1969).

In my own research on the evangelical movement in Colombia, these types of analyses alone have proven unsatisfying, if for no other reason than that they do not address the central question of motivation for converts themselves. As Stoll puts it, blaming evangelical growth on agents of the United States "suggests a deep distrust of the poor, an unwillingness to accept the possibility that they could turn an imported religion to their own purposes" (Stoll 1990:xvi).

The decentering of anthropology and the challenges to feminist theory by women of color have created an opening for new explanations. U.S. feminists have started to take seriously the problems intrinsic to the individualistic framework of their goals. The 1980s, decade of the double day for working women in the United States, dramatically illustrated that the family and children would continue to be an issue for women, and that simply wishing them away was no solution. African American feminist theorists challenged the ethnocentric and classbound limitations of mainstream feminist writings and forced a reconsideration of how ethnic identity and community alliances intersect with and shape feminist commitment (Hooks 1984).

The study of Latin American evangelicalism has begun to be transformed. New studies of the grass-roots experience of converts challenge the conclusions of macro-level analyses, and anthropologists are more willing not only to listen but to let the people speak for themselves in anthropological writings.

Finally, the evangelical movement in Latin America has proved to be not merely a curiosity or anomaly, not just a thorn in the side of the Roman Catholic church. Its success and durability are evidence of the fact that it provides something desirable for its adherents and that— whatever it is—it is increasingly sought after.

✚
RESEARCH QUESTIONS:
THE DOMESTICATION OF MEN?

This study deals with the effects of conversion to evangelical Protestantism on the domestic lives of converts in Colombia. My approach centers on understanding religious change through the examination of social process within households. Recruitment to evangelical religion most often takes place along kin lines, and the major proselytizing activity is located in small Bible study and prayer meetings held in members' homes. Women are often the first to convert and later bring in husbands, brothers, and sons along with female kin. In a sexually segregated society such as Colombia's, the household is perhaps the most important locus of social interaction between males and females and, as such, is surrounded by deeply ingrained beliefs and values, which themselves are manipulated by family members to their own advantage. A focus on household activities provides a unique insight into individual motivation in the context of the dynamic process of family interaction. It also allows us to see how decisions made in the "private realm" and activities carried on there generate social change in the public order.

The research for this study was initially oriented around the question: Does evangelical Protestantism in Colombia provide, among other things, an ideology used by women to improve conditions in the household by "domesticating" men? The asceticism required of evangelicals brings about changes in the behavior of male converts, particularly in relation to the machismo complex in Latin America. Drinking, smoking, and extramarital sexual relations are forbidden. By redirecting into the household the resources spent on these things, such changes have the effect of raising the standard of living of women and children who are in varying degrees dependent on the income of these men.

My data on Colombian evangelical households support the conclusion reached by virtually every other analyst of Latin American Pentecostalism, that is, that conversion of both a woman and her husband improves the material circumstances of the household. Quite simply, no longer is 20 to 40 percent of the household budget consumed by the husband in the form of alcohol. Ascetic codes block many of the other extrahousehold forms of consumption that characterize masculine behavior in Colombia: in addition to drinking, smoking, gambling, and visiting prostitutes are no longer permitted. Furthermore, an emphasis on male as well as female fidelity within marriage prohibits a man from keeping a woman other than his wife, and so a man's limited resources are no longer split among two or more households dependent on his wage.

In some ways, Colombian evangelicalism can be seen as a "strategic" woman's movement, like Western feminism, because it serves to reform gender roles in a way that enhances female status. Specifically, it promotes female interests not only in simple, practical ways but also through its potential as an antidote to machismo (the culturally constructed aggressive masculinity characteristic of the male role in Colombia as well as in other parts of Latin America).

The growth of evangelicalism in Colombia coincided with a period of social change leading to an increase in female dependence on a male wage earner and the devaluation of women's role in the domestic sphere as peasant household production declined. Modernization has brought about a breakdown of the articulation of male and female roles, with women segregated in a devalued private realm, and men identified with an extrahousehold world regulated by the laws of machismo. Because their access to resources is primarily through men, women suffer from the lack of correspondence between their own and male values. In reforming male values to be more consistent with female ones (i.e., oriented toward the family rather than toward individualistic consumption) the movement provides a "strategic" challenge to the prevailing form of sexual subordination in Colombia.

✛

DATA COLLECTION

The research design for the field study was shaped by my interest in documenting the "private realm" experiences of evangelicals within a wider social context. I conducted anthropological fieldwork in the capital city of Bogotá from July 1982 through February 1983, and in El Cocuy, a small highland agricultural community some fourteen hours by bus to the north of Bogotá, from April 1983 through December 1983. Methods included participant observation, survey questionnaires, closed and open-ended interviewing, the collection of life histories and family histories, and archival research. The dual focus, on an urban area and on a rural one, provided a vital comparative dimension to the study and yielded a wealth of important data on the changing structure of evangelical families, including geographical and social mobility and the maintenance of rural-urban networks, as these data relate to the growth of the movement in a context of rapid social change and urbanization.

Although the research concentrated primarily on evangelical households and families, I also conducted numerous interviews with church leaders, local officials, and nonevangelical members of the community. Participant observation included attendance at church services and other religious functions as well as involvement in secular and Catholic community activities throughout the course of my field stay.

I was fortunate to have been invited to accompany the representative of the Colombian Bible Society on many occasions, as he traveled around the southern part of Bogotá visiting evangelical pastors. I used these opportunities to interview pastors, their wives, and other family members. Evangelical chapels are usually located in a front room of the pastoral couple's house, and so through these visits (which were ostensibly oriented around the business of selling and buying Bibles and the added agenda of my conducting formal interviews) I was able to survey a wide range of evangelical households. As the result of these initial visits, I was almost invariably invited to return to attend a service or a meeting of the women's association of the church. Thus, I attended services at churches from the whole spectrum of the evangelical movement—Unitarian and Trinitarian "Pentecostal," historical Protestant, and independent "charismatic." Three of these were of particular interest: the Canaan Church (Iglesia Canaan), the Charismatic Christian church (Iglesia Cristiana Carismática), and the Lutheran Church of the Redeemer (El Redentor). I attended their services regularly during my first six months in Bogotá, and subsequently whenever possible until I left Colombia in December 1983.

In Bogotá, I collected overview data on the evangelical movement and interviewed the national directors of the United Pentecostal church, the Four-Square Gospel church, the Assemblies of God, the Evangelical Lutheran Church of Colombia, and the Presbyterian church. In El Cocuy, I collected archival materials from the Catholic church's parochial records.

During my first six months in Colombia I also made three trips outside Bogotá, including traveling with the Bible salesman through the Magdalena Valley and attending the weeklong Four-Square Gospel church convention in the oil center of Barrancabermeja, Santander. I administered a survey questionnaire to forty-five people (twenty-six

men and nineteen women) attending the convention. Another questionnaire was administered at an interdenominational tea given by the
women's association of the Lutheran El Redentor church in Bogotá, on
the occasion of the Day of Love and Friendship (and to raise money
for chairs purchased for the fellowship hall of the church). Forty-three
women responded to this questionnaire.

I was intensely involved in the day-to-day activities of evangelical
households during all phases of field research. The core of my sample
of households consisted of two large "nonresidential extended families"
comprising about 115 people in 25 households. One group was based in
Bogotá and the other in El Cocuy. The history and composition of these
families and my relationship to them is described in the Appendix. Data
collection focused in large part on the effect of conversion on household activities and organization. There is existing literature on changes
in the socioeconomic conditions of families after conversion and comparing evangelical and nonevangelical households in the same community (e.g., Hine 1974; LaRuffa 1971). Intrahousehold differences, however, that is, the differences in standards of living of husband and wife,
had not been considered.

✠

THE DIFFERENT LEVELS OF MEANING
IN THE CONVERSION EXPERIENCE

Although a major component of my research was attendance at church
services (including the recording of sermons, testimonies, prayer, and
hymn singing), the focus of the present work is not the analysis of religious belief. I. M. Lewis has noted that "once they have shown what for
secular ends is done in the name of religion, some anthropologists na-
ively suppose that nothing more remains to be said." This means that
we leave relatively unexplained "the characteristic mystical aspects
which distinguish the religious from the secular" and fail completely to
"account for the rich diversity of religious concepts and beliefs" (Lewis
1971:36). While I wish to clarify from the outset that this study of Colombian evangelicalism pursues a level of explanation linking religious
behavior to mundane activities and needs, I recognize its limitations and
do not assume, as those criticized by Lewis may have, that I have the

whole picture. The pragmatic function of evangelical conversion is to reform gender roles (and, by extension, marital roles), thereby dramatically improving the quality of life within the confines of the family. I hope to show that this process has implications also for spheres other than family groups. In illustrating the changes that take place, I have examined several aspects of the meaning of conversion to individual believers (men and women), and to family life. I also discuss what conversion means to the "male role," which, as it represents a level of abstraction from observed behavior, can be viewed as the observer's (my own) meaning. There is another level of meaning to conversion that explains why people have chosen to risk the ire of their friends and families, ostracism and persecution by the community, and even death. That the present study dwells on the mundane affairs, individual strategies, and interests that are connected to evangelicalism is not to slight the passionate emotion and the fervent faith that are the "true" meaning of evangelical Christianity for the followers of that path.

✛
GENDER ANALYSIS IN CONVERSION STUDIES

I did not set out to prove that women were dominant in the evangelical churches: that was unnecessary. Nor do my findings, both empirical, based on the Colombian case, and analytical, based on the feminist approach, negate most of the formulations of other students of the topic. The major explanations for conversion—marginalization, deprivation (status and other), and even individual deviance—could be fruitfully reworked in light of the gender issues involved and incorporated into a comprehensive theory of evangelical movements. As they are currently formulated, however, these theories suffer from having left gender out of the picture entirely, or from having proposed separate explanations for male and female conversion and then taking the male explanation as the more inclusive because it usually pertains to a "supradomestic" level of social organization. The goal of the present study is to illustrate that essential explanations of the movement emerge by not rising from the household level to some "more inclusive" social arena (from which, in all likelihood, women are excluded), but by retaining a focus on gender relations and domestic organization regardless of the arenas being considered.

✠
PLAN OF THE STUDY

Chapter 2 presents an overview of Colombian evangelicalism, including the early history of the movement and its contemporary scope. The meaning of *evangélico* (evangelical) is explored in terms of unifying and divisive factors within the movement as a whole. Colombian evangelicals are united across the spectrum of denominations by a rejection of Catholicism and the centrality of the Bible in their religious belief. The primary split among them derives from a doctrinal dispute over the unity or trinity of God (God in three persons, or three manifestations of a single God). The larger, trinitarian faction is further divided regarding style of worship: the "radical" groups manifest the charismatic gifts such as speaking in tongues and divine healing, while the conservative groups believe that these gifts were limited to earlier times. Chapter 2 concludes that this division is being transcended as charisma pervades even the "conservative" or historical Protestant churches.

Chapter 3 deals with the intersection of religion and politics in Colombian history. The overwhelming power of the Catholic church in Colombia is of primary importance in understanding the position of evangelical converts. Constitutional reforms during 1991 culminated in a clear separation of church and state in Colombia and the limitation of the power of the Roman Catholic church over areas such as marriage, the family, and education. A brief description of these reforms in included here. Included in chapter 3 is a discussion of La Violencia and its impact on the growth of the evangelical movement. The experience of religious persecution during that period is recounted in the words of an evangelical pastor. This chapter illustrates that the politico-religious climate contributed to the "household" orientation of Colombian evangelicalism, which was essential in promoting its rapid growth and endurance.

Chapter 4 describes the evangelical experience in a small rural town in Colombia. The "progress-minded" attitude of prominent evangelicals in the town is illustrated with case material, and the way this can be interpreted as a projection of family values into the wider community is suggested.

Chapter 5 reviews the literature on machismo and specifies that the theme of domestic abdication is the one clear thread running through the range of definitions. In chapter 6, the impact of machismo on family life is explored. Sex roles and the different values and aspirations of men and women are related to patterns of status acquisition in the public and private domains. Changing consumer patterns associated with class mobility are discussed in terms of a shift from individualistic status markers to those encompassing families and located in the household.

Chapter 7 concentrates on how this male-female dynamic relates to the conversion process. The implications of the radical change in sex roles, particularly machismo, that follows conversion are considered in terms of the household economy and class mobility. In the conclusion of this chapter I relate the household analysis back to the churches by examining the "feminine ethos" of Colombian evangelicalism.

In the conclusion (chapter 8) I propose that Colombian evangelicalism can be seen, in one regard, as a "strategic" women's movement, aimed at fundamentally altering sex role behavior to women's benefit. I expand this point to suggest that notions of "progress" held by converts reveal a "prosperity ethic" that is consistent with a female view of family well-being. I contrast this idea with existing literature on Latin American conversion, both Weberian and Marxist, which uncritically utilizes Western notions of progress. I show that Weber's Protestant Ethic in particular is misapplied to the Colombian case, which has its own social-historical trajectory. The relationship between Protestantism and capitalist development must be understood in its local manifestations and not preconceived from our models. A better understanding of the prosperity ethic will expand our discussion of how evangelicals are positioned in terms of competing class interests within a dependent nation-state.

The Evangelical Movement in Colombia

✛
EARLY MISSIONS

On June 20, 1856, the first evangelical missionaries to Colombia, Dr. H. B. Pratt and his wife, Presbyterians, arrived in Bogotá. Although the earliest evangelical influence in the country dates back to a visit by James Thomson of the British and Foreign Bible Society in 1824, it is the Pratts' arrival that is considered by evangelicals to mark the beginning of the movement in Colombia. In particular, the later occasion was more convenient when it came to setting the date for the celebration of the centennial: in 1925, the number of Colombian evangelicals was insignificant, whereas by 1956 their ranks had swelled to the point that a major public event was desirable.

Pratt began conducting services in Bogotá in 1857 and published the first Colombian edition of the New Testament. Shortly thereafter, the couple was joined by another missionary, Thomas Wallace, who took over the Bogotá mission so that the Pratts could travel and evangelize, and another missionary couple, the Sharps, who started a night school for workers, with eighteen pupils. The Sharps taught their students to read the Bible, write, and do arithmetic. Since that time, the Presbyterians have been very involved in developing educational facilities in Colombia, and their high schools, the *colegios americanos* in Bogotá, Cali, Barranquilla, Ibague, Bucaramanga, Giradot, and, formerly, Armero, are prestigious institutions that attract a large number of nonevangelical students.

The first small congregation was subjected to stonings, and the Catholic clergy was clearly disturbed by the presence of the missionaries. Evangelical lore has it that after the archbishop of Bogotá published a tract condemning the Protestants as "heretics and Masons," the first Presbyterian congregation grew from 36 to 150. It became impossible for the missionaries to meet the demand for the Bibles they were publishing. Outraged by the distribution of the Bibles, the archbishop decided to hold a public burning of Protestant Bibles in the Plaza de Bolívar, in front of the archbishop's palace. The Presbyterians learned that this was being planned and were extremely careful not to give the Bibles to suspicious people. When the fires were finally lit, it is said, the only Bibles they had to burn were two copies of the Catholic version of Padre Scio de San Miguel.

During the early years of the Presbyterian mission, a bookstore was opened, and Pratt wrote several important tracts. In 1859 Pratt returned to the United States to attend to the publication of his book, *Nights with the Romanists*. While he was home the Civil War broke out, and Pratt served as a chaplain for a Confederate mounted division. In 1869 he returned to Colombia and started a ministry in the Caribbean coastal city of Barranquilla. His wife became ill in the tropical climate, so they moved to the more temperate city of Bucaramanga.

Until the beginning of the twentieth century, the Presbyterians were virtually the only evangelical mission in Colombia. The establishment of churches began very slowly, with only a handful of missionary groups joining the Presbyterians during the first three decades of this century. In 1908 the Evangelical Missionary Union came, followed by the mission of the Evangelical Alliance in 1918, the Christian and Missionary Alliance in 1923, and the Cumberland Presbyterian Church in 1925. It was not until after 1930 that Colombia really began to attract the attention of foreign missionaries. Then, between 1930 and 1946 the pace of foreign missionary activity accelerated, and fourteen more groups appeared on the scene. This sixteen-year period of slow but steady expansion was brought to a halt by La Violencia (1946–1966), during which most foreign missionaries left Colombia for their own safety. Only one new mission was formed during those years, the Panamerican Mission, in 1956.[1]

Evangelical leaders in Colombia divide their history into four main periods. The Period of the Pioneers lasted from 1856 to around 1930, and was followed by the Period of the Establishment of Churches, from 1930 to 1946. The period during La Violencia, from 1946 to 1960, during which the movement really started to take off is called the Period of Awakening. After 1960, when relative peace had been restored, came the Epoch of Organized Evangelization, from 1960 to 1977 (SEPAL 1981:5).

It is extremely interesting that the "explosion" coincided with the period of least foreign missionary involvement. The persecution of evangelicals during La Violencia drove the movement behind closed doors and, as a result, it experienced a transformation: it became more closely adapted to the Colombian reality. This point will be discussed in more detail in chapter 3.[2]

✛

THE CONTEMPORARY PICTURE:
THE SIZE OF THE MOVEMENT

Estimates of the number of evangelical converts in Colombia at the time of my research vary widely. Evangelical churches rarely keep good records of membership; this may be due in part to fear of persecution. At a banquet in honor of the 500th anniversary of the birth of Martin Luther, held in Bogotá in November, 1983, one speaker estimated that there were approximately 2 million evangelical Christians in Colombia (of a total population of about 29 million), served by 4,000 pastors in 3,500 congregations. One of the evangelical service organizations, SEPAL (*Servicio Evangelizador para América Latina*) is currently compiling statistics on membership nationwide, but it is finding this a difficult endeavor. The organization estimates that in 1981 there were 1.2 million evangelical members in Colombia. The Catholic church estimate for 1979 was 900,000 (Secretariado Nacional de Pastoral Social 1981:111).

The evangelicals are divided into approximately 2,500 congregations served by no fewer than 3,000 Colombian pastors. SEPAL verified in 1980 the existence of 190 established evangelical churches in Bogotá. It should be noted that this figure leaves out the single largest evangelical sect, the Iglesia Pentecostal Unida de Colombia (the United Pentecostal Church of Colombia), as well as the Seventh-Day Adventists, the Jehovah's Witnesses, and the Mormons. These groups are not part of any of the Colombian evangelical confederations because of serious doctrinal differences.

✛

THE MEANING OF "EVANGELICAL"
IN COLOMBIA

In this study, the term "evangelical" is used to designate a religious movement and group of believers who, despite having developed significant differences among themselves over the years, manifest a number of common traits and share a common identity vis-à-vis outsiders. Perhaps the most compelling rationale for adopting this term is that it is simply a translation of the Spanish word *evangélico*, which is what they call themselves. Within the considerable array of denominations, missions, and splinter groups that may argue over issues of doctrine and styles of worship, and whose historical development has followed substantially different trajectories, similar positions on certain basic issues contribute to a common identity as evangelicals. The Colombian Lutherans, Baptists, or Presbyterians, along with more theologically "radical" adherents of the Assemblies of God or the Four-Square Gospel church, identify themselves as "evangelicals" and apply the term to those of the other denominations as well. In fact, one rarely hears the denominational labels used. In the little Lutheran church in El Cocuy, which dates from the 1930s, the young vicar, on the occasion of Martin Luther's 500th birthday in 1983, waged a concerted campaign to instruct his flock that they were, in fact, Lutherans. Neither the members themselves nor the townspeople had ever identified them as anything other than *evangélicos*.

The nature of evangelical identity in Colombia deserves considerable attention because it is not accurately glossed by any of the religious categories commonly found in the United States. The categories "Protestant," "Evangelical Protestant," "Historical Protestant," "Pentecostal," "Fundamentalist," "Charismatic Christian," and so on, are either irrelevant in the Colombian context or are used in substantially different ways than in the United States. A discussion of the unifying as well as the divisive factors in Colombian evangelical identity will be useful for delineating the focus of this study.

Unifying Factors

REJECTION OF CATHOLICISM

The evangelical movement in Colombia exists within a nation-state that has given tremendous power to the Catholic church. The privileged position of the Catholic church in Colombia and its influence on Colombian society will be discussed in the next chapter. For the moment, however, it should be noted that in the past, and in contemporary Colombia to a very great extent, to be Colombian meant to be Catholic. No other alternatives existed—the religious affiliation was as much a birthright as was citizenship. To be human was to be Catholic.

Excommunication meant not only damnation in the afterlife, but in the present life as well. Since church and society were unified, leaving or being expelled from one excluded you from the other. The enormous gravity of the step taken by the early evangelical converts must be understood within this context. Renouncing their Catholicism, risking the ire of the priests and the contempt of their neighbors, they separated themselves, voluntarily and involuntarily, from the mainstream. The relative cohesion of the movement, then, can be viewed in part as an outcome of their status as renegades. In many respects evangelical religion in Colombia was and is an opposition movement. This status was further solidified by the persecution during La Violencia, which will be discussed further in chapter 3.

THE *EVANGÉLICO* AND THE *EVANGELIO*: THE IMPORTANCE OF OWNING AND READING THE BIBLE

One of the main distinguishing characteristics of evangelicals in Colombia is the centrality of the Bible in their lives and as the focal point of their religious beliefs and practices. This feature in particular marks them as something apart from ordinary "Catholic" Colombians, and indeed from truly devout Catholic Colombians, because until quite recently Bible reading and Bible owning by lay people were subject to severe sanction by Catholic clergy. The latter believed that, in the wrong hands, the Bible was a dangerous and potentially evil document, and only those trained in its correct interpretation should be allowed access to it. It would be impossible for the laity to understand the Bible by themselves, and its truths could be revealed only through the doctrine and the explication of the authorities of the Catholic church.[3]

Thirty years ago the Bible was all but unavailable to the Colombian populace. At a breakfast given for evangelical pastors in Bogotá by the Colombian Bible Society (SBC) on the occasion of "Bible month" (October), a Colombian pastor reported how thirty years ago his father, who lived in a small town, was very much interested in the Bible but could not find one. He knew a person who owned one and asked him to sell it to him, but the man replied that the Bible was "*muy mía*" (very much mine). When he tried to trade his horse, which was worth considerable money, for the Bible, the man still refused. Finally, he agreed to lend him the Bible for three months, and the pastor's father hand-copied large portions of it by candlelight each night after his full day's work.

Bibles are still not easy to acquire, especially outside of the large cities, where bookstores do not exist. The Colombian Bible Society is a key organization providing Bibles and tracts for the myriad of evangelical sects (with the exception of the Jehovah's Witnesses and the Mormons, who use a different text). The Bible Society is also the oldest evangelical influence in Colombia, dating from the first visit of an agent of the British and Foreign Bible Society, James Thomson, in 1824. The SBC sells Bibles directly to pastors and to Christian bookstores, which in turn sell them to members. A little bookstore attached to a thriving Pentecostal church in a working-class neighborhood in Bogotá sells one hundred Bibles a week. The clerk explains that people get converted and immediately come in to buy two or three Bibles. The pastor asks his congregation during the services how many of them have Bibles, and in response people hold their Bibles above their heads. A forest of arms holding Bibles aloft is a common image in Colombian evangelical churches. Then from the pulpit, the pastor tells those people who are without a Bible to go buy one.

The purchase of a Bible is the first major commitment by those considering conversion. The "discovery" of the Bible or the truths in the Bible figures prominently in the testimonies of believers. Despite the fact that, as Catholics, they have never owned or read the Bible, a major concern for people considering conversion is often the difference between the Protestant Bible and the Catholic one. A number of converts reported that they had purchased a copy of each version and spent a long time comparing them. They were gratified to find out that the Bibles are the same—the Protestant Bible was not full of heresies as the priests had claimed. The only difference between the two was that the Catholic Bible contained the books of the Apocrypha, but beyond that the two Bibles corresponded.[4]

Despite a major annual fund-raising effort in October, only 3 to 4 percent of the operating costs of the SBC are met by the offerings from Colombian churches, and the Bibles themselves are sold below cost. The SBC is heavily subsidized by the American Bible Society (ABS) and pays the ABS what it can for the Bibles. Perhaps for this reason Bible Society representatives do not say that they "sell" Bibles, but rather that they "distribute" them. In 1981 the SBC distributed 131,000 Bibles and 76,000 New Testaments.

Although particular congregations may take up special collections to buy a number of Bibles for free distribution, the Bible Society itself almost always requires at least a nominal payment for its Bibles. The SBC field representative explained that this was to make people appreciate and respect the Bible they acquired; if they received it completely free they would just take it for granted. It is only with reluctance that the field representative sells the cheapest, paper-bound version of the Bible,

Dios Habla Hoy, and then he instructs the buyer to obtain a plastic cover for it so that it will not fall apart from the heavy use to which most evangelicals' Bibles are subjected. The SBC offers a whole line of Bibles, from very inexpensive ones to more costly and elegant ones. They urge pastors who can afford them to buy the highest-quality Bibles, because the sale of these subsidizes the sale of the cheaper editions. There is a highly developed appreciation of these "*Biblias finas*," and Roberto (a pseudonym), the SBC field representative, turns into quite a salesman when enticing his customers with the fine Moroccan leather and the gilt-edged pages. But he is also an evangelist and hands out free tracts to many of the people he meets on his circuit.[5]

Roberto has worked for the SBC for nearly twenty-five years. He is a member of the Evangelical Lutheran Church of Colombia, as are the president and the secretary of the SBC. Roberto has been put in jail and harassed innumerable times for selling the Bible. Until a few years ago he completed his arduous circuit on buses, but the Society finally got him a Nissan jeep, which is his pride and joy. Even now, however, his job is not an easy one, considering the perils of overland travel in Colombia, the severe changes in climate to which he must constantly adjust as he visits cities high up in the frigid mountains and then, two hours later, smothers in the heat of the valley towns. About every two months he makes a wide loop, heading west out of Bogotá down into the Magdalena Valley to the city of Ibague at the foot of the central *cordillera*, up into the mountains through the heart of the coffee-growing region to the cities of Pereira and Manizales and crossing the Magdalena Valley again on a more northern route back to Bogotá.

I accompanied him on one of these trips. He works a very long day, and has developed an astonishing capacity for consuming with equanimity and graciousness the meals, snacks, and "refreshment" that are offered to him in a stupefying barrage at his scores of stops. Passing through the high *páramo* (the highest point in the mountain pass), he is greatly amused by the fact that people at a wayside stop call him "*padre*" because they mistakenly assume that since he is handing out religious tracts and talking about God he must be a priest. Nowadays, his business brings him into contact with a few Catholics, priests, and nuns, but he is convinced that the Catholic church has failed in Colombia and believes that the current interest the church is showing in promoting Bible reading is no more than hypocrisy. When he parks the jeep outside a parochial office in order to pay a visit to some nuns who want to buy Bibles, he turns and says sardonically, "If the police come, tell them that the '*padre*' is upstairs talking to the bishop."

His main purpose on the circuit is to stop in every small town and pay a visit to all of the evangelical pastors in each, checking on their supply of Bibles. Occasionally he will sell a Bible out of the back of the jeep. Someone will ask to buy a "book," and he will say, "What kind of book? A Bible or a New Testament?"

Roberto's knowledge of the various evangelical groups in Colombia is encyclopedic, and he moves among competing sects imperturbably, always addressing his customers as "*Hermano*" (brother) and "*Hermana*" (sister). In return, he is always called "Hermano Roberto" or simply "El Hermano," and it would be unthinkable to speak his name without this honorary title. People closer to him sometimes refer to him with the diminutive "El Hermanito," poking fun gently at his universal appeal within the Colombian evangelical community.

As he passes through one of the numerous *retén* checkpoints that dot the Colombian highway system, seven police armed with automatic weapons stop the jeep to search for contraband. It is dark now and Roberto is trying to make it through a difficult stretch of mountain road to the city where he will spend the night. The police at these stops are notorious for demanding payoffs for imagined infractions. Roberto, who is usually a meticulous driver, brings the jeep to a jerky halt and stalls it out. He is clearly nervous. The police ask him what he is carrying and he replies "books." He stays in the driver's seat, staring straight ahead, as they rummage around among the boxes in the back. There is nothing to keep them from deciding to make problems, to delay us, to charge us a fine, but they seem to lose interest after a few minutes and walk away from the jeep. Roberto, who is now free to go, calls out to one of the police, "Brother, how many of you are there?" and the policeman replies that there are seven. He reaches into a plastic bag on the seat beside him and finds seven *porciones*, reprints of the Gospel of John, which he hands out to the police with instructions that they should read them. For a man who has been dragged off by police for selling the Bible, this takes courage.

EVANGELICAL VOCABULARY AND PRACTICE

As is true for any other specialized group within society, evangelical Protestants in Colombia have developed a particular vocabulary, a new way of using words—new words describing old things, old words describing new things. Evangelicals talk about when they became *cristianos* (Christians), but they do not mean that they were nonbelievers before. They use the term "Christian" to describe themselves and their fellow believers, and this does not include Catholics. Evangelicals do not perceive of themselves as being "religious." The words "religious" and "religion" are used to refer to Catholic practices; they connote something that has to do with rites and rituals. An evangelical describing her nonconverted mother as "a very religious woman" might be implying something that, from an evangelical point of view, would be considered quite negative, for example, that her mother had many statues of saints around the house, she attended mass and confession regularly, and she owned and believed in the efficacy of religious objects that had been blessed by the priest. Other words that might occur in the context of such a description are *fanático* (fanatic), *idolotría* (idolatry), and *Romano* (Roman Catholic). One of the main features of conversion to evangelical Protestantism in Colombia is a strong rejection of what is seen as the meaningless ritual of the Roman Catholic church. Becoming a Christian is seen not as changing one's religion, but rather as changing one's entire life.

The guidelines for this change are laid out in the Bible. Converts claim that Colombian Catholicism does not make the text and its contents accessible. Only very recently has the Catholic clergy in Colombia encouraged or permitted the laity to own and read the Bible.[6] Although *evangelio* literally translates as "gospel" (the story of Christ's life, crucifixion, and resurrection), a *creyente* (believer) usually thinks of the Bible in general when he or she refers to the time when "*conocí al evangelio*" (I first came to know the *evangelio*). For insiders as well as outsiders, the identifying feature of evangelical religion is the centrality of the Bible in worship, in belief, and in dictating a code of personal conduct for believers.

Evangelicals in Colombia will refer to themselves and others like them as *creyentes*, *evangélicos*, or *cristianos* (more generally, any group of believers is referred to as *hermanos*, brothers and sisters). They never refer to themselves as *Protestantes*, and even among the bulk of Pentecostal churches, rarely as *pentecostales*. *Protestante* is a word used exclusively by Catholics, and has a negative and subversive connotation.

One of the largest Pentecostal groups in Colombia is the Iglesia Pentecostal Unida de Colombia (the United Pentecostal Church of Colombia—IPU), and people almost always confine their use of the label *pentecostal* to that group. Other Pentecostal groups do not identify with the word, partly because few of them started out historically as Pentecostal, but rather tended to become so as they were adapted to the Colombian setting. Moreover, the IPU is quite unpopular with the wider evangelical community because of doctrinal differences (they are unitarian; see below) and ethical conflicts. Specifically, other evangelical groups resent the IPU pastors' "no-holds-barred" attitude toward winning new members. Pastors of trinitarian evangelical groups report that because the IPU pastors and members believe that all other evangelical groups suffer from the "erroneous doctrine" of the trinity, they are compelled to win (or steal) members from already-established trinitarian evangelical churches. The relationship of the IPU to other Colombian evangelical churches, its independence from foreign missionary influence for many years, and its spectacular growth and organizational development is a fascinating story, aspects of which are discussed in Flora's work (Flora 1976). The church has changed considerably since Flora's study and this group will be discussed further below.

Another category of people are the *inconversos*, the unconverted. People use this word to refer to themselves before they knew about the *evangelio*, and to nondevout people generally, that is, nominal Catholics. People's involvement in the Catholic church in Colombia varies greatly, and identifying as a Catholic, especially for men, may essentially mean little involvement in organized religion.[7] It is one of a number of ascribed characteristics, and since it is perceived as being pan-Colombian, it may in fact have less to do with a person's identity than with the fact of being a Liberal or a Conservative, or a *boyacense* (from the Department of Boyacá) or a *costeño* (from the coast). An evangelical woman, in a sermon instructing members about methods of evangelization, pointed out that it is of very little use to ask a prospective convert the question, "Are you a Christian?" because they will most certainly reply, "Of course I'm a Christian—I'm not an animal!"

In the nonevangelical population, then, "Christian," like "Colombian," is a characteristic that is taken for granted. It is a status, like "human," that one does not have to work to achieve. In this conceptualization, Christian also means Roman Catholic. This stands in marked contrast to the way evangelicals use the word *cristiano*, and they are frustrated by the fact that such a response says nothing about the individual's degree of religiosity and the extent to which his or her life is guided by religious precepts.

Finally, the most important religious terms have been renamed by evangelicals. In keeping with the rejection of the cult of the saints, San Pedro and San Mateo (Saint Peter and Saint Matthew) become el Apóstolo Pedro and el Apóstolo Mateo (the Apostle Peter and the Apostle Matthew). An evangelical praying is *orando*, never *rezando* (reciting by rote), as a Catholic would do.[8] A Catholic goes to *misa* (mass) and an evangelical to *culto*. The eucharist as celebrated by the Catholic priest is *comunión*, while the evangelicals participate in *santa cena* (holy supper). This takes place in a *templo* as opposed to a Catholic *iglesia*. (The word *iglesia* [church] is used by evangelicals, but not usually to refer to the building itself, which may in addition to *templo* also be called simply the *casa evangélica*. *Iglesia*, when used by evangelicals, usually refers to an entire denomination.)

It is not simply that the evangelicals want to differentiate themselves from the Catholics; these terms really do refer to radically different activities. On every level the evangelical churches are less hierarchical than the Catholic, there are very few religious trappings and a much greater participation by the congregation in the service itself. The extreme reaction on the part of evangelicals against what they see as idolatry in the Catholic church (particularly in terms of the cult of the saints) has rendered most evangelical *templos* practically bare of ornamentation. It is not unusual for the altar to consist of no more than a speaker's podium, although frequently the wall behind the podium will be decorated with a painted mural. These murals tend to be artistically primitive in style, rendered by a talented *creyente*, and characteristically portray a landscape with a flowing river or waterfall, trees, and in many cases an open Bible suspended over the scene amidst a radiant cloud. Sometimes a ray of light is painted in, strategically descending from above in such a way that whoever is at the podium is directly under it.

The water imagery recurs in association with the Bible, which provides "streams of living water" to the believer (from Revelations 7:17: "and he will guide them to springs of living water; and God will wipe away every tear from their eyes"). The Bible replaces the cross as the central visual symbol in the evangelical churches, and it is only the more traditional historical Protestant churches (such as the Lutherans, Presbyterians, and Baptists) that have defined altar areas on which there may be a simple cross. Even in these churches, however, the cross is empty; one never sees a crucifix, that is, the cross with the body of Christ hanging on it. Also, in the historical churches, there are sometimes candles on the altar, but this is a point of controversy because of the strong Catholic association. In the Lutheran church in Bogotá in 1983, there was a discussion in progress as to whether the pastors should be made to wear vestments. Evangelical pastors in Colombia as a rule wear regular suits or even more casual clothing, and the instances in which they wear clerical robes and collars can be traced to the influence of foreign missionaries or foreign training. In a country where every group has its *uniforme* (uniform), it is significant that evangelical pastors choose not to set themselves apart by any distinctive dress. If there are other adornments in the *templo* they will usually consist of Colombian flags and church flags, vases of flowers, and perhaps several ornate chairs.

MARTIN LUTHER'S 500TH BIRTHDAY PARTY

In November, 1983, Martin Luther appeared on the cover of the Sunday magazine sections of the two major Bogotá newspapers, *El Tiempo* and *El Espectador*. A retired Presbyterian minister who had suffered through the long years of persecution recounted how, when he saw this, tears came to his eyes. Martin Luther's 500th birthday was a big event in what is considered to be the most Catholic of all Latin American countries. Colombian evangelicals celebrated the anniversary with an air of guarded relief, recognizing a degree of public acceptance of their beliefs that is still only tenuously established. The memory of persecution will always be vivid in the minds of the evangelicals who lost family members during La Violencia, and who themselves suffered stoning, beatings, and the constant threat of death.

The major event of the anniversary celebration was a banquet at the Bogotá Hilton, organized jointly by the Association of Pentecostal Churches (ASECOL), the Confederation of Evangelical Churches (CEDEC), the Association of Christian Professionals, and the Lutheran Church of Colombia. Tickets cost sixteen hundred pesos each (about twenty dollars), a healthy sum by Colombian standards. The choice of the Hilton as the location for the event, rather than one of the larger evangelical churches, which could have easily accommodated the approximately six hundred people in attendance, was an expression of respectability and desire for public recognition that marks a new trend among Colombian evangelicals. It was a symbolic representation of the fact that the exclusive identification of evangelical beliefs with the lowest classes is no longer appropriate. The president of the republic, Belisario Betancur, was invited to attend, and although he sent a very cool letter declining the invitation, he did send as his representative the minister of development, who delivered an all-purpose address concerning the need to provide jobs and training for Colombians, with no specific references to religion.

A whole spectrum of Colombian evangelicals was in attendance and represented among the speakers. When the closing prayer was led by the pastor of one of the larger independent Pentecostal churches (the Cruzada Cristiana Colombiana), the majority of the crowd raised their hands above their heads to pray, Pentecostal-style.[9] The choir of a Bogotá Lutheran church presented part of a cantata of the hymns of Martin Luther, sung in Spanish, and the entire assembly joined in singing "Castillo fuerte es nuestro Dios" (A Mighty Fortress Is Our God). As the speeches ran on for several hours, no one smoked (there were no ashtrays on the tables), and no alcohol was served. The last speech, delivered by the

Cruzada pastor, departed in tone from its predecessors, which had focused on the success of the evangelical movement and emphasized that the great gains that the movement had experienced must prove that it is right and God's will. The Cruzada pastor reminded the listeners of the death toll, and that they were still under the gun, his passion quickened by the murder of one of the Cruzada pastors not quite a week earlier in a small town in Boyacá. He invited everyone to the funeral and demonstration against the continuing persecution the following Thursday.

That among their numbers evangelicals count doctors, engineers, and other professionals, that they can hold a major event in the Hilton, which symbolizes wealth, progress, and, for them, upward mobility, that their choirs can negotiate a Bach chorale, and that a high government official would see fit to grace the event with his presence, all indicate a new status for evangelical religion in Colombia that requires something better than the "opiate of the masses" explanation that Protestantism in Latin America has sometimes received in the social science literature. It is not only that the rate of growth in evangelical churches has been astonishing, over the past century the movement itself has undergone a series of transformations, and the individuals and families involved have been affected dramatically by their participation in the movement.

Around the time of Martin Luther's anniversary celebration, El Tiempo reported that four Protestant organizations (the same ones that sponsored the banquet) had petitioned the government for an abolition of the Concordance with the Holy See. Colombia remains the only country in the world that has an agreement in force with the Vatican (see chapter 3 for a discussion of the Concordat). The head of the Presbyterian church in Colombia articulated the impatience of evangelical leaders with the stubborn refusal of the Colombian government to recognize evangelicals as an important force in the country. He complained that Belisario had not invited a single evangelical to be on his Peace Council, despite the fact that evangelicals had been preaching peace for the 126 years that they have been in Colombia. He pointed out that the heads of the evangelical confederations were intelligent and educated men, and that Belisario's failure to consider them as representatives of a significant portion of the population was evidence of his flat refusal to admit that evangelicals exist in Colombia.[10]

Despite what amounts to a cultivated ignorance on the part of non-evangelical Colombians, particularly among the more educated, toward a national movement affecting more than a million Colombians, their perception of evangelicals occasionally appears in a sort of romanticized eulogy. This attitude is consistently connected to diatribes about Colombian national character, in which negative qualities of "the Colombian personality" are enumerated and the failure of the Catholic church to rectify the situation is bemoaned. An article in *El Tiempo* in November, 1983 listed the psychological and sociological characteristics of the Colombian personality as "a tendency toward disorganization, a notorious lack of individual and social discipline, an exaggerated interest in vices, a lack of respect for others, an overriding interest in the easy life." The Colombian journalist who authored this article presented his view of evangelicals as the exact opposite:

> An analysis of the human values inherent in the non-Catholic Christian groups that operate in Colombia demonstrates the weakness of traditional Catholicism in this subject. The faithful Protestant, perhaps because he pertains to a minority movement, is above all a dedicated militant, proselytizer, consistent in his faith, given to respect the values of the family and look for worldly inspiration in the Bible. He practices solidarity, brotherhood and sisterhood, he is a friend to dialogue and always observes a profound respect for others. He is philanthropic, a model of good behavior, mystical, an enemy of vices and excesses, modest, thoughtful, peaceful, genuine. Is not this kind of behavior something diametrically opposed to that of a great number of Colombians who belong to the Catholic community? (Sabogal 1983; translation mine)

The author goes on to predict the continuing success of the evangelical movement in Colombia due to the failure of the Catholic church. He points out that, although the Catholic church is the national spokesman, this is true only at the high levels of power, while in middle and lower sectors the penetration of Catholic influence has been in name only.

Divisive Factors within the Colombian Evangelical Movement

THEOLOGY: UNITARIANS AND TRINITARIANS

The Iglesia Pentecostal Unida de Colombia (United Pentecostal Church of Colombia, the IPU) is the largest single Pentecostal denomination in Colombia. Although a relative latecomer to the evangelical scene in Colombia, the denomination now has some 850 churches in every department of the country.[11] Other evangelical groups refer to the IPU as the "*Jésus Sólo*" (Jesus Only), because they are unitarians, believing in a single unified God with three manifestations, as opposed to the other denominations, which are trinitarians. This doctrinal difference is enough to isolate the IPU from fellowship with the rest of the movement; they are not, for instance, part of any of the national evangelical associations such as CEDEC and ASECOL. In the national organization publications the IPU is conspicuously absent from nationwide evangelical membership estimates, which is quite a sacrifice, since the publications are losing one of the largest churches which would certainly swell the numbers in the movement when the accounting is done. In many cities, evangelical pastors have weekly or monthly breakfast gatherings, but the IPU pastors do not take part in these. (Other sects that are excluded are the Jehovah's Witnesses, the Seventh-Day Adventists, and the Mormons.)

At first glance the IPU does not seem to differ very much from the other churches. The rough outlines of the services are identical with those of other Pentecostal churches. When they talk about the Holy Spirit, it is in much the same way that trinitarian groups do, but, to the best of my understanding, they believe that the Holy Spirit is not a separate part of the triune God, but rather is a manifestation of Jesus. The trinity is a difficult theological concept at best, and perhaps part of the wide appeal that these churches have is due to the fact that dispensing with the notion of the trinity simplifies things.

Although all Colombian evangelicals reject Catholicism and do everything they can to distinguish themselves from the Catholics, it is possible to argue that the IPU has made the more radical break from the old religion. While trinitarian evangelicals uniformly reject the pantheon of saints, they still share a belief in the triune God with the Catholics. The unitarians, on the other hand, at least on the level of formal doctrine, have carried this trend of streamlining the number of divine personnel to its limit: not only the saints are cast out, but also the multiplicity of God's personalities. At the same time, in terms of its administrative organization, the IPU is at least as hierarchical as the other evangelical churches. The national leadership body, the council of elders, has considerable power over the local congregations, including the appointment and removal of pastors.

At any rate, because of these differences the trinitarians and the unitarians identify one another as having "erroneous doctrine." Members of trinitarian evangelical groups assess other denominations in terms of whether or not they have *doctrina sana* (healthy doctrine). To the trinitarians (who are numerically in the majority, but boast no individual denomination as large as the IPU), healthy doctrine means a belief in the trinity and the conviction that the unitarians are sunk in *"errores."*

One of the sources of antagonism on the part of the evangelical community toward the IPU is the accusation that IPU pastors were responsible for splitting many of their churches. It is stated this way: Because the IPU identify the trinitarian churches as having erroneous doctrine, they think that they have the right to recruit new members from among the ranks of other churches. A pastor of the Four-Square Gospel church says that when he first began mission work in the coastal city of Barranquilla, he made the rounds of all of the other evangelical pastors who were already established there to learn where the best places would be to begin evangelizing without stepping on anyone's toes. The response of the IPU pastor he visited was that it did not really matter to him where the Four-Square started its mission, because for his part he would open up a church right next door if the Spirit led him. The Four-Square pastor said that the IPU would try to steal his members away when they were on their way to church, riding down the street in a car and yelling to the people walking along on their way to church that they should come to the IPU instead.

The IPU is one of the most purely "Colombian" of the evangelical churches because there are at present no foreign missionaries either serving as pastors or on the board of directors. The church as a whole is economically self-sufficient, and the members love to report that they are now sending Colombian missionaries abroad, to Canada and Ecuador. In 1983 there were approximately nine hundred Colombian pastors belonging to the IPU, the majority of whom had received no formal training.

Despite the size of the denomination, and unlike most other Pentecostal groups in Colombia, such as the Assemblies of God, the IPU has no Bible institute for training pastors and teachers. It is the duty of the local pastors to keep a lookout for promising prospects, dedicated young men who seem to have the potential for making good pastors, and to recommend them to the district leaders. The first appointment will be to an unevangelized sector of the same municipality, and the local church will support the new pastor for two years while he proves his dedication. After that he will be licensed to preach, but not to officiate at marriages or baptisms. If the young pastor does well, that is, if he makes converts, he may be rewarded by transfer to a more promising spot. Many times the first appointment will be to a *campo blanco* (white, or blank, field), that is, to an area with no converts.

The local churches are expected to be self-sustaining, so what goes into the offering plate, at least most of it, goes to sustaining the pastor and his family. This is not unlike the way the Catholic church in Colombia operates, wherein the local priest is supported by his parish and not normally by outside funds. In this sense a wealthy parish is truly a reward and a poor one is a punishment. Sometimes if nothing at all is coming in, the national church will provide a small stipend. The really large churches make enough money to support the pastor's family in style and still have some money to contribute to the national church for mission work. So a transfer to a more fertile or established area is tantamount to a raise. After three years the licensed pastor can have his case reviewed by the council of elders, who can recommend that he be ordained. The only requirement to be a pastor is to have the calling.

The importance of the role of the pastor's wife in these churches is quite striking. In many ways, her influence in the church is equal to that of her husband. The woman is the leader of the women's part of the church, which usually is the majority of the membership. She is in a sense the "copastor." This is also true in many other evangelical churches, and will be discussed in more detail in chapter 5.

STYLE OF WORSHIP: "RADICAL" VERSUS "CONSERVATIVE" SECTS

The "Problem" of Charisma in the Historical Churches

Gilberto Vargas, the director of the Colegio Americano in Bogotá and a prominent Presbyterian minister, visited the United States in the 1970s, and says that when he returned to Colombia he hardly recognized his church. He reports that the Presbyterian church in Colombia has been greatly affected by the charismatic movement. The pastors as well as the laypeople are speaking a new language, and it has Vargas worried. In the past, he says, the Presbyterian church in Colombia was very serious about doctrine. Now the sacraments are no longer considered to be as important as before, and the whole style of worship has changed.

The Pentecostal influence has had a tremendous impact on both the historical Protestant churches and the Catholic church in Colombia. Vargas said that in 1982 there were 380 evangelical sects in Colombia, and that at least 20 percent of the Catholic churches have turned charismatic. The numbers are growing. The historical churches are in a precarious position. They are the oldest evangelical groups in Colombia, the ones responsible for putting down the first roots in the face of what appeared to be insurmountable opposition. Now, in comparison to the charismatic churches, such as the Pentecostals, they are so small that no one takes them seriously. He says, "If you ask a pastor of the United Pentecostal Church who the Lutherans are, he'll tell you, 'Oh, they're a tiny little church.' This is because the only thing the Pentecostals consider important is the growth rate. They think there is something wrong with a church if it doesn't grow." But he believes that just because a church grows does not mean it is the true Church, and he is angry because the Presbyterian church is not remaining faithful to its principles. He quotes the Bible verse, "Many are called but few are chosen" and points out that even though the Jews were numerically in the minority, God chose them.

Despite their skepticism about the Pentecostals, the historical Protestant churches, like the Catholic church in Colombia, are compelled to come to terms with the attraction that Pentecostal-style charismatic belief holds for a large segment of the Colombian populace.

Although the charismatic movement is affecting Christian churches throughout the world, the factors that fuel this particular religious expression should be analyzed in their cultural setting. I do not know if foreign missionaries in general have had a tendency to move in the charismatic direction, but this certainly has been true in Colombia. Although these missionaries originally come to reveal "the truth" to Colombia, it would seem that Colombia has a very powerful effect on them. An example of this is a very well educated Presbyterian missionary, who, when she came to Colombia, was quite conservative theologically. Her charismatic conversion occurred some years after she had been in Colombia. Now she is creating quite a stir within the Presbyterian church because of her dramatic success in establishing churches in the northwestern region of the country. It is generally recognized that her success is tied to her charismatic teachings, and some Presbyterians complain that she establishes little churches in the jungle region of the Chocó and leaves them to develop on their own, whereupon they become indistinguishable from the Pentecostal churches.

✛
CONCLUSION

Protestant missionization in Colombia has not been a simple process of indoctrination of converts and the implantation of a new, imported religious system. Wherever evangelical missionization has been successful, there has been a great deal of mutual accommodation between missionaries and missionized. Conversion must serve the needs of individuals in the specific social and cultural context of their lives, or else why would they take such a dramatic step? In so doing the doctrine itself is transformed in culturally appropriate and meaningful directions. There is little doubt that in Colombia, as well as elsewhere in Latin America, the "radical" aspects of Pentecostalism, for example, speaking in tongues, healing, prophecy, and exorcism, are compelling in ways that more somber, conservative Protestant forms are not.

✛ 3 ✛
Religion and Politics

✛
INTRODUCTION

This chapter concerns the turbulent political and religious context within which evangelicalism in Colombia took root and grew. This history is essential to an understanding of both the complex motivations that bring about individual conversion and the position of evangelicalism as a dissident religious movement within a theocratic state. There are notable differences between Colombia and other Latin American countries in terms of religion and national politics.

First, I will discuss the Catholic church as a national institution, its especially privileged status in Colombia, and its role in the life cycle of the individual. An important shift in the status of the Roman Catholic church in Colombia occurred after my study was completed. The 1991 constitutional reform ushered in a profound change in relations between the Colombian government and the Roman Catholic church. I report on these developments here, but the real impact of them on Colombian evangelicals has yet to be assessed.

Next, I briefly describe the fusion of religion and politics in Colombian history and the conflict between the two dominant political parties over defining the role of the Catholic church in the country. The rest of the chapter deals with the impact of La Violencia on the evangelical movement. I have included here, as an especially vivid illustration of the impact of these historical forces on the individual, the firsthand account of an evangelical pastor of his experiences as a young man during that period.

✛

THE POWER OF THE ROMAN CATHOLIC
CHURCH IN COLOMBIA: THE CONCORDAT

The proliferation of denominations within Protestantism is taken by Colombian Catholics as evidence for the argument that evangelicals do not have the "true" faith. The word preferred by Catholics in this debate is "sect," which is explained as coming from the Latin *sectare*, which means to cut off, "as a branch is cut off from a tree" (Salesman 1982:14).[1]

The fact that, to this way of thinking, religious plurality is incompatible with religious truth needs some explanation. In the United States, at least on a certain ideological level, religious pluralism is valued. A small town may boast about the number of churches of different denominations existing within its boundaries. Such a situation would usually be taken as an expression of one of the fundamental values of U.S. society—freedom of worship—rather than as an indicator of hopeless theological confusion.

Freedom of religion, however, has not been a basic value in Colombian society, but rather has long been a matter of controversy, both on the level of constitutional legislation and in the attitudes and behavior of people in everyday life. In Colombia, there has been a complete fusion of the (Roman Catholic) Church and the State, the society of (Roman Catholic) believers and society. The Catholic church in Colombia has a reputation throughout South America as being particularly powerful and influential in national life. The Colombian state has been remarkably willing to delegate public authority over major areas of the lives of its citizens to the Catholic hierarchy.[2] Levine (1981) describes the legal status of the Colombian church as "unusually favored." In 1887 the Colombian government signed a Concordat with the Vatican that stands as "a model of the traditional ideal of Christendom—complete Church-State integration" (Levine 1981:70). The provisions of the Concordat define a major role for the church in many aspects of social life, recognizing it as "an essential element of the social order" (p. 70). It is in the public regulation of personal life that the church's authority is most absolute; that is, major junctures of the individual's life cycle are under the control of the church hierarchy. For example,

> The Church also received the predominant role in registering births, with parish records having preference over civil records. In addition, the management of death was placed in Church hands, as cemeteries were turned over

to the ecclesiastical authorities. Marriage, another step in the life cycle, was also placed firmly under Church control. Civil divorce did not exist, and civil marriage for baptized Catholics was made contingent on a public declaration of abandonment of faith. (p. 70)

Levine points out that the requirement of public declaration of abandonment of faith worked as a powerful discouragement to those considering civil marriage, since the outcome of such an act would surely be ostracism.

Education at all levels was to be maintained "in conformity with the dogma of the Catholic religion" (Concordat, art. 12), and religious instruction was obligatory. Catholic control of "public" education still exists in Colombia, a situation that creates problems for evangelical students.

Levine contrasts the Colombian situation with that in neighboring Venezuela.[3] There, it would be unimaginable for the church to play such a predominant role. Secular, governmental control of registry, education, marriage, and death keep the Venezuelan church "strictly a junior partner" (Levine 1981:71). Besides Colombia, Spain and Haiti were the last remaining countries to maintain Concordats with the Vatican, but these countries abolished their agreements some time ago. The Colombian Concordat was renegotiated, amidst intense public debate, in 1973, but Levine claims that the only changes immediately visible were the possibility of civil divorce and the elimination of public apostasy as a prerequisite for civil marriage of baptized Catholics. Levine claims that in some areas the power of the church actually increased, notably due to special provisions for the church's missionary role.

Colombian evangelicals experience the privileges awarded the Catholic church by the state as a limitation of religious freedom. They are frustrated and affronted by the fact that devout evangelicals must still come under the authority of the Catholic hierarchy simply because of their status as Colombian citizens. They resent it when their children enrolled in public colegios are required to attend mass or to participate in Catholic religious celebrations. Before the 1973 revision of the Concordat, children were required to present a Catholic baptismal certificate in order to be allowed entry into the public schools, and many evangelical converts, against their will but for expediency's sake, had their children baptized in the Catholic church.

A similar situation held for marriage. During the period when civil marriage was equivalent in the public mind to the pathway to damnation, many evangelicals found it easier simply to go through the Catholic ceremony, allowing the priests this temporary jurisdiction over their union more as representatives of the Colombian state than as religious authorities. In contemporary Colombia, only Catholic and civil marriages are recognized as legitimate (in the eyes of the state), and hence the couple who goes through a marriage ceremony in an evangelical church must also be married by a civil authority for the union to be considered legitimate. This is, of course, unnecessary for Catholic marriages. Ironically, given the relative stability of evangelical marriages compared to Catholic ones, an antievangelical rumor is that "they don't marry; they just live in sin." This statement reflects the attitude that nothing short of Catholic marriage is truly marriage, and certainly a ceremony in a tiny Pentecostal church does nothing to legitimate the couple's status in the eyes of the wider community. Hence, many evangelicals when asked about their marital status will say that they were married "*a la civil*" (in a civil ceremony), sometimes neglecting to mention the accompanying evangelical church ceremony.

In November, 1983, four of the leading Protestant organizations used the occasion of Martin Luther's 500th birthday to call publicly for the abolition of the Concordat. Although the petition was reported in the major Bogotá newspapers, the government failed to respond.

The complete exclusion of evangelicals from national politics and the status of the Roman Catholic church as a state religion came to an end eight years later. Along with many other groups that formerly had been marginalized from the centers of power, evangelicals had a voice in the drafting of the new constitution. Although the Concordat was not abolished, as evangelical leaders wished, it was substantially weakened, and church and state were for the first time legally separated.

✠

CONSTITUTIONAL REFORM AND THE CONCORDAT

In November, 1992, Colombian President César Gaviria Trujillo and a Vatican representative signed a revised Concordat that substantially curtailed the Vatican's legal authority over the personal lives of Colombians. This step was a direct outgrowth of a new Colombian constitution promulgated on July 4, 1991. The new constitution separated church and state and declared all religions equal.[4]

Colombia's attorney general subsequently declared that all Colombian laws derived from the papal treaty were unconstitutional. The nationally elected assembly that drafted the new constitution afforded Colombian evangelicals a significant political voice at the national level for the first time. Two evangelical leaders sat on the seventy-member assembly as representatives of a new political movement called the Christian Union, which was organized about a month before the elections for representatives to the constitutional assembly.

The revised Concordat takes away the Catholic church's long-standing right to legislate family law. One of the most significant changes is the legalization of divorce for Catholic couples. It also ends obligatory Catholic education in public schools and cancels the rights of priests not to be tried in state courts when charged with crimes (Anonymous 1992b).

Evangelicals still feel the government has not gone far enough in ending Roman Catholic hegemony in Colombia. They would like to see the Concordat scrapped completely. The Rev. Héctor Pardo, of the evangelicals' Christian Union Movement, was quoted in a *New York Times* article as saying, "They have held the reins of power for centuries, and the results are evident: A nation with fewer moral values and more out of control every day" (Anonymous 1992a).

Even before the weakening of the Concordat, the extremely powerful and conservative Colombian Catholic church had been undergoing changes in response to the reforms of Vatican II and the increasing visibility and viability of the evangelical movement. These changes have been slow to come about, however, and in the consciousness of both evangelical and Catholic Colombians, issues of faith are still interlaced with political loyalties and conflicts. To provide a background for understanding the place of evangelicals in the national context, it is useful briefly to examine the politics of religion in Colombian history.

✛

LIBERALS AND CONSERVATIVES AND THE SEPARATION OF CHURCH AND STATE

"*En el tiempo del Partido Conservador, era pecado ser uno Liberal*" (During the time that the Conservative Party was in power, it was a sin for one to be a Liberal). This statement by a longtime evangelical convert vividly illustrates the fusion of religious and political thinking characteristic of the period during which evangelical missionaries in Colombia attempted to make their first converts. The dominant political parties in Colombia, the Liberals and the Conservatives, which grew out of the early period of independence, differed on many issues, including the relative rights of temporal versus spiritual authorities. The Liberals, following Santander, hero of the independence struggle and Bolívar's second-in-command, were federalists, while the Conservatives, following Bolívar himself, were devoted to the concept of a strong centralized government. Specific issues on which the two parties differed included the following:

> What jurisdiction the Church courts should have, whether ecclesiastical appointments were to be controlled by the Church or the state, whether non-secular schools and non-Catholic cemeteries would be allowed. Although the lines were not entirely clear cut, Liberals generally upheld the power of the state in these matters and Conservatives the power of the Church. (Holt 1964:28)

Throughout the nineteenth century, as Liberals and Conservatives struggled for control of the government, Liberal administrations tried to limit the prerogatives of the church, only to have these reinstated when the Conservatives came back into power. A Liberal victory following a civil war that ended in 1861 put them in power for two decades. Holt describes this period as "the highwater mark of official anticlericalism" (p. 29). He describes the somewhat peculiar measures taken by the Liberals in an attempt to ensure religious freedom:

> The Constitution of 1863 suppressed all religious orders and decreed separation of church and state. Paradoxically, it authorized the government to exercise "supreme inspection over public worship" at the same time that it provided for freedom of worship. This was not, however, as contradictory in Colombia as it would be in the United States, where church-state relations are based on total non-participation of the state in church affairs and vice versa. In Colombia, there has been, as a practical matter, only one church and one state, each of which felt that it must either control the other or be controlled. Thus, it probably seemed perfectly natural to mid-nineteenth century Colombian Liberals that the way to guarantee freedom of religion was to inspect public worship; if the state did not do this, the church would—to the detriment, in the Liberal view, of freedom. (p. 30)[5]

The reforms lasted only as long as the Liberal government, and during the long period of Conservative rule that ensued (from 1887 to 1930), the church prospered and in return regularly supported that party's candidates and positions. From 1930 to 1946 the Liberals took over again; "old conflicts over ecclesiastical privileges were reopened, and a visible threat was posed to the status and image of the Church as a central institution of national life" (Levine 1981:64).

Rarely were these changes of government peaceful. Political violence of massive proportions was endemic in Colombia throughout the nineteenth and twentieth centuries, usually accompanying the transfer of national power from one party to another. The most recent, and also the most extended and bloodiest, episode of civil violence is the period known in Colombia as La Violencia.

✚

LA VIOLENCIA

Like almost everything else in contemporary Colombia, the evangelical movement cannot be understood without reviewing the history of La Violencia. Between 1946 and 1966, Colombia was the scene of "one of the most intense and protracted instances of widespread civilian violence in the history of the 20th century" (Oquist 1980:101). It is estimated that about 200,000 people were killed, 112,000 of them between 1948 and 1950. The beginning of La Violencia is usually dated as April 9, 1948, the day that the Liberal Party chief, Jorge Eliecer Gaitán, was assassinated and rioting and police retaliation in Bogotá left the city looking like Dresden after the bombing.[6] The worst of the ensuing violence took place in the countryside, and it was during this period that the rural areas of Colombia emptied out as people sought the relative safety of the cities.

The history of La Violencia is complex, and no monocausal explanation is sufficient.[7] Although the political issues involved are generally identified as the conflict between the Colombian Liberal and Conservative parties, the details of the violence in the countryside suggest in many instances that the conditions of social upheaval and the institutional support of aggression toward those not in power were often an excuse for a kind of brutality that took the form of vendetta feuding, banditry, and persecution of what was defined, for many reasons, not all of them readily evident, as the opposition. What is particularly frustrating in trying to understand this political clash is that the real differences between rural people who identify themselves as Liberal and those who

identify as Conservative are virtually indiscernible beyond their identification with the label and their hatred for the opposite side. Hartlyn's
work on coalition rule in Colombia draws parallels between the social
divisions caused by party affiliation in Colombia and those generated by
ethnic, linguistic, or religious differences in Western Europe (1988:27).
One Colombian analyst states that "in the Colombian case the traditional
political parties do not clearly represent social sectors, since they divide
society vertically rather than horizontally. They are types of primary
identification; people are 'born liberal or conservative.' They are more
like, therefore, deeply rooted *subcultures* than distinct programs for
the conduct of the state or economic development" (Sánchez 1985:796).
Another Colombian writer, cited in Dix's classic work on Colombian
politics (Dix 1967, citing Hernández 1962:168), remarks that "among
the most remote childhood memories of a Colombian are . . . those of
political parties similar to two races, which live side by side but hate
each other eternally."

Although there were originally fundamental philosophical differences between the Liberal and the Conservative factions of the ruling
elite, it is unclear to what extent the campesinos themselves, who were
the ones attacking each other with machetes, were motivated by these
concerns. Although originally the party affiliation of the campesino
probably derived from attachment to either a Liberal or a Conservative
patrón, by the time of La Violencia, among the rural population, party
affiliation was virtually an ascribed characteristic. Liberal campesinos
may have been somewhat more tenuous in their devotion to the priests
than their Conservative counterparts were, but they were not uniformly
anticlerical (see the statement by Don Pedro Merino at the end of the
chapter.) The fact that party affiliation is not class-based, in that both
Liberals and Conservatives can be found throughout the class strata,
from the landless peasantry to the ruling elite, is another factor that contributes to the difficulty of constructing a straightforward analysis of La
Violencia. Again, the complexity of the motivation for all the killing
extends beyond a single explanation, and individual animosities and
long-standing vendettas were not minor factors.

Virtually all evangelicals over the age of about forty contextualize
their faith within the framework of La Violencia. Evangelicals were severely persecuted during that time, many lost their lives, and the survi-
vors relate stories of stonings, being thrown in jail, hiding out for long
periods of time in caves in the mountains, or escaping to cities. Churches
were closed down. The large majority of Colombian evangelicals are Liberals, so they were doubly damned during a time when Liberal Party
affiliation alone was sufficient for getting oneself killed by the police or

officially supported vigilantes. Reading the Bible or evangelizing was
courting death. Evangelicals were routinely denounced, many times
from the Catholic pulpit, as Communists and as subversives, which is
ironic because they tend in general to be relatively middle of the road in
their political beliefs.[8]

La Violencia was the worst of times for Colombian evangelicals, but
it was also the best of times. Churches were shut, and foreign missionaries, for the most part, abandoned their fledgling congregations and fled
back to the United States (with notable exceptions—a number of very
dedicated U.S. missionaries stayed throughout La Violencia and suffered
along with their congregations). Yet during this time, when to publicize
one's faith meant risking one's life, the evangelical movement exploded.
The scenario repeated time after time was that when a church with one
hundred members was closed down, the home of each of those members
then became a church in itself. When the doors to the main church were
reopened, one hundred new congregations united in a church that now
had one thousand members.

That the dramatic growth happened during the years of most intense
persecution can be attributed to a variety of factors, but it is certain that
in the eyes of the evangelicals the experience of the church in Colombia
has a worthy precedent: the persecution of early Christians as written in
the books of the Apostles. A text that is often cited with regard to this is
Matthew 5:11,12, in which Jesus said, "Blessed are you when men revile
you and utter all kinds of evil against you falsely on my account. Rejoice
and be glad, for your reward is great in heaven, for so men persecuted
the prophets who were before you." Thus, although stories of evangelical persecution are still recounted with horror and sadness, there is also
often a distinct note of pride in the voices of the narrators.

The persecution has almost disappeared, although there are occasional incidents. While people are generally grateful to be able to worship in peace, the experience of La Violencia left them with a deep animosity toward the Catholic church. Many of my informants recount
stories of priests actively inciting the people against the evangelicals.
Also, evangelicals who survived the violence are skeptical about the
strength of commitment of new believers. They are afraid that their children will stray from the path because they were never "consecrated" by
having their faith tested under such difficult circumstances.

Colombian evangelicals, who are primarily identified with the Liberal
Party, provided me with their perspectives on La Violencia. A few years
later I researched Conservative Party newspapers in the Boyacense regional archives in order to get the opposite perspective on the terrible
events of that time. During the late 1940s through the mid-1950s, a Con-

servative Party newspaper called *El Demócrata* (The Democrat) was filled with reports of violent acts carried out against innocent Conservatives by the hated Liberals. The language used in these accounts is identical to that used by Liberals in oral history accounts of Conservative atrocities: "persecution" of "the martyrs of the party" by "criminals" or "vandals"; the "injustice," "barbarism," and "infamy" of "Liberal terrorism" and "Liberal hegemony"; the "villainous" nature of their "banditry"; and their inclination toward "subversion." As Riches (1986:5) has observed, "Violence differs from conflict in that violence is about structures of integrity while conflict is about structures of control." In the case of La Violencia, the intersection of ingrained and immutable party affiliation, the dominion of the Catholic church over the individual in mundane as well as moral and religious respects, and the denunciation of Liberal peasants by the clergy created a fatal polarization around the issue of legitimacy.

✠

THE EFFECT OF LA VIOLENCIA ON EVANGELICALS IN EL COCUY

The following account illustrates the meaning of the preceding history to an individual believer. Graciliano Azucena is the youngest son of one of the first evangelical converts in El Cocuy, Teófilo Azucena.[9] Teófilo's sons and daughters and their children form a large nonresidential extended family that remains at the core of the evangelical community in both El Cocuy and Bogotá. Graciliano still lives in El Cocuy. He is an ordained Lutheran minister, having been sent to study in Argentina during La Violencia, after his brother was murdered by the police and his own life was repeatedly threatened. His story illustrates how the roots of evangelical persecution during La Violencia extend to the existing animosity between Liberals and Conservatives, which itself was one of the factors predisposing certain individuals (Liberals) toward accepting the "other religion" being offered by the early missionaries. Graciliano's words also eloquently recount the experience of early missionization of El Cocuy.

> My father had had some arguments with the Roman clergy. In those days, the Roman clergy didn't have a single competitor. They had very strong domin-

ion over all the people of this region; everyone was compelled to obey them. They used to say that if you didn't follow their orders, if you didn't do what they commanded, you were damned. They'd excommunicate you. Also, there were two political parties, the Liberal and the Conservative. After the War of a Thousand Days some of the priests became extremely fanatical. The majority of priests always came from the Conservative Party. They used to say in their sermons, "Why don't you Conservatives defend yourselves against the Liberals? By chance don't you have an arm up to the shoulder blade?" That's a quote from a priest in those days. And when they killed the Liberal hero General Uribe, a priest here in Cocuy said from the pulpit, "Look, you see? That's how those who are against the church die—they get it in the head with an ax." That's just an example, but it was typical of many other priests. They were very political. There was an extremely strong fanaticism against the Liberals. So my father no longer believed the priests, because he had suffered so much opposition from them for being a Liberal.

You could say that the beginning of the *evangelio* in this region dates from when Juan Galdames came. He was a salesman. I don't know what region he was from. We thought he was probably from the coast because of his accent. He went from house to house selling the Bible. Finally he showed up at our house. The first thing my father said to him was, "If this is any of that stuff that has to do with priests, don't bring it to me because I don't like it." And Galdames answered him, "No, this is about the word of God." So my father listened to him a little and said, "Yes, what this man is talking about really seems very good, because he is really talking about the things of God." When you really understand what God is saying, he isn't ordering you to hate and detest anyone. After that time my father became very interested in studying the scriptures. That same day he bought the Bible and we began to read it. But at that time it was very much prohibited to read the scriptures, because the priests disapproved of it. So people went and told the priest that we had the Bible, and many people began to criticize us for this.

Well, Galdames had noted down the names of the people who had bought the Bible, and later, around 1938 or '39, a man of European origin came. He was Norwegian, and his name was Andrew Larson. He paid a visit to all of the houses where Galdames had sold the Bible. And he spoke about the Gospel. I remember when he visited our house, my father asked him a lot of questions, and he answered them all, and so my father liked him. We had already heard said of Protestants that such a thing existed, but the word *Protestant* to our minds was something bad. That was because we hadn't ever met a Protestant. But it seemed to us that this man was humble, and he read some parts of the sacred scriptures, and it all seemed pretty good to us. I remember that he also sang a hymn, "Rock of Ages," and he explained it to us. And one of the things that seemed most curious to me and to everyone was when he bowed his head and he started to pray to God. It was the first time that we ever saw a man close his eyes and bow his head and start to talk to God. This made us laugh, and we sort of made fun of him at first when we saw this. And I especially remember the women who were there in the house at the time. They didn't come out to be with him, but instead watched from where he couldn't see them, and they were sort of making fun of the way he talked, the way he closed his eyes, and since he didn't pronounce Spanish very well, they were also criticizing him for that.

At first, when this missionary, Andrew Larson, began to hold meetings, they were like lectures, and he held them in the town theater. A lot of people came, mostly out of curiosity, because it was a new thing. People had heard about Protestantism, but only as something very remote. One would hear it said that there were people of other religions, but we never thought that we would meet them. Still, the criticism against those who read the Bible and those who were showing hospitality to the missionaries was very strong right from the start. There was no way that it was going to pass unnoticed because many people took it upon themselves to take messages to the priests saying that certain people were getting involved in other religions. And the priests delivered a lot of sermons that were no more than tirades against the Protestants. It seems that God wanted it that way because it awakened a lot of interest in many people.

So Pastor Larson visited the homes where they had bought the Bible, and later he rented a house in El Cocuy. We heard that he was holding services in the house, and that you could hear singing coming from there, but we didn't know yet what a service was. His wife was with him, and she used to sing hymns in the services. When he invited us to one of the services, we went, and we continued going, although at first there were very few who went. Other people whom Larson had visited, those who were on the original list of Galdames, converted in the same manner.

After a short time the missionaries, Larson and his wife, started a small school. They were very good teachers, and the evangelical school at first was somewhat welcomed. But there were always the attacks, more and more frequent. They used to attack people who enrolled their children in the school, and also the children themselves. And later when the children would go on to the higher grades in the public schools, they were reproached by the teachers and also attacked by the other students. The other students would say to us, for example, "Devils! These are Devils!" and "Most Holy Virgin, protect us from the Protestants!" and other things like that. But those of us who knew the Gospel from the start, we would always talk about it no matter where we were. Because there was a lot of interest, and people were ready to discuss it, even if it was just to contradict us. One would talk with one's friends, with the field hands, and with lots of different people, because even if one wasn't talking about the *evangelio* they would always argue with you and laugh at you, some with ridicule in their voices, others because they were simply interested in asking about it, and others out of anger because you had another religion. They were always talking to you, and all that was a help in truly consecrating us in the *evangelio*.

In order to be a believer in those days, you really had to believe, you really had to accept the Gospel. You couldn't be mixed, because they themselves, the nonevangelicals, wouldn't allow it. You had to declare yourself definitely—either you were a part of the Lutheran church or you weren't.

During the early years of the church, it was attacked a lot, and continued to be attacked up until a few years ago. There was book burning, people were attacked, stoned, some of us were put in jail, and some Christians were sacrificed. Mostly during the time of La Violencia.

But the work of the Lord is not in vain, and many of those people who have attacked us have brought their children to study in our little *colegio* CELCO, which has always functioned in this town since the days of the missionaries, except for a few years during the time of La Violencia.

I and my brothers in the flesh, and also those in the faith, have suffered some things. For example, on one occasion during the time of La Violencia, some people arrived at our house before dawn. We saw that they had not come to look for arms, but to look for books. They took some books with them after having killed my brother and wounded me. They also took me and another brother and some companions away. In the entrance to the jail they burned the books they had taken from our house, and when the smoke went up they said, "It smells like Protestants—that smoke smells like Protestants."

They persecuted me. I came home one day. Most of the time I was hiding out, I was always fleeing from them so that they wouldn't kill me. When I got home that day I found that they had taken all the books out of my room and strewn them all around. Some of them had gone, but others had stayed behind hidden behind a wall. I was writing a letter to send to Bogotá, telling about what they had done with the books, when the police who had been hidden came out. They asked me if my name was Graciliano Azucena, and I told them yes. They asked me, "Are those your books?" I told them yes. They spoke to me with very coarse words, saying, "You have to come with us and bring those wicked books." So they picked up some books, some Bibles and commentaries, and they took me down to town. When we arrived in town they told me I had to go to the rectory. The mayor was there. He met me in the doorway of the rectory and he said, "Oh, you're the Protestant?" And I told him yes, and he called the priest right away, and a priest came out whom I had never seen before. I said hello to him, but he didn't respond. Instead he said to me, "Are you the owner of these damn things?" And I asked him, "What damn things?" And he said "These damn books. Don't you know that they are forbidden?" I told him, no, that this is the Bible and it's sold anywhere. You can get it in Bogotá. And he said, "But don't you know that it's prohibited, that you don't understand it? Don't you know that you shouldn't be doing that?" And with a good deal of fury he called the other priest, who already knew me, and when he came out he said to him, "Look at the Protestant." The other priest hardly paid attention to him, but instead said to me, "Hello, Azucenito, it seems strange to me that you're getting into these things. One swallow does not the summer make. Why are you messing with that? Come over here." So I went over to where he was, and they started to examine the books. And a policeman grabbed a Martin Luther's catechism, and said, "Look, it's Martin Luther, the one that used to steal the nuns and married nuns. Look, that man was so evil, and right here it says 'Martin Luther.'" I had the urge to answer him, so I said, "Yes, that's a catechism written by Martin Luther, but if you know the word of God, look, I'll show you. Here is the Lord's prayer, and here are other explanations of the Holy Scriptures, which is the word of God." Then the mayor grabbed a text on which was portrayed a cathedral, and he said, "Look at this cathedral, they're probably planning to put a bomb in it." And it went on like that, and finally the priest asked me if it were true that I had a piano. I told him no, I didn't have a piano. And the policeman said, "That's buried up there with the other little priest," making reference to my brother whom they had killed earlier up at my house. Then I couldn't stand it any longer, and with anger and fury I answered him, "If that's why you've brought me here, why don't you go ahead and murder me, right here in the patio of the rectory. If it's for that that you've brought me here, I'm ready. If for the word of God you want to kill me, go ahead and do it." Then the priest made a sign that they should shut up. So then some of the police withdrew, and one policeman struck a match and started to burn some books, but finally the priest made a sign that he shouldn't burn any more.

And one of the things that preoccupies me a lot is this: About three years ago I was in the veterinary drugstore that I own, and a priest came in and asked me if I was Graciliano, and I said yes. He said, "Look, they tell me that you sell Bibles here, and it's that we're having a meeting, we've been having them all week in the rectory, and I want the people to buy Bibles. Could you send me some Bibles at about 7 o'clock tonight?" I told him yes, and that if he wished I could bring them myself. So some of the evangelicals and myself went, we brought the Bibles, and after the priest had spoken to the people he asked them who had Bibles. He asked them that, and then he said, "How can you know Christ if you don't know the word of God?" Then after he had talked some more about the importance of the Bible, he called to me to bring the Bibles and sell them. And this took place in the same patio of the same rectory where before I had been attacked for selling Bibles, and for having a

Bible, by order of the priests. And later by order of another priest, there I was selling the Bible in the same place. So I have seen that truly, when one fulfills the Gospel, one can only triumph. When one no longer triumphs in things it's because we have gotten away from doing the will of God.

The role of the Catholic clergy in fueling anti-Liberal sentiment, and the status of Liberals as stepchildren of the Catholic church, was reiterated by other evangelicals. An elderly campesino, Don Pedro Merino, who is also a longtime member of the Lutheran church in El Cocuy, explained why more Liberals than Conservatives accepted the *evangelio*:

Back in the days when I still attended mass, I heard the priest say from the pulpit that by the mere fact of being a Liberal you were already body and soul in hell, and the fact of being a Conservative you were already body and soul in heaven. That's why terrible things would happen. If the Conservatives killed a Liberal they had gained heaven. We Liberals were the bastard children of the Roman church. But even as a Liberal you had to continue to be a Catholic and obey the clergy or you'd be damned. People have a natural instinct, an inclination to look for salvation, to look for God, and since there wasn't any other church, we were stuck with the Catholics. There weren't any other religions around. So we tolerated it even though they shouted insults at us.

In earlier times, the campesinos in El Cocuy had a very real fear of excommunication. As a prominent lawyer in the town, who himself is not evangelical, recounted:

In those days the Roman Catholic priests had a method of frightening the people, and that was excommunication. The guy whom they excommunicated did not even deserve to live in society, and no one would accept him because they knew that he was already body and soul, from this life onward, in hell. And actually, you could see how those people began to decay, because everybody began to look badly upon them and no one wanted to have anything to do with them, and they would stop helping them in every way. Then the priests would say from the pulpit, "You see what excommunication does to you? There you have it, now you see how it is."

The divisions and animosities between Liberals and Conservatives, and between evangelical and Catholic, affect the dead as well as the living. There are at present three cemeteries in El Cocuy: the Catholic one in the center of town, a lay cemetery on the outskirts, and the evangelical cemetery up in the *campo*. The priests tried to refuse the burial of Liberals in the Catholic cemetery, so the lay cemetery was founded by the grandfather of the prominent lawyer just quoted. The evangelicals were in the same straits, and so a bit of rocky property was donated by one of Teófilo's sons way up in the countryside for evangelical burials. The situation has changed substantially, however, and in 1983, when an elderly woman who was a devout evangelical died, her funeral was held in the Catholic church and she was interred in the Catholic cemetery. Although this woman had attended evangelical services faithfully for many years along with her daughters, her eldest son was an aspiring *político*, and it was he who made the decision to have her buried from the Catholic church. The Catholic priest took the opportunity to make the point that although people may stray from the fold and enjoy the company of the evangelicals, in the end there is only one church, the Catholic church, to which everyone was born and to which everyone must return.

Needless to say, the evangelicals were not pleased by the decision. Pastor Graciliano, whose account of persecution during La Violencia is quoted earlier, saw the situation as a good lesson for Cipriano, the young vicar, whose attitude toward the Catholics had been much more open and friendly. Graciliano said that it was good for him to learn what it was like to suffer at the hands of the Catholics, because he was too young to remember La Violencia. Cipriano's ecumenical bent, his budding friendship with a radical young Catholic priest, and his receptivity to the incorporation of evangelical young people into the Catholic youth group illustrate the attitude of younger evangelicals, which is very much at odds with the older generation, who lived through La Violencia.

✛

CONCLUSION

Stories of persecution during La Violencia could fill several volumes. In addition to my examples, Flora (1976) has also documented the experience of Pentecostals during this period. The tensions between Liberals and Conservatives, culminating (but not ending) in the warfare of La Violencia, along with the opposition of the Conservative-identified Catholic clergy to their Liberal parishioners are important to understanding the early growth of Colombian evangelicalism. As an initial step toward developing an explanation of the spectacular growth rate of the movement, which is based on the level of social process within households, the following points derived from the foregoing discussion must be stressed: (1) the Catholic church in Colombia was and is extremely powerful; (2) conversion to Protestantism was a drastic step requiring enormous commitment; (3) conversion separated people from the mainstream and allowed for the development of an ethos divergent from the norm. I would emphasize the fact that much of the Catholic church's involvement in the lives of individuals (as designated in the Concordat) concerned matters relating to the family: marriage, baptism of children, and education. The evangelical convert rejected the hegemony of the Catholic hierarchy over these affairs, and this allowed for a new system of regulation to flourish, one that was grounded more in individual responsibility; (4) the retreat of foreign missionaries during La Violencia allowed for the "Colombianization" of evangelical churches to an extent not previously realized; (5) persecution forced evangelical activity out of the public realm and reinforced its identification with the household.

It is no coincidence that the greatest growth rate in Colombian evangelical history coincided with the enforced establishment of the household as the incubator for new congregations. Nor is an explanation of this phenomenon based on anomie and cultural disruption sufficient. If we confine our analysis to examining how national and even local-level political events affected evangelical growth, we miss some of the prime motivating forces behind conversion. The fact that evangelical religion in Colombia was jolted out of its relative stagnation during its closest association with the household is yet another indicator that a focus on household-level activity will be fruitful in understanding conversion.

✛ 4 ✛

El Cocuy: Colombian Evangelicalism on the Community Level

✛

RURAL LIFE IN URBAN COLOMBIA

In Bogotá I was told that I would never understand the Colombian situation until I had traveled to the countryside. The converse would be true if I had started my fieldwork in a rural area, as I did in an earlier research project.[1] I would not have understood what was happening there until I had gone to the city. Rural and urban as categories in contemporary Colombia are less than discrete—in the thriving city of Ibague in the Magdalena Valley, cows graze from garbage cans attached to lightposts in the center of town. In Bogotá itself, carts drawn by burros are a not uncommon, if a somewhat incongruous, sight. Despite a great deal of urban sprawl, as one travels toward the perimeters of the city, urban zones seem to dissolve quite suddenly into *campo* (the Spanish term for rural countryside, which in Colombia, tends to be quite rugged and underdeveloped rather than benign and pastoral). Lacking are the suburban zones buffering the transition from city to countryside that typify the geography of the U.S. landscape.

A high rate of rural-urban migration has transformed Colombia from a predominantly rural country to a predominantly urban one in the space of forty years. In 1938 about 70 percent of the country's population lived in rural areas, while by 1973, 60 percent of the people were living in urban areas (Mohan 1980:10).[2]

This means that most city dwellers have spent their formative years in the *campo*, and they have been faced with the task of adapting the values and behavior patterns of the countryside to city life. This process has been no simple shedding of the old skin, but rather has resulted in a kind of amalgam of rural and urban. The relatively tiny percentage of people who think of themselves as "true" Bogotanos—those whose families have been urban for several generations—display a degree of cosmopolitanism that sets them off from the masses. For many city dwellers, the countryside is idealized as a sort of enchanted place—

despite the fact that numbers of people were driven out of their villages by the horrors of violence and rural poverty. There the milk is pure, the food is nutritious and abundant, the people are wholesome, healthy, and honest. Although the work is hard it is seen as rewarding; there is no need to pay for entertainment when the performance of one's daily duties carries as compensation the excitement of seeing a calf born, or of riding a horse up mountain trails, or simply of existing in a landscape of astounding beauty.

✚
CHOICE OF EL COCUY
AS THE RURAL FIELD SITE

I took the advice about visiting the countryside to be sound, and, conveniently, it corresponded to my original research plans. Selecting the appropriate site for the rural part of the study was a complicated process, which I discuss in the Appendix. After about six months in Bogotá, during which time I had also traveled to other areas, I became acquainted with some evangelicals who talked a great deal about a town called El Cocuy, in the northern reaches of the neighboring department of Boyacá. El Cocuy was the incubator for the Lutheran church in Colombia. The original Lutheran missionary activity took place there in the 1930s, and the Bogotá church was formed as the result of numbers of families migrating to the city to escape the violence in El Cocuy in the early 1950s. Three other evangelical groups were established in El Cocuy after La Violencia: the United Pentecostal church, the Trinitarian Pentecostal church, and the Church of Branham. The family of the wife of the pastor of the Bogotá Lutheran church still lived in El Cocuy, and this generous woman facilitated my move to the town.

El Cocuy intrigued me for several other reasons. First, Boyacá is the department that has contributed the greatest number of migrants to Bogotá. To understand Bogotá, one must understand Boyacá. Second, the perhaps most famous ethnographic study of Colombian peasants was carried out by Orlando Fals-Borda in that department in the 1950s. Although other parts of Colombia have been investigated by anthropologists and rural sociologists since that time (notably the Department of Valle de Cauca), virtually no other study of Boyacá has been published since Fals-Borda's (1962). Finally, from what I had been told, El Cocuy seemed geographically remote. It is high up in the eastern cordillera, a good distance from any central roads, still overwhelmingly agricultural, and hence a place where I might encounter some remnant of a more "traditional" Colombia. I wanted to see what the evangelical experience was like in such a place. Much has been written connecting conversion to the anomie of modernization, the dislocation of peasants migrating to cities, and the experience of people who are marginal to a larger system; it intrigued me that a church existed in an area where none of these factors were present.

I lived in El Cocuy from April through December of 1983. El Cocuy's history in many ways makes it unique among Colombian towns. The experience of evangelicals in the community is also somewhat different from much of what has been written concerning the backgrounds of Protestant converts in Latin America. An examination of some of these differences and how they articulate with the wider movement provides a fresh perspective on conversion in Latin America.

✚

DESCRIPTION OF THE TOWN

The small highland Andean community of El Cocuy, Boyacá, lies 480 kilometers (298 miles) to the north of Bogotá, and is connected to the capital city by regular bus service over mostly unpaved roads. A local police department information sheet estimates that the population of the municipality of El Cocuy was 18,000 in February 1983: 3,500 in the town itself and 14,500 in the nine outlying rural neighborhoods, or veredas. Similar figures were cited in much older documents, and town officials vacillated a great deal when asked to estimate the current population of the municipality. The 1973 national census figures are quite different, counting the total population to be 6,569, with 2,595 in the town and 3,974 in the outlying veredas. Without a doubt El Cocuy has experienced a dramatic depopulation, and out-migration continues. The lower figures seem more accurate at present, and perhaps the higher figures of the police department (which I believe derive from an unrevised estimate of a much earlier time) indicate the severity of the population loss.[3]

The economy of El Cocuy is agricultural; potatoes, wheat, corn, and beans are the main crops. The raising of cows for dairy products and meat, and sheep for wool and meat, also constitutes a major source of income. The town itself is 2,749 meters above sea level (slightly over

9,000 feet) and has a cold climate, averaging 13 degrees centigrade (55 degrees Fahrenheit). The mountains that surround the town reach altitudes above 5,000 meters (over 16,000 feet). One of the most extensive ranges of snow-capped peaks in Colombia, the Sierra Nevada del Cocuy, Chita y Guicán, is located a few hours from the center of population, and in the summer months of December and January a few hardy tourists visit the area.

The *cabecera* (head town) of El Cocuy lies cradled in the palm of a small highland valley, with the mountains sloping sharply upward all around it. The majority of houses in town are built in the colonial style. The exterior façades of the houses face the street as one continuous wall, each house distinguished from its neighbors only by slight variations in the painting of details and doors, or in upkeep. Almost all of the roofs are made of clay tile in various states of decrepitude. Glass-paned windows are almost nonexistent. My house, which had been constructed in recent years, was one of the few that could claim such luxury, and visitors constantly exclaimed about how *"abrigadita"* (warm; *abrigo* means overcoat) my house was. Other houses had windows closed off with wooden shutters. With the open central courtyards that typify older houses, the spacious but drafty rooms are rarely comfortable, and people sleep under many heavy woolen blankets.

The *cabecera* of El Cocuy is marked at the north end (the entrance) by the small hospital and at the south end by the high school. Such head towns are defined in the national census as "urban," which presumably has to do with settlement density, since their flavor is much more that of the countryside than of the city. Although in comparison with the jagged mountains that rise above it and descend below it, the *cabecera* rests in a level valley, many of the streets are sharply inclined, and hence the town can be divided into several upper and lower sections. The government offices of the municipality, including the mayor's office, local judges' offices, and the registry, are housed together in the upper section of the town. The Catholic church dominates the central plaza in the lower part of town.

Several developments in the past three years or so have altered the town's appearance. Directly in front of the Catholic church a lighted basketball court has recently been constructed. During the past few years, the weekly market has been relocated from the central plaza to a large, covered, open-air shed, constructed especially for that purpose. A cement butcher house with tiled counters was built adjacent to the market.

The relocation of the market was part of a plan to improve the appearance of the town. The center plaza underwent a beautification effort for the regional provincial fiestas of December, 1982, which El Cocuy hosted. Cement benches were built, each bearing an inscription of the name of the local personage or Cocuyano colony in various distant cities who donated money for the materials. Low cement walls were built to define paths across the square, and flowerbeds were put in. Construction was still under way when I left the field, and one project was a lighted fountain contributed by the colony of El Cocuy migrants in Bogotá. In fact, a recent photograph shows that a scale replica of the Sierra Nevada has been built on that spot.

The town has electricity and running water, although both are erratic. In the 1980s about sixteen houses or stores had telephones, but most people placed calls to distant cities from the national telegraph office, TELECOM, and it was more often the case than not that "no hay línea para Bogotá" (there's no line to Bogotá). When it was possible to get through, a five-minute call to Bogotá cost about 130 pesos ($1.60). Although there were three doctors in the town, their ministrations were usually limited to prescribing antibiotics, and for any serious illness the person was sent to the departmental capital of Tunja or, more likely, to Bogotá. New medical school graduates who are performing their *año rural* (rural year of service required to get a license to practice medicine in Colombia) staff the hospital clinic. Anyone who can afford to, and certainly anyone who travels to Bogotá regularly, has medical needs attended to in the city. Medical emergencies are terrible crises in El Cocuy—people frantically try to arrange for transportation of the sick or wounded to Bogotá, all the time wondering if they are strong enough to withstand the rigors of the journey. Although the hospital has an ambulance that was bought for this purpose, it disappeared soon after its purchase and was said to be "in the shop" for the entire nine months I lived in El Cocuy.

About fifty years ago, El Cocuy was first connected to the lowlands by a road that winds down in a seemingly endless series of hairpin turns to Capitanejo, in the Department of Santander. This road, which is fifty-three kilometers (thirty-three miles) long, was constructed without the benefit of machinery, entirely with picks and human labor. Local people say that the road was made "con las uñas" (with the fingernails). Before the construction of this road, loads of potatoes and other produce destined for market were hauled by men and burros over the high mountains on rough paths.

Most Cocuyanos express love for their town and its exceptional beauty, notwithstanding how many leave for the ugly urban sprawl of Bogotá—a fact that may partly explain their continuing ties to their hometown. The exodus of people that began with La Violencia has left visible reminders. In the *campo* there are numbers of empty houses that are falling down. At the time of my fieldwork there was considerable discussion among local people about developing tourism in the area. Various plans to obtain money from the government tourist agency to build a hotel were hotly debated—the exact location, the price of the land, the design and contracting of the building were a favorite topic of conversation among the town activists. Tourist facilities at the time were nonexistent. The sad "hotels" that put up the bus drivers who ended their trips in El Cocuy and the occasional stalwart European or American visitor to the Sierra Nevada consisted of a few bare rooms behind a greasy kitchen. The town offered nothing that could be expected to meet the needs of tourists.

Unfortunately, the fundamental problem with developing tourism in El Cocuy was not the lack of comfortable accommodations, but something much less easy to solve: few people were willing to make the twelve- to fourteen-hour bus trip over mostly unpaved roads to enjoy the splendors of the scenery. Bus travel was dangerous as well as arduous. There are cases of entire buses being held up by bandits in the isolated mountain passes, and buses are also the center of attention for thieves, who will relieve passengers of possessions should their vigilance stray for a moment. There are also, of course, terrible accidents on the perilous roads. Although some people made the journey in private cars (always jeeps), the condition of the roads was very destructive to vehicles and, in a country where cars are scarce and highly valued, the few people lucky enough to own them were usually unwilling to subject their prize possessions to such abuse.

Most nights, and sometimes during the day, the town is submerged in clouds. At 9,000 feet (about 2,700 meters), El Cocuy is one of the highest towns in Colombia. The snow-covered range lies some distance from town, and during the rainy season it is almost constantly hidden by clouds. The snow line lies several thousand feet higher than the town, and breathing is very difficult at that altitude. The whole area is extremely well watered: gushing rivers and waterfalls and little streams are everywhere. Mud is also very abundant. Local people are accustomed to traveling most places on foot. Even for horses the terrain is difficult to negotiate, and it is sometimes safer to walk than to risk breaking a horse's leg or suffering a bad fall on the steep, rocky mountain paths.[4]

The lands around El Cocuy are said to have been very fertile, although in recent years the use of chemical fertilizers and pesticides reportedly has had an adverse effect on productivity. Local people blame the government for failing to control the quality of fertilizers sold to farmers. They claim that the fertilizers brought in burn the natural fertility out of the land and leave it sterile after a year or two. An evangelical view of this situation is that an increase in crop diseases followed La Violencia as God's punishment of the people for having burned crops and store-rooms full of grain.

The mayor of El Cocuy is much respected by local evangelicals, even though he is not evangelical or a native of the town. As was the practice prior to constitutional reforms in 1991, he was not elected by the town's citizens but rather appointed by the governor of the department.

He has considerable power. For example, he decides the schedule for irrigation and sets prices for milk and meat for local sale. His presence is very much felt in the town, primarily because of a powerful loud-speaker set up in his office in the municipal headquarters. It is rarely silent.[5] Most of the time it blares music, but this is interrupted by fre-quent mayoral messages to the general population, especially on Fridays (market days) and prior to major holidays or special community events.

One of the mayor's innovations was to require the citizenry to sweep the streets in front of their houses each Sunday and Wednesday night. This ruling applied to all streets within the perimeters of the town, whether paved or not. Failure to comply meant a fine, which at one time consisted of a bag of cement to be used in the project to improve the town's central plaza. Moreover, the guilty party would be summoned, by means of the loudspeaker, to the mayor's office, thus publicly announc-ing the crime. The mayor himself would often accompany the troop of men who made the rounds early on Monday and Thursday mornings to collect the little piles of trash that had been dutifully swept up by the residents. It was not uncommon for his ferocious banging on the door to awaken any laggard who at 6:00 A.M. had not managed to sweep in front of the house. The mayor pledged to the town (over the loudspeaker) that it was his duty "to God and to country" to see that El Cocuy was clean and orderly. In fact, compared to many other towns in rural Colombia, El Cocuy appears immaculate. The façades of ancient houses that are falling in on themselves are neatly whitewashed, at least the part that faces the street. El Cocuy was entered in the "Pueblo más lindo de Bo-yacá" (Most Beautiful Town in Boyacá) contest in 1983, and leading up to the anticipated visit by the judging commitee, the mayor exhorted the populace almost constantly over the loudspeaker, ordering citizens to remove every blade of grass growing through the cracks in the cement or between the cobblestones that paved the streets in front of their houses. All their efforts came to nothing because the judging committee never appeared in town. They apparently were "indefinitely delayed" in a town lower down, after allegedly getting drunk and not being able to proceed further. El Cocuy finally did win the contest in 1985.

Evangelicals were very proud of this progress-minded and disciplined mayor and were concerned that the newly appointed Conservative governor of Boyacá would remove him from office. The political involvement of evangelicals at the community level is discussed below.

Male and Female Occupations

In the countryside, men are occupied with farming and the raising of livestock. Few men have not spent some time outside of El Cocuy working as wage laborers. At the present time, most families have kin connections to an urban area, usually Bogotá, and younger people often leave, either temporarily or permanently, to live with their urban relatives while they study. Later they find work in the city. In the town of El Cocuy, many men are occupied in "middleman" business dealings, buying and reselling agricultural produce and livestock.

Probably the majority of women in the municipality of El Cocuy, certainly those who live in the outlying rural neighborhoods, are farm wives. They are engaged in the ceaseless activities required of women as their contribution to the household economy. A major task is cooking, especially when day laborers are hired for major farming tasks such as plowing, weeding, or the harvest. Cooking the five meals, which in addition to approximately two hundred pesos constitute the pay of a day laborer, and transporting the food to the field where the work is being done is an enormous job and one of the key contributions women make to production. Food processing, such as shucking corn, baking bread, making cheese, butter, *cuajada* (the milk curd that is a staple food in the countryside), and *chicha* (a mildly fermented corn beer that is traditionally provided for the workers), is a labor-intensive activity. A number of gasoline-operated grinding mills now function in the town, so women no longer have to use the traditional *mano y metate* to grind grain, but these worn stones are still evident around rural households and the *metates* are now used for slopping pigs or other animals.

Rural women also spin wool to be taken to weavers to be made into blankets or *ruanas*. An especially valued gray yarn characteristic of the region is called *entripulada*. It is made by blending the wool of black and white sheep by pulling apart the fibers with the fingers. The time-consuming labor of scrubbing clothes by hand on cement scrubboards occupies women in both the countryside and in town. Milking is often a woman's job, although men also milk, and traveling to whatever distant mountainside the cows are pastured on makes the task an especially tiring one. Rural women also keep chickens and pigs, and the income from these ventures is often their own to do with as they wish. Given the fact that male support of the household may be erratic, women usually use these funds to pay school fees for their children or to buy them the uniforms or supplies they need.

In town, women engage in a range of occupations. Many women run small stores. The stores that double as cafes more often belong to women than to men. The larger general stores in town are run by men, with their wives (and children) assisting. The two drugstores in town are run by women, one by a doctor's wife and the other by a woman who also serves as a midwife. Both women also prescribe drugs and give injections. The Institute of Family Welfare day care center is run and staffed by women, and there are numbers of female teachers in both the elementary and the secondary schools. The switchboard at the Telecom office is run by both female and male employees, and many of the clerks in municipal offices are women. The largest percentage of market vendors of fruits and vege-tables and of prepared foods are women, while the meat stalls are run almost entirely by men.

There are a few women who occupy important formal public roles. There is a female judge in town, and a woman who is head of the Insti-tute of Family Welfare is also very active in local politics, serving on a number of committees and on the municipal council. Among the evan-gelical women, the most prominent are Doña Lucía, who holds no for-mal office but is politically involved (see below), and her adopted sister, Marta, who is the director of the Lutheran primary school and also fills the role usually occupied by "pastor's wife" in the Lutheran church.

Many of the occupations that women pursue are of a part-time nature, and they identify themselves primarily as *amas de casa* (housewives) when asked their profession. Poorer women offer their services as part-time domestic servants, and many women work as seamstresses or bake small rolls or make sweets or cheeses for resale in the local stores to supplement the family income.

✠
EARLY HISTORY OF EL COCUY

In 1540 or 1542 Hernán Pérez de Quezada and one hundred soldiers passed through what is now El Cocuy looking for the "Casa del Sol." Some accounts recognize this event as the founding of El Cocuy. Other accounts state that the town was founded by German conquistadores

Federman, Jorge Spira, and Ambrosio Alfinger, who came over the mountains with an expedition from Venezuela. A good number of people in the area are tall and fair-skinned, with blue eyes and blond or red hair. It is rare that people are able to trace their ancestry back more than a few generations, and people of this physical type are not distinguished in any other way from other campesinos. In fact, a family with several children whose looks more closely approximate the "Indian" type that prevails in Colombia—that is, dark eyes and hair, trigueño (wheat-colored) skin, and shorter stature—frequently also has a mono (blond or fair one). It is believed by local people that this atypical physical type is the heritage of the German conquistadores.

It is generally agreed that the early conquistadores encountered a tribe known as the Laches, who were part of the Chibcha. According to local history, rather than become slaves of the oppressors, the native population committed collective suicide, throwing themselves off of a high peak, which today bears the name El Peñón de los Muertos (the Cliff of the Dead).[6] The first night that they spent in the region, the conquerers noticed a strange light illuminating the banks of the river that flowed down from the snow-capped peaks. They discovered that this phosphorescent light came from fireflies, which bore the aboriginal name chochue; Hispanized it became cocuyo. From this came the name of the town.

In the beginning El Cocuy was a small hamlet that served as a rest stop for those who were traveling to the salt mines of Las Salinas, the major source of salt for the entire northern region, especially Santander. In 1673 the parish of El Cocuy was founded and the church was constructed.

In the first half of the seventeenth century, El Cocuy was divided into a three-tiered class system. The jailudos, or upper class, lived in the town and owned vast expanses of land, which provided them with the income to support an elite life-style that included trips to Europe, the purchase of fine imported goods, and a social life embellished by fancy dress balls and string orchestras. The small middle class comprised mostly artisans, who also lived in town but were not wealthy. The majority of people, the campesinos, inhabited the outlying rural areas and made their living by working the lands of the elite in combination with small private plots they were able to acquire and by raising livestock.

El Cocuy has produced a number of distinguished native sons, the most significant being General Santos Gutiérrez, who was the president of Colombia from 1868 to 1870.

During this century, the town has undergone a complete change in its class structure. The upper class sold its property and began to leave, preferring life in the capital, and those who remained by the late 1940s were driven out by La Violencia. As a Liberal town in the center of a Conservative region, El Cocuy was particularly hard hit.[7] Oquist, in his comprehensive analysis of La Violencia (1980), uses El Cocuy and its Conservative neighbors as "a particularly important case study" of the role of traditional village rivalries and vendetta fighting in fueling the fires of violence. What remained of the upper class left during the late 1940s and early 1950s, as did large numbers of individuals and families from the countryside. The epoch of La Violencia marked the beginning of a surge of out-migration, which has continued until the present. Most have gone to Bogotá, but there are colonies of Cocuyanos in other urban centers.

Such emigration had several effects. First, land became plentiful and relatively cheap, making it possible for the campesinos who remained in El Cocuy to accumulate moderate-sized to extensive holdings. Some individuals of campesino origins have become quite economically successful, mainly through cattle raising. Second, there has been an acute labor shortage. Lands that used to be cultivated have been converted into pasture, since cattle raising requires much less labor input. Third, people in El Cocuy have developed networks that provide various benefits for both the rural-based and the urban-based branches of extended kin units. (A similar pattern has been identified in Peru by Bourque and Warren [1981].)

✛

RELIGION IN EL COCUY

The vast majority of Cocuyanos, like Colombians elsewhere, are Catholic. Catholic feast days are public events that engage most of the community. Processions of the decorated saints through town on their holy days are still focal points for the community. The month of May, which is dedicated to the Virgin Mary, is marked by special masses, the daily ringing of the church bells, and fireworks. Corpus Christi day, which is celebrated on June 2, is a major community event. Special *arcos* (arches) are constructed around the central plaza, each arch the responsibility of a different rural neighborhood or community organization (such as a school). These arches are elaborately decorated with foodstuffs, such as strings of potatoes, bananas, and specially decorated breads. Also mixed in are store-bought items such as bars of drinking chocolate or even a jar of Tang. The arches are also decorated with boughs and flowers, and hanging from some are cages of birds or wild animals such as foxes. In earlier times, it was explained to me, the animals were killed and hung from the arches, but the government has forbidden this practice. The priest proceeds around the plaza, saying prayers at each arch. He is followed by the local band. Many fireworks are set off. I was unable to get any explanation of this event beyond the response that it is "traditional." This may have to do with the fact that evangelicals refused to admit that they knew anything about it, and Catholics, identifying me with the evangelicals, were reluctant to appear "backward" in my eyes.

Another major Catholic procession occurs on the day of the Virgin of Carmen, the patron saint of drivers. Car and truck owners move in procession around the streets behind the priest and the image of Carmen, ending in the plaza in front of the church. There, the priest sprinkles holy water on the hoods of the vehicles and blesses them. Needless to say, the two evangelicals in town who owned vehicles did not participate in this ceremony, and, in fact, they mildly ridiculed this blessing of inanimate objects as typical of the misplacement of Catholic faith.

The history of Catholic-evangelical relations in El Cocuy and the role of politics in religious affiliation were elaborated on in chapter 3. It is important to reiterate that El Cocuy is unusual in the region in being primarily a Liberal town. Despite the severe persecution during La Violencia and the much milder harassment at present, evangelicalism has managed to endure as a minor but established religion in El Cocuy for the past fifty years. In contrast, nearby Conservative communities, such as Guicán and El Espino, have tolerated no evangelical presence to speak of.

At the time of my fieldwork in 1983, four evangelical groups existed in El Cocuy. As mentioned at the beginning of this chapter, the oldest and most enduring influence has been that of the Lutherans. The Pentecostal churches, which are split along unitarian/trinitarian lines, began in the early 1970s. The Church of Branham is a more recent development.

I attended services in all four of the churches, interviewed their pastors and members, and spent time in their homes. Both because of my contacts and because of its predominance in the town, the bulk of my work was carried out with the Lutheran church.

There is some integration among the churches; occasionally Pentecostals will attend services at the Lutheran church. The Pentecostals have a great deal of respect for the Lutherans and especially for the quality of the primary school, where they send their children to study and get "a Christian education." I will briefly describe two of the three smaller evangelical churches before going into more detail about the Lutherans. The Branham church had only a few members, and will not be described here.

The United Pentecostal Church

The IPU does not like to leave pastors in their home towns, because, as it was explained to me, "people there remember how badly one acted before one converted." The pastor and his wife are both from outside of El Cocuy: he is from the Eastern Plains and she is from the coast. They have been assigned to the congregation in El Cocuy for two years and are still finding it difficult to adjust to life in the highlands. Since they are both from hot, flat regions, the environment in El Cocuy is a real change for them and they are somewhat depressed by the situation. The food is unfamiliar and making the rounds requires exhausting climbs up and down the mountains. They have three preschool children, the older two of whom spend the entire day, from 7:30 to 5:00, in the day care center run by the Institute of Family Welfare. This pattern is endorsed by both husband and wife. The little living space they occupy in a house that they share with another couple and the chapel is extremely neat and the children are clean and beautifully dressed.

The pastor counts about sixty members in the area, including those who attend services at the little chapel in their house in town and those who gather at members' houses in the distant rural neighborhoods. The IPU in El Cocuy was founded around 1971. The IPU is suffering from the same problem in membership that the Lutherans complain about. Although the goal is to build membership—and in the IPU especially, the number of souls he wins is the standard by which a successful pastor is judged—emigration to Bogotá is keeping the numbers low. The pastor complains that a family will join and be active in the church for a while, but after a time the whole family pulls up stakes and moves to Bogotá. The loss of entire families at one blow is badly felt by the small church.

The Trinitarian Pentecostal Church

The Trinitarian Pentecostal church was founded on February 13, 1972. At the present time, it is loosely affiliated with the Assemblies of God, receiving periodic visits from Colombian missionaries of the Assemblies. At one time the church had an active membership of about thirty people, but because of migration, the membership has fallen to about eighteen or twenty. For the past three years they have been without a permanent pastor, and the members take responsibility for conducting the services themselves.

Members recounted stories of persecution in recent years. One story involves an evangelical wedding that was performed around 1976, which was disrupted by an angry man. The female judge who was present at the ceremony called the man in the next day and fined him so that he would stop harassing the evangelicals. Another man commissioned the local fireworks maker to make some bombs for him to kill the evangelicals, but, as the story goes, he was later killed when he slipped on a rock and fell down a mountain path.

The Trinitarians are perhaps the strictest group in terms of behavioral standards. Women are not allowed to wear pants, earrings, necklaces, or makeup. Men are forbidden to drink, smoke, play billiards or *naipes* (a card game), or use vulgar language. Dancing is not permitted, and, although members can watch television and listen to the radio, they are urged to be selective about the programs: soap operas, love songs, and other secular music are not permissible. Christian radio programs and cassettes are available, and are approved.

These strict behavioral codes are motivated by the desire of church members to "present a living testimony." Trinitarian Pentecostals emphasized how their behavior set them apart from others in the community, of whom they were very critical. They are concerned that others notice their behavior and believe that the "good impression" that each member makes will attract people to the Gospel. Accompanying this attitude is the belief that one should be hospitable to one's neighbors. "That's how you conquer humanity," said one man. "Show them affection, gratitude, friendship, hospitality." It is interesting that, despite strict codes of asceticism, Trinitarians are still intensely social in their orientation and eager to participate in community life as long as it is "wholesome." I will develop this point further in a discussion of the peculiarities of Colombian evangelical asceticism vis-à-vis the notion of "otherworldliness," which has usually been associated with ascetic religions.

A married couple now occupies the house in town that belongs to the mission. Since they are filling in for the pastor, the mission offered to pay their utilities, but they refused because they did not want problems with the other members. Pedro is a native of El Cocuy, and his wife, Consuelo, is from the neighboring town of Guicán. He is forty-two years old and converted in Bogotá at age thirty. His wife converted two days after him. Pedro's father was murdered during La Violencia, and his mother married a man who did not treat the family well. He has had only two years of formal education, his wife, three. Pedro did his obligatory military service from 1960 to 1962, and married in the Catholic church shortly after coming out of the army. He lived in Bogotá for a year and a half, but he could not get accustomed to it, so he returned to El Cocuy. He owns no property in El Cocuy and makes his living through a variety of strategies. He runs an uncle's farm and rents some land on which he pastures livestock. He works as a middleman, traveling around in the countryside buying livestock (pigs, goats, sheep, and occasionally cows or horses) for resale in the weekly market. The couple has four children ranging in age from eleven to seventeen. The oldest two are studying in Bogotá.

According to Consuelo, the Gospel has worked a miraculous change in Pedro's life. Before he converted, he was a cruel man who drank heavily, beat her, and was having difficulty supporting his family: "When we were recently married we weren't Christians—we were unconverted. And then the home was a disaster area, because we didn't understand each other [no nos comprendíamos], there wasn't affection, there wasn't friendship, there wasn't love or anything. Everything was a disaster."

By the time he left for Bogotá, right before he converted, she had decided to leave him, although she was very worried about how to support their children. Pedro's sister, who lived in Bogotá, was a convert. He reported that when she spoke to him about the Gospel he did not like it because he thought it was evil. But while he was in Bogotá he attended a service in her home.

I said to myself, well, out of decency I have to go and hear what those people have to say. And that night the Lord spoke to my heart and I saw the condition that I was walking around this world in. I acknowledged it, and I said to myself, the mistake of Catholic religion is that one isn't saved there. I said to myself, is that a religion? What happens is that in the evangelical church they teach one the Bible and they apply that to their lives, and in the Catholic church they don't teach you the Bible nor do they apply it.

Apparently, Pedro was already predisposed to the Gospel when he was cured of an illness:

According to the Bible it was impure spirits that I had. I went to have X-rays taken in Bogotá and Málaga, and eight doctors met there and nothing came of it—there were no results. Then my sister said to me, "Let's go to services and there you will be prayed for and you'll get better." And that's how it was, that night, thanks be to God. The pastor anointed me with oil and put his hand on my head and cried out to God. I felt something that went out of me from the mouth of my stomach, and I've never felt that pain again, nor will it come back. So then that was the basis for me to like the *evangelio* even better.

The unconverted members of both Pedro's and Consuelo's families criticized them sharply for converting. Only one brother refused to interfere. When the family spoke about "ridding Pedro of these evil customs," that is, his evangelical practice, the brother replied, "But what evil customs? Now he doesn't get drunk any more, nor does he smoke, nor does he fight, and he's responsible for his home . . . what do I have to say to him?" Pedro is gratified that people recognize an extraordinary change in him and believes he is providing a proper testimony to his family.

Pedro had been very interested in politics, and when he converted one of his main concerns was to see how the evangelicals conducted themselves around a presidential election. The pastor of the church announced that the day of the elections the church would be open from six in the morning, that people could come in to pray, and that "God, who knows the hearts of men," would elect the next president to govern the country. Pedro was very impressed that that was all he had said, because he remembered the priests dictating from the pulpit for whom people should vote. He claimed that the politicians would bribe the priests for their endorsements.

Pedro's experience with the gift of tongues seems to be limited to his stay in Bogotá. There the words of the tongues speaker would be interpreted by someone else who had the gift of prophecy. Pedro felt that this was a very useful gift specifically for admonishing the church or particular individuals who were walking in sin.

Another devout couple who belong to the Trinitarian Pentecostal church live in the distant rural neighborhood of Llano Grande. Francisco is a farmer renting land from a wealthy cousin. He also watches over the renters on neighboring farms of the same *patrón* and arranges for the marketing of the produce. The couple has been married for twenty-three years and they have seven children. They converted, more or less at the same time, in 1976. Both of them spoke about how conversion had transformed their married life. Inez said: "There didn't used to be understanding ["*no había habido comprensión*"], nor was there happiness in our home, and I used to say, 'Lord, how long will my life go on?' My husband used to get drunk a lot, and he'd spend everything that he had worked to earn, like we used to say, 'What is earned in one year is spent in one day.' "

Inez's phrasing is identical to Consuelo's, in terms of the former lack of understanding that conversion has corrected. This same phrasing is used pervasively by evangelical women. The significance of "mutual understanding" in evangelical households is developed in chapter 5.

All of the members recognize the need to evangelize in order to build up the church, but they feel hampered by the lack of a full-time pastor. There are a number of women, especially in the countryside, who members think are interested in attending but whose husbands are preventing them from doing so.

The Lutherans

Exact membership figures for the Lutheran church in El Cocuy are not available. I was told that the church records were among the books burned during La Violencia. The church council estimates that there are now about thirty members. During the best times there were well over one hundred, and many more "sympathizers" who attended periodically. During the past twenty years or so, the church has been losing two or three families every year to emigration to Bogotá.

An attempt has been made to reconstruct the records, and I had access to baptismal records from 1941 to 1983. These showed a total of 125 baptisms for those years. Unlike the Pentecostals, the Lutherans do not believe in rebaptism. Therefore, those who converted as adults (and had already been baptized in the Catholic church) would not appear in the baptismal records. The records of confirmations for some years from 1957 to 1978 showed a total of 130. According to these records, the people who were confirmed up until about 1965 had all been baptized as Catholics. After 1965 they were all baptized in the El Salvador church, which means that they are almost exclusively the sons and daughters of members.

✠

THE IMPACT OF FOREIGN MISSIONARIES IN EL COCUY: THE LUTHERAN CHURCH OF OUR SAVIOR

The first missionaries to the area, Andrew Larson and his wife, came to Colombia from Norway in the late 1930s. The Larsons entered an area that was completely dominated, in terms of both religious ideology and political influence, by a strong Roman Catholic church. One explanation for the presence of the Lutherans in Boyacá is that during the early days of missionary activity, the historical Protestant churches divided the territories among themselves, and the Lutherans drew Boyacá. The department has a reputation among evangelicals as being a difficult region to evangelize because most towns are dominated by the Conservative party, people are highly traditionalistic, and a particularly intransigent machismo flavors interpersonal relations. At the time of the Larsons' arrival in El Cocuy, local people were only vaguely aware that other religions (besides the Roman Catholic) existed. As noted earlier, the Larsons began their ministry by visiting the houses of people they knew had purchased Bibles. At that time, owning a Bible was sufficiently heretical (in the eyes of the Roman Catholic clergy) that these individuals could be expected to have a more open attitude toward religious ideas than was generally the case. The original list was provided by the Bible salesman who had visited the area earlier. It seems that the families who were positively disposed toward the message the visitors brought were those who harbored anticlerical feelings and were identified with the Liberal party. Other factors must also have come into play, since El Cocuy is a predominantly Liberal town, but not all Liberals converted. Party identification is important for a number of reasons (see chapter 3), and it is notable that the missionaries had no success whatsoever in the surrounding Conservative towns.

The major period of growth for the Lutheran mission in El Cocuy was during 1938–1950. Larson seems to have been a very dedicated and ingenious evangelist who managed to attract a solid core of families to the church. An early convert reminisced that "the Gospel entered wrapped up in agreeable things." Larson organized games and sports activities aimed at attracting young people (the Mormons in Bogotá are using the same tactic, although basketball seems to have replaced soccer as the game of choice). Children and teenagers who were inured to the endless drudgery of farm work delighted in the sack races, games of blindman's buff, and soccer matches to which the Larsons invited them.

Although clearly aimed at the youth, the goal of these events was to make them family affairs. The idea that leisure activities could be sexually and generationally integrated was something new in El Cocuy. As we shall see below, this continues to be an issue. The Larsons also organized outings and picnics, and members brought along musical instruments to accompany the hymn singing. It must be remembered that such events must have rated as major entertainment in the isolated mountain regions of El Cocuy in the 1930s.

In the early days, Larson held some public meetings in the town theater that were well attended, and he also sold religious books in the street on market days. Some people were drawn in because of intellectual curiosity. They describe their attendance at initial meetings or their attraction to the books that were being offered (including the Bible), saying, "I felt that there must be something more." One convert continued to attend Catholic mass while he began to become involved with the Lutherans. "I would come down to town on Sundays to go to mass, and then I'd come out of mass and go to the evangelical service. Many times in both places they'd be discussing the same part of the Gospel, the same chapter. But in the Catholic church the explanations were very twisted, very different from what the chapter was trying to say." The accounts of early converts suggest that a yearning for some sort of intellectual satisfaction played an important role in their conversion.

The Larsons started a small day school that offered the first few years of primary-level education. It continues to function.[8] In the early days the children of believers were sometimes refused entrance in the public schools in town, or if they were allowed to attend they were subjected to abuse from both the teachers and other students. The evangelical school also suffered numerous attacks, although it eventually developed a good reputation based on its quality and the discipline and dedication of the teachers. Eventually, nonevangelicals began to enroll their children in the school, and in 1983 the majority of pupils were from nonevangelical families.

A series of missionaries served the congregation in El Cocuy during the period 1938–1950. During La Violencia the missionaries left for their own safety, and the members of the congregation were subjected to persecution, as described by Graciliano Azucena in chapter 3. Graciliano's older brother Tomás, who had been very active in the church, was murdered by vigilantes, and the building housing the evangelical school in the outlying rural neighborhood of El Carrizal was burned down.

As noted earlier, many evangelicals spent this time hiding in the mountains, or eventually left the town for the relative safety of Bogotá or other big cities. It was during this time that the Lutheran churches in Bogotá and other cities were established. Although many of the refugees from the violence returned to El Cocuy, once things calmed down, others migrated permanently. The church in El Cocuy continues to lose members through migration. Its small size may make its contribution in terms of the growth of the movement seem minuscule compared to much larger and more active churches elsewhere; however, an impressive number of evangelicals in Bogotá, among them some of the most prominent people in the national church, originally came to know the Gospel in El Cocuy.

The Missionaries and the Notion of Progress

The early missionaries were also involved in what might be viewed as small-scale development work, and this interest in "progress" was a main selling point of the doctrine that continues to characterize evangelical activities in Colombia. An early convert in El Cocuy recalled that Larson was very concerned with improving the quality of life of the people:

> He tried to show people how it was possible, despite the fact that they were poor, to improve their situation in the *campo*, because he was a campesino in Norway. So he used to teach people things like how to make a stove, how to make a bathroom, how to cultivate corn better. He even helped us with the agricultural work at times. And it was clear that that man was a big help, because once he went to an area near El Espino, and later when we went to visit there we found all the houses where that man had been received very changed—now they had bathrooms there in their houses, and they had stoves, and people were eating better and living better.

These kinds of home improvements very much characterize the evangelical lifestyle in El Cocuy. Many women still prefer to cook over the *fogón* (an open fire surrounded by three stones for supporting the pots), but in evangelical houses there is usually at least a wood stove, so that the smoke does not fill the room and blacken it.

Larson also tried to encourage the cultivation of vegetable gardens. He first had to teach people "how to eat vegetables" (such as lettuce, beets, cabbage, and carrots) because this was unheard of within the normal campesino diet. When Tomás Azucena obediently started to cultivate vegetables at the instigation of the missionary, his father criticized him for planting the garden so far away from the house, where crops might be stolen. Tomás answered ironically, "Well, if they steal them, I've accomplished something, because that would prove that the neighbors have finally learned how to eat vegetables." When evangelical women included cooked vegetables to supplement the mandatory meals for the field hands during harvest, the workers would be disgusted and complain, "We're not cows that we can sustain ourselves on grass."

This kind of teaching was aimed more generally at the larger population and not simply at evangelicals, although it would appear from current practices that the evangelicals have been more diligent in applying these ideas. Graciliano dispenses seeds for vegetables in his tiny veterinary drugstore, and on market day the campesinos may come in to buy a tablespoon of carrot or beet seed, which he measures out precisely from a large can and wraps in a twist of newspaper. Malnutrition is a widespread problem in Colombia, and even in the *campo*, where fresh milk, eggs, and grains are available, people often prefer to sell their produce and buy *panela* (slightly refined sugar) or chocolate with the profits. Evangelical households do tend to eat better, partly as a result of the missionary influence and also because of the reorientation of consumption priorities—if the money is not being spent by the husband on beer, more of it is available to buy food for the family.

It seems that this "progress-minded" attitude existed in certain families before the advent of the missionaries, but the missionary influence served to reinforce it and provided a context for its expression. This point will be developed further by a discussion of the history and political activities of the Azucena family, an important evangelical family in both El Cocuy and Bogotá. This case material will illustrate how Colombian evangelical notions of "progress" stem from a concern with the prosperity and well-being of individuals and families. In this sense they are actually domestic standards writ large on the community as a whole. Modernization for its own sake, as well as class mobility and status achievement, are not the goals of these evangelical community activists. This is an important distinction, because it reveals something about the potential for social change inherent in evangelical conversion in Latin America.

Lucía Azucena and Community Development

Lucía Azucena is a woman in her early seventies, the middle child of eight siblings whose father and mother were among the first evangelical converts in El Cocuy. Lucía's father, Teófilo Azucena, lived his entire life in the countryside surrounding El Cocuy. He is described by his children as having been a thoughtful and enterprising man, concerned about progress. He continually made improvements on his small farm— digging irrigation canals, constructing a more comfortable house, devising an oven for baking clay tiles and a mill to grind wheat and corn. He put his children to work making tiles and sent them along the mountain paths to buy eggs from the housewives. The eggs were packed into boxes, transported to Soatá on the backs of mules, and then sent all the way to Bogotá by truck, where they were sold. When a Bible salesman appeared at his house up in the mountains in the 1930s, he purchased a Bible and began teaching his children to read it. His home was among the first to be visited by Andrew Larson, and his children grew up dedicated to the evangelical church. One son, Graciliano, became a Lutheran pastor after attending seminary in Argentina during La Violencia. Another son, Tomás, was murdered during that time. A daughter (Clara) married a boy from another town who went on to become pastor of the Lutheran church in Bogotá. An adopted daughter is the director of the Lutheran school in El Cocuy. His grandchildren and great-grandchildren (numbering about fifty) are involved in the church to some degree.

Teófilo passed on his enterprising spirit and an attitude that life could be improved to his children. There is something about them that distinguishes them from other Cocuyanos. Lucía Azucena is in many ways an exceptional Colombian woman. Dressed in pants, a brown *ruana*, and a straw hat, she is perpetually bustling through the town on her way to some important rendezvous, or engaged in conversation on political topics with anyone who will listen. Lucía has a vision of a paradise on earth, which centers around a cooperative run by women. It would have fruit trees, clean water from an aqueduct, and electricity. Women would learn to raise rabbits for sale and engage in other sorts of small-scale projects for improving their lives. While I was there, she was planning to start a cement block business, anticipating a big building boom with the development of tourism.

Perhaps Lucía's most important contribution to the town was the electrification of the *vereda* (rural hamlet) of El Carrizal. Her brother Graciliano attended an international Lutheran conference in Dar es Salaam in the 1970s, during which representatives from the Lutheran World Federation (LWF) in Geneva solicited from those in attendance ideas for development projects in their various countries. The support of the LWF for projects in Colombia was particularly secure due to the fact that the secretary of the Latin America desk at the LWF is Colombian, a former Colegio CELCO teacher from the region around El Cocuy. Graciliano thought of the electrification scheme, which was greeted with enthusiasm, and was told to return to Colombia and develop a proposal so that the LWF could provide the necessary funding.

On his return he reported this possibility to the congregation, but months passed without any progress. Lucía kept pestering him about it, until he finally turned the papers over to her and told her to do the legwork and the paperwork. This was an involved procedure, because the LWF wanted at least a symbolic amount of local financial support for the project. Lucía ran herself ragged climbing up and down the steep mountain paths in El Carrizal, trying to convince people of the advantages of having electricity, and that the rates they would have to pay for the service were relatively low because of the LWF subsidy. She also managed to convince the national, departmental, and municipal governments to put up a small fraction of the money to cover the installation of the lines.

Along with her brother Graciliano and the town priest, Lucía gave lectures at the high school and at various Junta de Acción Comunal meetings in the early 1980s on the origins of the political parties. This was motivated by El Cocuy's very bad reputation for political violence, for, with the December fiestas approaching, the town leaders were afraid that there would be trouble. The lectures were aimed at presenting a more rational view of politics that would "defanaticize" the people. This was the first time that she had had anything to do with the priest. "*Uno siempre tenía como cólera*" she said ("One was still angry somehow," referring to the persisting resentment and anger the evangelicals feel toward the Catholic clergy for having persecuted them during La Violencia). Her attitude has mellowed considerably, and she now chats with the priest quite amiably when they meet in a store or in the street. In fact, she has a sort of "bootstrap" politics, believing that the poor are that way because they do not want to work. She has no patience for the Catholic youth association, which is quite radical in its views and vocally denounces the rich while ennobling the poor. She believes that there are no longer any rich people in El Cocuy, that those who have money are hard-working people who simply are reaping the rewards of their labors.

She has an undefined political influence in the town because of her determination in talking to the powers that be. She frequently travels back and forth between El Cocuy and Bogotá or Tunja (the capital of the Department of Boyacá), often for the purpose of speaking to important men in politics. When she returns from such a visit, the mayor asks her solicitously for the latest news. She is angry that she has not been elected to serve on the ten-member municipal council, even though her two brothers do.

I first met Lucía at a women's conference held by the Lutheran World Federation in Bogotá. This was the first such conference to be conducted by the LWF in the northern part of South America (others had been held in Chile and Brazil). While she consumed with gusto a plate full of raw onions, explaining that they were very good for the health, she told me the story of the first missionary's visit to their home in El Cocuy.

The possibility of attending international conferences is one of the side benefits of membership in the Lutheran church, and the Colombian Synod regularly receives invitations to send a representative to meetings in other parts of the world. Of course such opportunities are highly coveted, and when a letter arrived in El Cocuy saying that the churches had to select a woman to represent Colombia at a meeting of Lutheran women in the United States, it created a stir. The pastor read the letter to the congregation and explained that they had to select someone to compete with the candidates from the other churches. Lucía was cynical about the whole situation. Although she would dearly love to have gone, she said that the "señores" in Bogotá would no doubt select one of their ladies to have the privilege of traveling to the United States and that, although it would certainly be more valid to send a person who knew the countryside and was articulate about the problems people faced, there was no chance that they would send a mere campesina (such as herself) to the United States.

Graciliano Azucena and the December Fiestas

Graciliano Azucena, Lucía's younger brother, is also unusual in many ways. He has the same "progress-minded" attitude as Lucía and is constantly trying to think of ways to improve things. He has done quite well with cattle raising. He does not tie his cows or milk them, but allows the calves to have the milk so that they will grow faster. Since cattle raising for beef is mainly for export to the cities, while dairy products tend to be sold only locally, he is sacrificing the small, short-term gain for a more delayed, but larger, profit. He also feeds his cows corn cobs mixed with molasses, a habit that the other farmers ridiculed at first until they saw how fast and well his cattle grew. He is also responsible for starting a cooperative to combat livestock rustling. Members contribute one hundred pesos to belong, and if any animals are stolen, the organization pays to announce the theft over the radio and mobilizes a search.

Graciliano was also very active in a committee set up to administer some land that was left to the town by a wealthy Liberal about forty years ago. During his service on this committee, he convinced the members to set up eighty scholarships for poor students to study at the high school in town. In an election in 1983, Graciliano lost his seat on this committee. Even though he really did not care to serve any longer because he was frustrated with the other members, it upset him because he said that the winners had been up in the campo buying shots of aguardiente for the campesinos to get their votes. He lost because he did not campaign that way. This incident illustrates his priorities and the kind of frustrations he faces in his public role in the town.

Graciliano has acquired quite a bit of land, much of which is used to pasture his cattle. Another portion is cultivated by his poorer brother, who gives him a share of the crop for use rights, in the fashion of a regular *aparcero* (sharecropper). Two of this man's sons, Graciliano's nephews, live with Graciliano in town while they attend secondary school. Another half-brother contributes his labor to the cultivation of this plot, and he is paid in potatoes at harvest time. Graciliano is clearly considered by his family to be the well-off uncle, and he regularly assists other family members when they need money. He has not, however, used his financial superiority to differentiate himself in terms of status from his family or from the rest of the community. He is typically modest about his holdings, and although he suffers from rheumatism that makes it hard for him to get around when the weather is damp, he takes great joy in visiting his herds, participating in the construction of irrigation ditches to keep his fields watered, and just spending time out in the familiar countryside where he grew up.

Graciliano was designated by the Municipal Council to act as "president" for the annual December fiestas in El Cocuy in 1983.[9] Since the fair and fiesta normally involve a great deal of public drinking as part of the celebration, Graciliano, as an evangelical, was in an equivocal position. He is an adamant teetotaler and identifies alcohol and drunkeness as the main factors that inhibit progress in the town. He is also a very reserved man, not given to dancing or any sort of public display. During the course of presiding over the fiesta, his standards constantly came into conflict with the wishes of the townspeople. He wanted to "reform" the fiestas, to try to reorient people away from the kinds of behavior he found objectionable toward more wholesome activities. In anticipation of the public disapproval he was expecting as a reaction to his new approach to the fiestas, he made a public announcement over the local radio station. This address is an excellent example of Colombian evangelical rhetoric and includes the essence of Graciliano's notion of progress, as well as his conceptualization of the problems that exist in the town.

Graciliano began his radio announcement by stating that the fiestas were going to be conducted in such a way as to give them a truly Boyacense flavor—they were going to characterize rural life in the countryside and be Cocuyano in their very essence. He said, "We don't need to bring things in from outside in order to have a good time, to enjoy ourselves." The message is clear: he values the traditional, things that are campesino, that is, common to the life of the rural cultivator. It is not unlikely that such a rural fair would be the opportunity for a show of farm machinery or agricultural technology, for the sake of showing the modern orientation of the community. Such things would be out of financial reach of the average farmer and have little applicability to the topography in a town such as El Cocuy. Graciliano expressed no interest in such displays, but rather his entire focus was on the enhancement of traditional values. *"Todo esto se hace con el interés de mejorar"* (All of this is done in the interest of improving things).

In his speech, he identified certain problems that he believed were inhibiting "progress" in the town and outlined the proper attitude needed to correct these problems and to achieve the goal. Juxtaposed were a family orientation and an individualistic one, sharing as opposed to selfishness, productive things (such as agriculture, livestock, flowers, crafts) as opposed to nonproductive things (such as alcohol and fireworks). Very early on he mentioned that the fiestas should have a family orientation, and he reiterated this point throughout the talk. The emphasis was on learning—children should be socialized into proper values. He was hoping that people would use the fiestas to instill an appreciation of productive rural activities in their children.

Again, the criticisms that he raised were not aimed at "traditional" values per se. He did not urge people to give up their "backward" ways or to adopt foreign characteristics. When he enumerated the things that could be enjoyed in the town, they were the simple foods of the region. His objective was to encourage productive, useful, wholesome things and to direct people away from those things that he perceived as wasteful, selfish, and even dangerous.

This year, our fiesta and fair is going to be conducted in a somewhat different fashion from other years. Above all, we want to have a fiesta and fair that truly brings progress to our municipality, and also to the other neighboring municipalities, because they are going to participate in the fair along with us. We must learn to rejoice in wholesome things. This fair and fiesta is aimed at progress. Come with your family. Teach them about progress. If they see the exhibition of flowers, and of agricultural products, and of crafts, and of livestock, the children will learn something and they'll get enthusiastic. If you don't win a prize, no matter. What's important, and what is truly a prize, is that we should get enthusiastic about the things that are truly useful and make our municipality progress. It will teach your children to cultivate the land, to do projects, to plant trees and flowering plants—in that respect it is really a school. There is no reason for you to come alone, just to drink beer, just to drink liquor and beer and get drunk, while your family is sad at home. Take them out. Come with them. Share with them. You shouldn't just drink alcohol, because alchohol is the scourge of our country and of our town. There are many other things to eat and ways one can amuse oneself. The amusement one finds in alcohol isn't a true amusement. It's an amusement that brings with it tears, that later brings pain and poverty. Give your children the many other things that you'll find in town—you'll find *mazato* [a thick corn-based drink], chocolate, meat, potatoes, and other things. Learn how to share with your family and with your friends. Don't just offer them something that really doesn't have any purpose, any result. Also, you should learn to rejoice in things that don't just leave smoke. Don't think that if you don't hear a lot of fireworks that the fiestas weren't any good. What are fireworks? What do they do and what do they leave behind? Many times what they leave behind are deaths and injuries, and fuzziness in the head. It's not necessary to shoot off a lot of fireworks in the fiesta. Help us to make it happy. Happy in a fundamental way, in a way that is based on forward-thinking principles. In advanced places, in those places that have progressed, they don't use these things to have a good time, and these are people whose lives are many times happier than ours. We believe that with shots and with thunder and with drunkenness we will be happy. But these things don't bring true happiness.

Relatively far along in his talk he mentioned religion, and he took special care to appeal to the Catholic population.

Our wholesome fair and fiesta, organized around wholesome principles, will truly bring progress. Happiness that is based on God's principles is happiness that will last a lifetime, while the empty happiness based on satanic principles will soon be followed by sadness. For that reason, we should begin our festivities by praising God. On the morning of the eighth of December, before the fair starts, each one of us should go to our church to worship God. The Catholic evangelicals go to their churches to have a special service, and the Roman Catholics go to their church to have a special service, worshiping God. I would hope that that day you would study more about the Virgin Mary, what were her desires, how did she act in front of her God, how she served her fellow man, and what was it that she wanted us to do. We should teach the children and the young people to be enthusiastic about the things that God has given us for our sustenance: with the plants, with the animals. And we should take care of them and then we will progress. Let's teach them to look at these things that God has created which are so beautiful, so that later they won't have to use narcotics or alcohol in excess in order to feel a false happiness that will bring them pain and end them up in the cemetery or in prison. God has given us many ways to be happy. What happens is that we don't understand the things of God very much. We don't know how to rejoice in wholesome things very well.

Finally, in a statement that very clearly illustrates the family and household orientation projected onto the community, he juxtaposed alcohol and milk. He emphasized the symbolic import of the distribution of milk during the fiesta as a representation of peace, progress, nutrition, and life.

> Although I know that some people aren't going to like this type of fiesta, from right now I'm going to tell you that the president of the fiesta isn't going to take it on himself to distribute alcohol in order to get people drunk. You're better off asking him for a white liquid that is nutritious, not for alcohol, which gets you drunk and makes you stupid, and this white liquid is milk, which even in its color is a symbol of peace. At the beginning of the craft, floral, and agricultural fair, we are going to distribute milk and bread to the children, as a symbol of progress, of nutrition, and of life. And as president, I'm not going to preside over fiestas for drunks, or for fighters, or for exploiters. Although some people won't like it, the majority will, and it will be something that is truly beneficial for our town.

That a man in the prominent public office of president of the annual fiestas would concern himself with the homely task of giving milk to children is perhaps not entirely beyond the realm of possibility in rural Colombia. But to imbue such a gesture with symbolic significance, as representing an alternative mode of thought and behavior to that which is expected at fiestas, is a radical departure from the norm. If we consider Graciliano's stance in the abstract, disregarding for a moment that it is "en-gendered" (in the sense of being given its particular gender valence) by his evangelical belief, it appears as an attitude profoundly anomalous to the Colombian masculine role. In fact, the bulk of his argument would be quite appropriate had it been presented by a woman.

The point that this case illustrates is a most significant one. Although evangelical conversion does allow women positions of prominence in the relatively "public" world of the church, it is not often the case that evangelicalism provides either the motivation or the means for women to attain public roles such as that which occasioned Graciliano's speech. The point here is that the transformation of the male role into nurturer has to do as much with women as with men. The Colombian evangelical movement may be generated by a dynamic located within the parameters of the household, but its repercussions reach out into the wider community. Within the confines of a strongly male-dominated society such as Colombia's, the revolutionary impact of evangelicalism is not that it transforms women's roles but that it has the power to change men to conform with female ideals and aspirations. This point will be explored in greater depth in the chapters that follow.

Finally, although Graciliano, throughout his address, used the words "progress," "development," "advancement," and so on, in fact what he was expressing was a concern with what we might call "prosperity." Progress or modernization in the way we think of them are by no means required to achieve the kind of prosperity and well-being Graciliano promotes. The meaning of this notion of "progress" to Colombian evangelicals and, more broadly, in the literature on Latin American evangelical conversion, will be discussed in chapter 8.

Domestic Abdication, Individualism, and Machismo

✛
INTRODUCTION

In this chapter and the next, I examine three closely interrelated aspects of Colombian family life that have special bearing on the subsequent discussion of conversion to evangelical Protestantism: sex roles, household support, and strategies of status acquisition. The key points I wish to illustrate are that (1) the machismo role that often characterizes male behavior is a public and not a household role, a fact that leads to an attenuation of conjugal roles in many Colombian households;[1] (2) under such circumstances, the lack of conjunction between male and female values and aspirations, combined with the dependency of women on male earnings in postpeasant society, poses the central problem for women in terms of providing for the household, which is their main arena; and (3) patterns of consumption relating to strategies of status acquisition for men and women often reflect distinct value orientations and are realized in different spheres. A lesser degree of sex segregation with regard to patterns of status acquisition appears to be associated with upward mobility and "modernization" in Colombia; in terms of cultural factors influencing these processes, machismo has been viewed by Colombian writers as a major impediment.

✛
DEFINING MACHISMO:
CONTRADICTIONS AND CONSISTENCIES

For some time now, the concept of machismo has found steady employment in the literature on mestizo Latin American kinship. Machismo has been the touchstone in studies of conjugal relations, as well as of household and family roles. The term has been axiomatic in discussion of the relative status, rights, responsibilities, spheres of authority, and decision making of men versus women, as well as their attitudes and values. In this chapter, I will review definitions of machismo and theories of its causes and propose a refinement of the term that will be helpful in understanding its connection to Latin American domestic life.

The degree to which machismo is originally an emic expression is debatable—it has only recently appeared in Spanish dictionaries and seems to be a term coined by social scientists, urban elites, modernizers, and journalists.[2] The most oft-cited definition of the term, perhaps because it is the most general, is that presented by Stevens in Pescatello's early collection of essays on female and male in Latin America. Stevens says that machismo describes a male personality and concomitant behavior pattern characterized by "exaggerated aggressiveness and intransigence in male-to-male relations and arrogance and sexual aggression in male-to-female relationships" (Stevens 1973:90). Other definitions abound that emphasize various aspects, some positive and some negative, of what is often called a "complex": hypersexuality, *cuatismo* (male camaraderie), violence, risk taking, courage or stoicism, authoritarianism, independence.

Within the range of phenomena included under the rubric of machismo, there are some noticeable contradictions. The Andalusian men described by Gilmore (1987) have a strong aversion to violence, and a man prone to fighting is likely to earn the disdain of his peers. In Colombia, where homicide is the number one cause of death for males between the ages of fifteen and forty-five, social commentators have blamed machismo for the level of murderous violence (Pachón de Galán 1981). Another contradiction was recently pointed out by Kutsche (following Paredes [1971] on South Texas), who divides definitions of machismo along the axis of those stressing male self-confidence and those stressing male self-doubt. Kutsche believes that the "self-confident" aspects of machismo are covered by alternate labels in the ethnographic literature: "*vergüenza, honor, formalidad, respeto*" (shame, honor, formality, respect), while such alternatives do not exist for machismo as self-doubt. Hence he would confine application of the term to situations of male inferiority (in power and prestige, whether economic, political, ritual, or whatever), which results in a façade of unrelieved masculinity in the absence of objective evidence (Kutsche 1984:6–7). Paralleling Kutsche's very useful distinction would be the variance between the notion of the male as sole provider for his household, on the one hand, and the attenuation of conjugality, high rate of abandonment, and female-headed households, which are often connected to machismo, on the other.

Feminist analyses that have assessed the meaning of machismo in terms of both male and female roles are also polarized into two camps. Many Latin American feminist writers identify machismo as the root cause of sexual inequality. They say that *machista* society is characterized by an excess of male power and privilege and the corresponding low status, inferiority, and powerlessness of women.

The female counterpart to machismo, *marianismo*, is in every way machismo's mirror image. Arrogance and intransigence in the male are mirrored by self-abnegation and submission in the female. A double standard of extreme proportions awards all of the spoils to men and reduces women to little more than domestic slaves (Latin American and Caribbean Women's Collective 1980). On the other hand, writers including Stevens (1973) and Jaquette (1973) believe that machismo entails a more equitable division of desirable attributes so that male physical and intellectual prowess is balanced by a moral and spiritual superiority on women's part, through which women are able to wield considerable informal power.[3] One analysis (Ehlers 1991:2) argues that the role of *marianismo* is closely tied to the relative degree of female economic dependence, which changes with the material conditions of women's lives and over the life span of each woman.

Clearly, the meaning and use of the term varies by context, whether applied to the Old or the New World, different social and economic classes, ethnic groups, generations, or stages in the developmental cycle of the family. The particular agenda of each writer (e.g., whether the writer is a feminist reformer, a family therapist, or a Latin American nationalist poet) also influences the meaning of machismo.[4]

I take as a starting point the theme of male domestic abdication, which appears to run through many approaches to the subject of machismo. First, I should stress that I agree with Paredes and Kutsche that machismo is best applied to the pattern emerging from male self-doubt, and that the self-confident macho role is described by other labels present in the ethnographic literature. A truly effective, honorable macho role is a definite variant of Latin American masculinity, and the ways in which machismo grows out of and articulates with this ideal male identity are important to consider.[5] Certainly age and class are factors determining the ability to fulfill this ideal.

Leaving aside the honorable macho for the moment, I propose that machismo is a useful concept in describing an aspect of sex-gender systems characterized by the alienation of men from the household (includ-

attenuation of their roles as husbands and fathers) and their
.....ation with the world outside rather than with their household
group. Key to the emic understanding of what we are calling machismo
is an extreme divergence of men and women from common goals and
understandings. During my fieldwork in Colombia, female informants repeatedly complained about their husband's lack of comprensión, while
males were most concerned about female betrayal. Both attitudes indicate a gulf that has opened up as a result of the disarticulation of male
and female household roles.

As a feminist anthropologist, I have marveled at the efficiency with
which the application of the term machismo to Latin American kinship
and family has rendered women invisible. That kinship and the family
are indisputably female domains in mestizo society has not diminished
the alacrity with which this has been done, rendering women as a sha-
dowy supporting cast. As soon as machismo enters the discourse on
mestizo kinship and family, women's main activities are reduced to two:
suffering the male presence and mourning male absence.

There are three points that I would like to consider here. First, although machismo has ramifications for the domestic realm, it does not
stipulate the content of any key relationships within the family, except
by default. Its striking characteristic is that it is a nondomestic (one
might almost say antidomestic) male role. The centrality of the concept
in studies of Latin American kinship, family, and household is therefore
surprising. It can be explained in part by ethnographers' widespread acceptance of statements made by male informants that emphasize ideals
about masculine prerogative and privilege. Descriptions of masculine
domains in such countries, such as the bars, public politics, or certain
occupations, do not start out with an extensive consideration of the
absence of women in these arenas. Yet the writing on Latin American
household and family has historically been hampered by this curious
tendency to begin descriptions and analysis of Latin American domestic
groups with a consideration of the male component. Most writers have
tended to present a model of male dominance and female compliance
within domestic groups that leaves us with only a vague notion of what
actually goes on within the household and neglects to examine the attitudes of other than adult male members of the group. A prime example
of this kind of treatment is found in Fals-Borda's study of a town in
Colombia (1962:206–207):

Men's and women's roles are clearly defined. The former are knights in
their castles, entitled to all prerogatives; they are at the same time respon-

sible for discipline, domestic respect, and the upholding of the family pride. He makes all the decisions which affect his conjugal family. He works hard in the field and, in recompense, has a right to become noted for his *tienda* demeanor and ensuing prestige. Women, on the other hand, are mainly to serve their husbands, to give them children, to wash and cook for the family, to help in certain farming chores, to haul water from the springs, and to spin wool.

It is notable that those elements assigned to the male role are all phrased in terms of values and prerogatives while the female role comprises actual domestic activities. The construction of this statement makes the degree to which it is based on observation of family life highly suspect: men "are entitled to" and "are responsible for"; women "are mainly to serve." The phrasing that describes women's role is particularly revealing: instead of "women are expected to serve" or "women are required to serve," we are told "women are to serve." There are no social circumstances compelling them to do these things; serving is simply the sum and the fact of their existence.

It is interesting that individual domestic strategies have appeared as a topic for consideration primarily in studies of the "matrifocal family," that is, domestic arrangements characterized by an absence of formal male authority, or, in studies that view machismo as pathological and discuss negative domestic symptomatology (e.g., drunkenness, wife beating) that is perceived as going along with it.

The second point that I would like to make is that machismo is not the same as male dominance or patriarchy. Our understanding of machismo has been clouded by a tendency to equate it with forms of male superordinance in quite distinct types of social systems. In feminist as well as nonfeminist literature, this assumed congruence between machismo and patriarchy leads to unwarranted conclusions about the centrality of masculine influence in domestic affairs. This is not simply terminological finesse; it has real implications for how we approach family and household dynamics, kinship, and women's status. Moreover, by distinguishing types of masculine prerogative, we enhance our understanding of how female subordination as opposed to sexual complementarity is created and maintained in sex and gender systems.

The third point to be made in this chapter is that machismo in all of its variations is best understood not as a static role but as a transitional one reflecting the enormous social change, including proletarianization and increasing economic insecurity, that has occurred in Latin American society over the period of twenty or thirty years during which the term has been used. Hence it is important to investigate how certain features, such as the negative symptomatology of abandonment, or the characterization of male personality by self-doubt rather than by self-confidence, grew out of earlier stages.

✣
DOMESTIC ABDICATION

The nondomestic nature of machismo is most succinctly summed up in a statement made throughout Latin America: "la mujer es de la casa y el hombre de la calle" (woman is of the house and man is of the street). A public and private division of male and female spheres has been given abundant attention by feminist anthropologists, especially those dealing with the Mediterranean (see Reiter 1975; Rieglehaupt 1967; Rogers 1975). In order to throw male abdication of the domestic realm into relief and thereby understand some of the essential features of machismo sex and gender systems, it is useful to consider a masculine role that is not alienated from the household.

A stark contrast to the equation female = house and male = street is provided by the Laymis, an Aymara-speaking people north of Potosí, Bolivia. The Laymi word for household, *chachawarmi*, is formed by combining the word for man or husband (*chacha*) and the word for woman or wife (*warmi*). Harris, who has written about the complementarity of male and female roles in Laymi subsistence production (1978), has further pointed out how the unity of man and woman is repeated in many ritual and symbolic contexts. Male and female are not represented in a series of antitheses, but are, rather, viewed as predominating alternately. At the same time that women are excluded from formal political roles, Harris reports, men spend a good deal of time in ritual drinking (a fact that is resented by women), wife beating is commonplace and there is little solidarity on the part of women to defend each other, maleness is associated with strength and daring and women are said to be lazy and cowardly, and inheritance and residence rules are biased toward males. Yet it would not occur to us to assign the term "machismo" to Laymi masculinity, precisely because of the complementary fusion of male and female identities and activities on the domestic level.[6]

Other examples of complementarity in Latin America could be cited, including Rothstein's analysis of Mexican peasant households (1983), which is discussed in more detail in the next chapter. She asserts that

male and female activities are determined by the primacy of
of labor in peasant household production rather than by ̤
masculine authority.

An intriguing paper by Weist (1983) based on work done i
municipio shows the absolute peripheralization of males to the household even with regard to the single aspect of the machismo complex that
might be taken as a domestic role: that of good provider. Weist argues
that migration to the United States by Mexican males is highly functional in minimizing role conflict generated by machismo ideals. Men
are able to send back enough money from the United States to keep their
wives dependent on them, thus fulfilling an important requisite of machismo. Away from home, men are free to pursue sexual liaisons with
other women. Wives tolerate their husbands' absence as long as support continues, and even express relief to be freed of their beatings and
excessive drinking. Far from requiring both male and female presence
for the household to function smoothly, as in the Laymi case, the husband's complete removal is a boon to both domestic life and the ethic of
machismo.

The evidence for male rejection of domestic involvement (in terms
of both activities and ideals) and corresponding female power in the
household is extensive. As far back as 1949, Oscar Lewis elaborated on
the illusory nature of masculine household authority in Tepoztlán. It
was impossible for men to maintain actual domestic control when their
"lofty" positions removed them from the family. The ramifications of
male domestic abdication in the face of the relative weakness of their
political and economic power in the public realm has been discussed for
several areas of the Mediterranean (see e.g., Reigelhaupt 1967; Rogers
1973; and Gilmore 1987), and it is a situation that certainly also pertains
in the New World.

✤

PSYCHOLOGICAL APPROACHES:
MACHISMO AND MALE DOMINANCE

The abdication of males from key arenas of social life seriously erodes
their impact on socialization. Psychologists, and psychologically oriented anthropologists, have repeatedly concluded that machismo inhib-
its the reproduction of effective masculine roles. These studies need to

be evaluated with great care to determine if their notion of what masculinity is or should be is implicitly Eurocentric. Likewise, if these conclusions are premised on the idea that the nuclear family is the optimal or necessary setting for the socialization of children, we can discount their relevance to cross-cultural understanding. For the purposes of the argument being presented here, masculinity is viewed as a culturally constructed bundle of roles, and it is the problematic nature of the social reproduction of male domestic roles (e.g., husband and father as actual domestic roles rather than as public statuses) in the Latin American setting that is of special interest. Whether or not biologically or psychologically intrinsic masculine predispositions can be identified cross-culturally is outside of the scope of this study. Likewise, I am not making any assumption about optimal family form. I am not advocating the position that the nuclear family is a better setting for the "proper" socialization of children than other types of families. It has been illustrated repeatedly that the male roles of husband and father, though differently constituted, are carried out quite effectively in other than nuclear family settings (see e.g., Gough 1959; Stack 1974). What is key here is the degree to which domestic involvement is tangential (or actually incompatible) with the particular masculine identity characterized by machismo.

Ideology and Experience in Male Socialization

The connection between male domestic abdication and masculine insecurity has received much attention from psychoanalytic and socialization points of view. David and Margaret Gilmore have elaborated on the ways in which Andalusian machismo results from an ideology of male dominance in the face of strong domestic matriarchy. The resulting insecurity is allayed by repeated feats of sexual conquest. Consistent with the view that machismo applies to male self-doubt, the Gilmores conclude that "Andalusian machismo is not a libidinal assertion of secure male identity, but is rather a compensatory attempt to resolve intrapsychic conflict between male and female identities" (1979:283).

Díaz (1966:92) has described how the distance between father and son creates a crucial distortion in the son's idealized picture of his father, which leads to the traits associated with machismo:

> The child does not observe his father's making of decisions within the walls of the house . . . the boy does not gradually learn the role as a result of observing how his father acts vis-à-vis other grown men, for the rules are such

that when his father is somewhere outside the house, he [the son] is not in the same place . . . the father tends to be seen as a free agent rather than as the representative of a nuclear family in reference to the outside world. As a consequence of these factors, the child sees authority as power shorn of responsibility and clothed in the symbols of the male role—machismo if you will.

Both Díaz and the Gilmores focus on a crucial gap: that between the ideology of male dominance and the actual experiential outcome of the division of male and female spheres in Latin American culture. In their analyses, machismo is a product of this contradiction. Such approaches have an advantage over the simple psychoanalytic axiom that boys need involved fathers in order to develop secure masculine identities. It is not the absence of the father per se that leads to the *machista* personality, but the contradictions between a societal idea that male influence and prerogative are completely pervasive, and the actual situation, which excludes males from domestic involvement.

By logical extension of their conclusions, we could say that an authoritarian father actually present in the household and making day-to-day decisions on the domestic front would not be as likely to produce a *machista* son. Such a domestic arrangement would resemble the patriarchal household in preindustrial Europe, in which the male was truly the household head, making daily decisions that affected women, younger men, and children (Eisenstein 1978). Thus we can begin to differentiate between machismo and male dominance or patriarchy.

Family Dynamics and the Macho's Mother

Psychotherapists who have been involved in the treatment of Hispanic families have contributed their insights about the process within the family that reproduces the *machista* personality. It is curious that women who openly disdain the *machista* behavior of their husbands and other adult men cannot break the cycle with their own sons. The statements of the Colombian women I worked with, as well as ethnographic reports from field-workers working with mestizo populations in other Latin American countries lead to the conclusion that women do not consciously socialize their sons into *machista* behavior. Colombian women (and men) admire a kind of behavior or person that they label *macho* (and also *guapo*, which can mean both strong and handsome). This entails physical strength, the ability to endure pain, and recognized control over certain arenas earned by proven effectiveness. This ideal, or the "true macho" of Hunt's study (1971), should not be confused with machismo. Women may respect and value "true macho" characteristics because they also benefit from them. They also clearly aim to reproduce this kind of masculinity in their sons, encouraging them to be strong, fearless, stoical, and so on. The behavior associated with machismo, on the other hand, is at best treated with an attitude of resigned tolerance by women, but more often is openly disparaged and condemned. Women identify such behavior as the immediate cause of their own problems and suffering. It is also significant that women see *machista* behavior as a threat to the well-being of their sons and other male family members who exhibit it. A mother, wife, or sister may attempt to "save" a male family member from the dangers of machismo.

This is not to say that women are irrelevant to the reproduction of machismo. The family therapy literature suggests a critical part for women in the construction of the *machista* personality. From this point of view, a feedback system, in which male infidelity and irresponsibility are countered by female resentment, is key to the process. The wife resists the *machista's* abuse and authoritarianism by forming alliances with her children in opposition to their father (see e.g., Bird and Canino 1982). The young boy, lacking a positive male role model, identifies with his mother, develops an antagonism toward men and a contempt for women, and, in order to establish his own adult masculine identity, proceeds to act out the "flight from femininity" (Goldwert 1985) through the pursuit of sexual conquests.

An interesting but problematic study by Fromm and Maccoby (1970) discusses the effects of the father's absence on female socialization. In their view, the absence of a reliable and loving father during her own childhood leads the adult woman to despise her husband and to try to undermine him. Her husband reacts to the threat of "psychological castration" with physical violence and abandonment.

This "blame the woman" approach would lead to the conclusion that a loving and supportive wife is what it would take to "cure" the *machista*. This theme is frequently reiterated in popular Colombian music. However, we might more readily conclude that the little girl is affected by the same family dynamic as her brothers. Both male and female children witness their mother's mistreatment or neglect at the hands of their father and are bound in an alliance with her against him.

Again, field data from Colombia support this conclusion. The system reproduces itself in the next generation with both male and female protagonists contributing to its perpetuation. It is interesting to note here a study by Browner and Lewin (1982), which shows the variable emphasis that Hispanic women place on their roles as mother or wife, depending on economic circumstances. Their study is useful in illustrating that the alliances women form with their children are strategic and variable, not an inevitable aspect of the Hispanic female role.

It is intriguing that machismo has received so much attention from psychologists and psychoanalysts, but actually assessing the relative weight of psychological determinants in the formation and perpetuation of machismo is not the task of this study. However, perhaps because of the interventionist and prescriptive nature of their work, the therapeutic literature does focus on female agency in the process of socialization. This is useful because it demystifies the ideology of male dominance, which allegedly permeates societies in which machismo is present. Hence, one very important contribution of psychoanalytic models of machismo is that they allow us to see women in a central position in the reproduction of identity and social roles, and thus as creators of culture. In considering women's responses to *machista* behavior, we are able to see the holes in male dominance created by male domestic abdication. How this works on a level beyond that of psychodynamics remains to be explored adequately.

✛
CHANGE OVER TIME

The third factor, change over time, leads us to a consideration of some of the wider social processes that have brought about machismo sex and gender arrangements and allows us to identify a set of predispositions that these changes act on.

The differential expression of machismo in Spain and in Latin America can be traced in part to the legacy of conquest and colonial domination in the New World. In this regard, a study by Ramos (1962) attempts a psychohistorical explanation of the origins of both Mexican sex roles and family patterns. Ramos emphasizes the fact that Spain's conquest of Mexico involved the exploitation of indigenous women by Spanish men. In his analysis, the offspring of these unions, the mestizo Mexicans, developed an inferiority complex because of their status as a conquered people. Mexican rhetoric sometimes refers to the creation of the Mexican nation through the Spanish conquerors' sexual exploitation of Indian woman as its "original sin." The child of mixed descent began to look on his mother as a devalued person and on his father as the exploiter. The father, as "Don Nadie" (Lord Nobody), expected to be waited on hand and foot by his wife and children, a situation he never could have enjoyed in Spain. Woman became the symbol of the conquered, subdued Indian and Man the symbol of the conquering, demanding Spaniard. According to this formulation, women, in Mexican mestizo society, come to be considered objects of violent and sadistic conquest and possession. Both creole and mestizo children find out that the woman who has given them warmth and love in childhood fills an inferior role. When the male child of mixed descent grows up, Ramos argues, he treats his wife as he saw his mother treated by his father. In this way, the specific family pattern dominated by machismo begins to be passed down from generation to generation (Peñalosa 1968:682).[7]

Ramos's argument brings to mind what must be the most poetic formulation of the *machista* personality, that presented by Octavio Paz in his essays on Mexican national character (1961). Paz's *machista* is cut from the same cloth as Ramos's conquerors, as revealed in his statement: "whatever may be the origin of these attitudes, the fact is that the essential attribute of the macho—power—almost always reveals itself as a capacity for wounding, humiliating, annihilating" (1961:82).

While Ramos's analysis and Paz's observations are convincing as a broad explanation for women's lowly status within *machista* mestizo culture, they lack historical detail concerning the expression of this pattern in various contexts during the several hundred years since the Conquest. Missing is a consideration of the fact that *machista* behavior is perhaps less common among men in positions of real power than among their social subordinates.

Several writers have concluded that economic insecurity or class oppression is a key component in the creation of machismo. The conflict between sexual identities in the male mentioned by Gilmore and Gilmore (1979:283) with regard to Andalusian machismo results from "external socioeconomic constraints . . . in the subordinate class of landless day laborers." The rich, politically dominant landowners do not exhibit the characteristics of machismo. Rather, the machismo complex results from "extreme conditions of male economic failure, matrifocal and matriarchal household patterns, and equally important, political oppression and exclusion."

Kutsche (1984) cites evidence from rural New Mexico and Costa Rica, which he sees as egalitarian societies and distinguished by an absence of machismo. He concurs that an oppressive class structure is a necessary component in Hispanic cultures for the development of machismo.[8]

Michaelson and Goldschmidt (1971:349) also connect machismo to situations of male economic insecurity. They have suggested that machismo may arise in response to a conflict between a cultural expectation of masculine authority and bilateral inheritance. They feel that machismo may be "the product of a role demand which does not have adequate economic support. Where male dominance is not buttressed by control of property, it may generate masculine doubt, expressed in the fear of impotence and the need to demonstrate virility through sexual conquests."

One psychotherapist has linked economic conditions and class relations with the machismo role. De la Cancela (1986) observes the function that machismo serves in mystifying the economic exploitation inherent in capitalist transformation. He maintains that machismo predates capitalism but has been instrumental in its development, obscuring the alienating effects of capitalism on individuals by embodying it in male-female interaction (1986:292).

The economic basis of machismo needs further clarification and development. While I agree with these writers that economic insecurity plays an important role in the development of machismo in the New World, a focus on economic insecurity alone is not sufficient to explain the origins and perpetuation of machismo. In societies and subjugated classes in which social organization operates within the constraints imposed by economic insecurity, a wide range of masculine roles, types of conjugal relationships, and household arrangements, including complementarity, can be found. While poverty or class oppression may be important preconditions for the development of machismo, alone they are not necessary or sufficient to explain its occurrence.

Hence, the additional component that needs to be considered for a more complete understanding of the phenomenon of machismo is how the processes of proletarianization and modernization differentially affect men and women.

✢

MACHISMO, PROLETARIANIZATION, AND INDIVIDUALISM

Many writers have noted that in Latin America kinship links have been of such strength that neither men nor women have been discerned primarily as individuals, but rather as integral parts of kinship groups—individual identity is merged with collective identity (see Bohman 1984 and Gutiérrez de Pineda 1975). As economic activity becomes more individualistically oriented, a family identification, especially for men whose labor becomes almost entirely extra-domestically situated, is undermined. With proletarianization, human action becomes a commodity, which can be bought and sold.

This view of human potential in society is aggravated by the expansion and consolidation of the nation-state, which is dependent on the development of the notion of individual identity—of the individual as free agent in articulation with the market and the state. In this regard, Wolf has noted the contrast between mestizo versus Indian notions of power in Mexico: "Where the Indian saw power as an attribute of office and redistributed it with care lest it attach itself to persons, the mestizo would value power as an attribute of the self . . . for the mestizo, power is not an attribute of the group. The group exists to back the individual; the individual does not exist for the group" (1959:239).

On an emotional level, fervent nationalism in Mexico, or passionate identification with national-level political parties in Colombia, which is often expressed in male gatherings, is understandable as compensation for the alienation of the individual from larger social groupings like the family or household. As Wolf puts it, "Nationalism allows men to transcend the limits of the separate self and to merge that self with a social body, the nation, to which they impute a magical collective strength" (1959:244).

We now understand that individualism is a Western ideological construct that has become worldwide only in recent decades (see e.g., Meyer 1986:208). Far from being a natural state of affairs, individualism must be systematically socialized. Meyer has asserted that individualism amounts to a social doctrine and is a public rather than private view of the person (1986:209). He further states that "all modern societies are individualistic . . . they locate the value of life in the social action of individual persons" (p. 209).

The implications of these observations in the light of what has been said about Latin American sex and gender roles and household organization are powerful. The difference between male and female notions of individual versus collective identities constitutes a major contradiction within which machismo flourishes. It is not that men are modern and women are not. This all takes place within the parameters of class oppression and economic insecurity, which keeps the majority from achieving the trappings of modernity. Yet masculinity in Latin America has surely been affected, perhaps excessively, by individualism whereas, by comparison, Latin American femininity has been especially resistant to it.

With this understanding of machismo in the Colombian sex and gender system we are now able to move on to a closer look at the arena in which it is played out: the household and family. The next chapter details the impact of the attenuation of conjugality on the household and on women's lives. Then in chapter 7, we look at the specific impact of evangelical conversion on the domestic realm.

✤ 6 ✤

Colombian Sex and Gender Roles and the Family

✤
INTRODUCTION

Anthropological approaches to household organization have undergone serious reevaluation in recent years. For some time now, the conceptual and empirical separation of family and household has been noted (Bohannan 1963:86; Keesing 1958:271). The concept of household has been further refined by distinguishing coresidence from domestic functions (Bender 1967). A refinement of special importance to the present discussion is the recognition that households are units of cultural meaning: "Households must be explicated as well as enumerated" (Yanagisako 1984:330). Analysis of changes in household composition or activity patterns must be accompanied by a cultural analysis, taking into account how people construe these units and the configuration of activities, emotions, and dilemmas they attach to them (Yanagisako 1984: 330). Consideration of these features is likely to reveal a picture that contradicts our idea of the household as a unity, equipped with a single consciousness and volition. In this approach, "strategy and struggle" can be seen to exist within households, not only between households and external institutional structures (Yanagisako 1984:342). Yanagisako criticizes the metaphor of household as human agent, "in which it is assumed that all members of a household share the same goals and strategies or, if they do not, that some (most often women and children) are so powerless as to have their actions determined by the goals and strategies of others (most often adult men)" (p. 342).

Directing attention to age and gender hierarchies within domestic groups is one way to reveal "the social process through which individuals negotiate the relations that give form to households despite different and sometimes conflicting goals, strategies, and notions about what it means to 'live together' " (p. 331).

Studies of domestic organization in Latin America have generally suffered from an adoption of the consensus model of the household (see e.g., Youssef's 1973 discussion of patterns of authority in the Latin American family). Most writers have tended to present a model of male dominance and female compliance within domestic groups that leaves us with only a vague notion of what actually goes on within households and neglects to examine the attitudes of other than adult male members of the group. It is interesting that individual domestic strategies seem to appear as a topic for consideration only in studies of the "matrifocal" family, in other words, domestic arrangements characterized by an absence of formal male authority. For more culturally legitimated domestic forms, such as the household formed around a couple married in the Catholic church, there often exists an ideal model, which tends to reflect a male perspective. Several excellent studies have appeared in recent years that attend to the female perspective on domestic arrangements (see, e.g., Benería and Roldán 1987; Bohman 1984; Bourque and Warren 1981; Browner and Lewin 1982; Gutiérrez de Pineda 1975; Rubbo 1975). These document women's strategic behavior on the home front and constitute a convincing argument against the consensus model or the acceptance of the male ideal as a true picture of reality.[1]

This chapter discusses the effect of Colombian sex and gender roles, beliefs, and behavior patterns on family and household organization. Although the pattern is slowly changing, a high degree of sexual segregation and a wide divergence between male and female goals and aspirations are still among the most salient features of Colombian domestic organization. Evangelical conversion dramatically restructures the pattern discussed here, as well as the meaning of the household to individual members, and the details of that change are presented in chapter 7. First, however, it is essential to understand the domestic arena on which evangelical conversion has a revolutionary impact, and within which we can identify some of the powerful motivations for conversion.

✛

SEX ROLES AND FAMILIAL ROLES

In discussions of the Latin American family, models of ideal male and female roles are frequently deemed to be the central features determining relations within families. These discussions range from (1) a belief in the complementarity and reciprocal nature of male and female roles (Stevens 1973:99) to (2) portrayal of the female role as ascendant in the household and machismo as psychologically pathological to (3) the conviction that machismo gives men the dominant role in the household, to which women respond with unquestioning subordination and submission. Stevens (1973) notes that mestizo culture (within which machismo is most prevalent) is not "traditional" culture but an amalgamation with a fairly recent history. As noted in the previous chapter, is also a cultural development that has taken place almost entirely within a situation of rapid social change and upheaval. In Colombia, as well as in other parts of Latin America, a variety of different family forms and household types exists; and although it is sometimes difficult to extricate the "ideal" from the "real" when we discuss families, it is always useful to consider the context to which certain forms must respond. Contextualizing machismo may also explain the disparity among the three views of how sex roles operate in the Latin American household.

Contemporary family life in Colombia is shaped by circumstances that clearly differ from those that affected peasant households during earlier periods. In order to understand how machismo affects household relations at present, it is helpful to consider, as background, male-female relations in the context of peasant family economy. This will also serve as background for a later discussion of how contemporary sex roles articulate with different patterns of production and consumption, especially in terms of the development of "separate spheres" of activity for men and women.

Sex Roles and the Peasant Household
Mode of Production

Rothstein (1983) has criticized the assumption of male dominance in Mexican peasant communities. She points out that this viewpoint results in part from a confusion of the real with the ideal, and in part from a projection of capitalistic notions of individual contributions onto peasant society. She proposes that male-female relations should be understood within the context of a family economy. She takes her model of family economy from Shanin (1971:30): "A peasant household is characterized by a nearly total integration of the peasant family's life and its farming enterprise. The family provides workers for the farm, while the farm's activities are geared mainly to production of the basic consumption needs of the family."

The projection of modern capitalist notions of individual economic independence onto peasant society is false because the basic unit of production and consumption, as well as the basic social unit in peasant society, is the nuclear family. Rothstein (1983:17) points out that in peasant societies that produce for subsistence, "consumption and production are two ends of a continuum, rather than two separate spheres." Earlier writers (such as Lewis 1963 and Beals 1946, whose material she uses) have made a false distinction between male productive activities and female nonproductive activities because they have assumed (with their modern industrial bias) that "domestic" means "nonproductive." Rothstein proposes, instead, that in peasant households in the three Mexican communities she discusses relations between the sexes are characterized by "cooperation and independence" (1983:20) and that "activities are dictated not by one's spouse but by the division of labor" (p. 12). Decisions are likewise made jointly and determined by family consumption needs rather than by an individual. Again, quoting Shanin (1971:241), "the individual, the family and the farm, appear as an indivisible whole . . . [and] the balance of consumption needs, available labour and the farm's potential, strongly influences a peasant's activities."

Rothstein's paper is valuable because it summarizes much of the discussion about male and female roles in peasant families (see, for example, Friedl 1967; Riegelhaupt 1967; Rogers 1975), which has criticized older literature based on idealized and male pictures of reality. With some modifications, Rothstein's model of family economy can be taken as a basis for comparison with the changed circumstances of modern, postpeasant families in Colombia.

In the Colombian peasant household, family roles were largely determined by the requirements of the domestic economy. What remains of or replaces these roles when the family economy dissolves (as peasants migrate to cities, become proletarianized in the countryside, or in other ways turn away from subsistence production) is our concern here. Massive changes in Colombian society over the past forty years have entailed a rapid rate of urbanization (70 percent of Colombians are categorized as urban), and even in the countryside very few independent peasant households still exist. The nature of the family and conjugal relations are no longer centered around access to land, nor is the division of labor embedded in a household production and consumption unit. Most people operate primarily within a cash economy, with the result that the main source of income is outside the household. The distinction between productive and domestic then assumes a certain validity. Because cash income is now the basis of subsistence, men and women are no longer interdependent. Women do not have the vital role in transforming produce into sustenance because the market economy and the service sector can provide that in exchange for cash.

The negative effects of modernization on women's status have been widely documented (see, e.g., Boserup 1970). In terms of the preceding argument it is important to note that machismo as it exists in contemporary Latin American society (as distinct from simple "male dominance") would have been incompatible with a peasant household family economy. The true *machista* role requires separate male and female spheres of activity, including production and consumption, the dependence of women on men but not the reverse, and distinctive (and often contradictory) sets of values and aspirations for men and women.

The Attenuation of Conjugal Roles

It is curious that discussions of Latin American domestic life center on male and female roles as reified in the stereotypes of machismo and *marianismo*, considering that neither type is defined primarily as a conjugal role. It might logically follow that it is precisely this weakness of conjugality as a factor in household organization that such analyses capture. Schneider and Smith (1973:7) point out that family and kinship roles are compound or conglomerate roles and are analytically separable into "'pure' kinship elements, sex role elements, and elements derived from the system of status and class differentiation." Machismo, as discussed in the previous chapters, is a public role and does not define how a man is to act as a husband or father, except by default. Indeed, machismo contributes to a man's lack of involvement in his roles as husband or father. Many writers say that the male role really changes very little as the result of marriage, while for women it is the major event in defining them as adults. *Marianismo* really describes the woman's role as mother and has bearing on the conjugal role only insofar as husbands have to be treated as demanding children. That women must be long-suffering in the face of male abuse may be interpreted as part of the conjugal role, but this has bearing only when the husband is present in the household, which, by definition of the *machista* role, is likely to be infrequently. It is significant that, although husbands are important because legal marriage gives a woman status and her children legitimacy in the public realm, the primary symbolic standard for Latin women's role is the Virgin Mary—a husbandless mother.

Despite the appearance of male dominance in Colombian families, when machismo defines the male role it is inaccurate to speak of the family as being "patriarchal." It has been noted (Secretariado Nacional de Pastoral Social 1981:93) that the male covers up his irresponsibility with an authoritarian attitude toward his wife and children. He gets respect by instilling fear. Carlos and Sellers (1972:104) point out that, "as the male becomes more absolute, he necessarily withdraws from the warm inner-circle of the family, and his distance (social and physical) from day-to-day events makes it possible—in fact necessary—for feminine power to prevail."

As illustrated in the previous chapter, the adult male role as defined by machismo is not a familial role. The husband may play an authoritarian role at home and his wife may declare him to be "boss," but his actual involvement in the household, including the degree to which his own aspirations are realized in the familial context, are not necessarily connected to this behavior. In fact, the household and family become very much the woman's domain. While the man's fulfillment of the standards of machismo must be carried out in the "public" realm, the household and family constitute the sole legitimate domain wherein a woman may realize her aspirations. Conjugal relations, then, are shaped on the surface by the dominance of the *machista* personality (just as it is supposed to be dominant in whatever context), and by the situation of female dependency on male income. Actual household arrangements and family relations may be determined in part by acquiescence to male desires, but the household belongs to the wife, who primarily creates it, shapes it, and keeps it running.

This divergence of ideal conjugal roles is centrally important. The "relative aspirations" (Oppong 1974:115) of men and women in Colombia rarely coincide and are most often in conflict. The intense conflict, insecurity, negotiation, and manipulation surrounding male household contributions has been documented by Benería and Roldán for women in Mexico City (1987). Their case material perfectly illustrates the problems arising from the disjuncture between male and female values, including how men tend toward individualistic consumption while the ideology of maternal altruism encourages women to devote their earnings to meet collective rather than individual needs. Even when a husband turns over his pay to his wife for household expenses, he still may claim a sizable allowance, which is usually spent on drinking and on consumer goods for his personal use (things that are connected to his status in the public realm). Benería and Roldán report on husbands' and wives' contrasting definition of what constitutes basic expenditures, or what the minimum acceptable standard is for children's clothes, schooling, and outings. In the working-class households they studied in Mexico City, "it is husbands who decide minimum standards; these are seldom shared by wives. Furthermore, couples often do not agree on the urgency of a given expenditure, but it is the husband who decides not only what is basic but when it is needed" (1987:122). Some household allowances afford only a bare level of survival, and men may "borrow" from the pool after they have exhausted the funds kept aside for their personal use.

Browner and Lewin (1982) note that women's restricted access to employment means that they must meet subsistence needs through relationships with others. They describe how women elaborate either their conjugal or their maternal roles in Colombia and among Latinas in the United States as a response to general economic scarcity and indirect access to the marketplace. Since women usually get access to resources through their ties to men, they are at a distinct disadvantage when their husbands' goals do not set the well-being of the household as a priority. A woman tries to bind a man to her through sexual attraction, and beyond that by bearing his children. Long after he has lost sexual interest in her, she hopes that his feelings of affection for their children will maintain his contributions to the household.

Machismo versus the "Breadwinner" Role:
A Comparative Case

Machismo stands in marked contrast to the male "breadwinner" role discussed by Ehrenreich (1983). As a journalist, Ehrenreich generalizes about "American culture" in a way that would generally be unacceptable to the anthropological approach, which tends to stress the significant cultural diversity within the United States. While recognizing that Ehrenreich overgeneralizes, I include this case as an interesting illustration of how standards of adult masculinity are ideological constructs, which vary both historically within one society and also between societies. Ehrenreich's analysis is also pertinent here because it relates to the following discussion on the degree to which the male identifies with his domestic group and fulfills his aspirations through it.

In Ehrenreich's portrayal of American culture of the 1950s, a man was expected to marry and support a family to be considered truly adult (and truly a man). "This expectation was supported by an enormous weight of expert opinion, moral sentiment, and public bias, both within popular culture and the elite centers of academic wisdom" (Ehrenreich 1983:12). In contrast, the *machista* individual is not tied down by any such well-developed sense of responsibility, nor does "society" generally try to impose it on him. If he is responsible to his wife and children, if he becomes a "family man," he is breaking with the norms of machismo. Although male irresponsibility is viewed with disgust by women and other defenders of the family, a man who has abandoned wife and children is in no way aberrant in the sense that Ehrenreich discusses:

> If adult masculinity was indistinguishable from the breadwinner role, then it followed that the man who failed to achieve this role was either not fully adult or not fully masculine. In the schema of male pathology developed by mid-century psychologists, immaturity shaded into infantilism, which was, in turn, a manifestation of unnatural fixation on the mother. (Ehrenreich 1983:20)

In Colombia, it is assumed from the outset that a husband's "maleness" makes it difficult for him to be faithful or responsible. When asked why men find it so difficult to adjust to domesticity, women respond that it is their nature to be sexually profligate. Gissi (1982:90), citing a study by Fromm, states that there is an inverse correlation of machismo with responsibility, cooperation, satisfaction in work, and productivity. The traits that are characteristic of machismo are aggressiveness and belligerence. This contrasts markedly with the standards for adult masculinity in the United States, as Gore Vidal phrases it:

> The thing that makes an economic system like ours work is to maintain control over people and make them do jobs they hate. To do this, you fill their heads with biblical nonsense about fornication of every variety. Make sure they marry young, make sure they have a wife and children very early. Once a man has a wife and two young children, he will do what you tell him to. He will obey you. And that is the aim of the entire masculine role. (Gore Vidal 1980, quoted by Ehrenreich 1983:29)

Clearly, the historical, economic, and cultural influences shaping masculine roles diverge greatly between Colombia and the United States. The family wage system and levels of consumerism in the United States as contrasted to the Colombian situation of general economic scarcity and the ongoing effects of rapid urbanization and modernization on a formerly peasant society in Colombia are issues of primary importance.

✠

THE CONSEQUENCES OF MACHISMO FOR WOMEN'S HOUSEHOLD ROLES

To reiterate, Colombian women are dependent on male income for support of the household, but the reliability of male support is eroded by the machismo complex. I will now turn to a brief examination of the implications of this statement for family and household organization from the female point of view.

Women's Work and Support of the Household

Because of pervasive discrimination against women in terms of employment, most Colombian women quite realistically recognize men as the primary source of household income. The average earnings of women characteristically range from about two-thirds to one-half of the average for men in most countries in the world. In Bogotá they are nearer half. The ratio declines with age: young women earn almost as much as men but older women earn less and less comparatively (Mohan 1980:82).[2]

Nevertheless, large numbers of Colombian women are engaged in income-generating activities. These include formal sector jobs, domestic service, and a wide range of informal sector activities such as giving manicures in people's homes, selling clothing on consignment to friends and relatives, or caring for the children of other women who work during the day. If a woman is not engaged in some sort of money-earning activity she is still constantly thinking of various possibilities for getting some income. The kinds of jobs available will depend on her class and education; and the amount of time and energy spent on income-generating activities will depend, in some measure, on her relationship to a man.

In Colombia, as in the United States, women with full-time jobs often work a double day. They are still responsible for running their households, and the addition of these duties to a regular full-time job makes for a horrendous burden. For upper-class women, domestic servants may take over most of the day-to-day running of the household; as Stevens (1973) has pointed out, professional-class women in Latin America benefit from the availability of cheap domestic labor. For the majority of women, however, the domestic work remains to be done at the end of the day. Older children and other female relatives sometimes take over some of the household responsibilities, but the double burden in many cases explains a woman's preference for male support as opposed to full-time employment.

The important point is that men are paid better than women, and not having access to any part of a male wage is a tremendous hardship for women trying to maintain a household. Women's pervasive concern with bringing in a few pesos as best they can reflects the insecurity of their claims on the male wage and their awareness that they had better see to it themselves that they can at least buy a pound of *panela* (a type of unrefined sugar that, dissolved in hot water, constitutes the standard baseline diet of the poor) and a few rolls for the children's dinner. With great resourcefulness and sacrifice, women may be able to earn enough to feed their families, but without access to a male wage they have little hope of providing for a better future for their children.

The Family and Women's Life Chances

As a direct consequence of this situation, for Colombian women, the destruction of a home is an incredible tragedy, similar to bankruptcy of a business for the entrepreneur or disbarment for a lawyer. In U.S. society, divorce is usually treated as tragic in terms of emotional factors—loss or failure of love. Divorce or separation and the breakup of a family are tragic because we imbue the family with a sentimentality reserved for nonmarket sectors of our lives, which are supposed to be less brutal than market-governed principles of behavior. It is this disillusionment of our sentimentality that gives family breakups their particular poignancy. It also is generally felt that the real victims of the dissolution of the family are the children, who presumably require, in addition to material necessities, a "loving atmosphere" in culturally defined terms, in other words, a household comprising a husband and a wife united by selfless dedication to each other and to the products of their mutual esteem and affection.

A difficult aspect of the family breakup tragedy, financial ruin, is more immediate, conscious, and compelling to Colombian women. While it is undeniably a component of our emotional response to the "broken home" in the United States, I think family breakup is more mystified in our society than in Colombia, where financial ruin unto itself is sufficiently tragic without having to provide further emotional embellishment. The terrible disruption and hardship caused by the failure of the familial corporation is, of course, the result of women's dependence on male income or the fact that an economic arrangement between men and women is the only generally recognized way for women and children to survive (or to maintain a hard-won level of family dignity, which is a woman's only avenue to social status).

A further consideration is the alternatives available to women after separation or abandonment. To a very great extent, Colombian women have a "one-shot" chance at forming a family. Hence, there is an elaboration of ideas surrounding courtship, and parents have an intense desire to control their daughters' choice of a mate. Starting a second family is difficult for women even in our own society, but in Colombia it is close to impossible. Although civil marriage is permitted, and since 1974 divorce has been allowed for those who married in this fashion, most Colombians still think of marriage in terms of Catholic marriage, and divorce, until very recently, has not been a possibility for Colombian Catholics.

The exception to this arrangement is the "matrifocal family/consensual union" pattern, which is based on the premise of men's basic undependability and assumes that a woman will have a sequence of mates during her lifetime. In this case the burden of family support falls more heavily on the woman. However, such support also depends on a woman's success at using the strategy of serial monogamy to maximum advantage by tying men to her who are willing and able to contribute to the support of the household and by getting rid of men who are economic drains or noncontributors. This pattern has been well described by Brown (1975) for the Dominican Republic, and its Colombian manifestation has been discussed by Rubbo (1975). Rubbo also points out the changing nature of marital ties with upward mobility. Lower-class women tend to have more flexibility in terms of their mating strategies, while lower-middle or middle-class women are bound to a single man.

✚

CONJUGAL ROLES
AND STATUS CONSCIOUSNESS

Individual Aspirations in Separate Spheres

Referring again to Schneider and Smith (1973), "elements derived from the system of status and class differentiation" also form part of conglomerate kinship roles. These status elements have a complex effect on conjugal relations. An analysis of how status issues differentially affect males and females in households, along with how and which status markers may be important in public as opposed to private realms, is of central importance here.

Payne (1968) has provided an interesting discussion of what he describes as "the all-engrossing struggle for status in Colombia." He maintains that Colombians are highly sensitive to status indicators and enumerates some of the plethora of characteristics and behavior patterns that affect status in Colombia.[3] These include styles of dress, titles of address, the cleanliness and state of repair of clothing, level and kind of education, where an individual is, and with whom, how he carries himself, whether he appears anxious or self-confident, whether he is alone or accompanied, whether he refrains from engaging in any manual labor including such things as oiling a squeaky hinge or changing a tire, and, of course, the more familiar status markers of type of residence, place of residence, skin color, and family background. Payne's assessment is that each Colombian is in constant competition with his neighbor for status. Payne cites the Reichel-Dolmatoffs' study of Aritama, where

> the ultimate goal of life is to be respected . . . to be attributed dignity in spite of skin color and poverty. . . . To have a family, to have sons who help in the fields, to have less work and more food, better clothes, to travel, to find a suitable match, were ambitions most frequently stated, but it was always understood that all these minor ambitions had value only insofar as they would contribute to personal prestige. (Reichel-Dolmatoff and Reichel-Dolmatoff 1961:441–442)

Status consciousness coupled with a relatively high degree of class mobility means that no one considers anyone else an equal. Because of this, claims Payne, it is futile to speak of "classes" in Colombia. Within any particular strata (his preferred word) there are gradations, and the stratification pattern lacks sharp divisions. There are no groups of "non-status competitive members one could meaningfully call a 'class' " (Payne 1968:44).

Payne cites a number of Colombian scholars who discuss the origins of this situation in the colonial period and who have noted the extreme importance of prestige or "honor" in Spanish-American culture: "It was the most status-conscious individuals of Spain, some argue, who carried out the conquest and colonization of the New World. The colonies therefore became heavily populated by quasi-, pseudo-, and would-be nobles all struggling for the titles they could not achieve in Spain" (p. 44).

As in Ramos's explanation of the origins of machismo, Colombian sensitivity to issues of status can be traced to particular features of Spanish colonization in the New World. The transplantation of Spanish notions of honor, the legacy of conquest and subjugation, the personal backgrounds of the individuals who left Spain and their aspirations in the New World, all influence the contemporary situation. A history of economic dependency and cultural imperialism have also affected sensitivity to status. Colombian writers frequently complain about the lack of national identity and cultural pride. They state that Colombians are at the same time very xenophobic yet immediately willing to believe that something foreign (in particular, manufactured goods but also styles) is superior to anything locally made. To Colombians, "*industria colombiana*" (Colombian industry) carries with it a connotation of inferior quality and likelihood of breaking down, while "*marca extranjera*" (foreign brand) designates high-quality imported goods. Employers who advertise in the newspaper for domestic servants will mention that they are "*extranjeros*" (foreigners) because servants prefer to work for foreigners, partly because of the higher status it infers but primarily because they believe that a foreign mistress will treat them better than a Colombian would.

The lack of class solidarity and the individualistic nature of status acquisition in Colombia affect family life and conjugal behavior. Men and women have very different experiences with regard to enhancing or maintaining status. In her study assessing the relative modernity of Bogotano women's values, Harkess (1973) points out that the differences between the lower middle class and the working class in Bogotá are social rather than economic. She adds that "maintenance of the family's recently or tenuously achieved social status requires constant effort" (1973:237). On a day-to-day basis, it is women who continually reproduce status (keeping clothes clean and mended, etc.). It is not uncommon for a husband to be much better turned out than his wife since he is the one who presents an image to the public world. He also has more disposable income to spend on himself, while his wife will most likely use whatever resources she has to feed her family or to clothe her children. According to the ideal of *marianismo*, the self-sacrificing mother receives more approval for spending her money on her children than for outfitting herself elegantly. In fact the attitude would be that her own elegant outfit means that she is in some way denying her children. An example of this is the inordinate attention paid to the school uniforms of children. Even very small children have uniforms. These are obvious status indicators, and a woman's compulsive fussiness over her children's uniforms contrasts with her often quite casual attention to her own appearance.

Women derive status from the men associated with them, but the converse is not necessarily true. While a woman can bring a man shame, she (or the conjugal unit they make up) is not usually the source of his pride. Again, a comparison with the situation in the United States is interesting. The male breadwinner in Ehrenreich's analysis kept his nose to the grindstone in part because the level of consumerism of his household (which could be enhanced only by his labor) was the most important illustration of his social status. The size and location of his house, where his children went to school, the kind of car he drove, and a multitude of less grandiose status markers such as ballet classes for his daughters and summer camp for his sons were all central to his social position. It is notable that all of these status markers are household-based. In Colombia, until fairly recently, such consumeristic status markers were not particularly important except among the very upper classes. This situation is changing.

It is very important to distinguish between consumerism that is household-based and consumerism that is individualistic and takes place outside the household. For the most part, this has broken down along sex lines—male versus female consumption patterns. The classic, and perhaps most prevalent, example in Colombia is the husband's drinking up the household budget in the local *tienda de la esquina* (corner store), while his wife wrings her hands helplessly at the prospect. Fals-Borda (1962) noted that *tienda* drinking was the primary avenue to personal prestige for men in the rural neighborhood of Saucio.[4]

The New Consumerism:
Household-Based Status Markers

Formerly, consumer goods were relevant as status markers only among the upper classes, who imported English woolens and grand pianos as impressive markers of their distinction. Currently in Colombia, certain types of consumer goods are becoming more widely available. Compared to the earlier generations in the countryside, contemporary Colombian families experience a relatively greater degree of material comfort, except among the extreme lower stratum. The markers of middle-class distinction tend to be categorized under the term "*electro-domésticos*": a refrigerator, washing machine, blender, electric coffee pot, television, and a stereo are all desirable status markers and essentials in the middle-class home. The phrase "*casa, carro y beca*" (house, car, and scholar-ship) appears on a billboard that is frequently displayed in Bogotá to advertise a lottery run by a national savings bank with account numbers of depositors, the prizes of which are a house, a car, or a scholarship (also on occasion less costly items such as a color TV). This billboard epitomizes the new orientation of Colombian consumer patterns in the direction of household-based items: goods that would be consistent with patterns of status acquisition beyond the individual, focused on the family and household.[5]

In Colombia, it is commonly accepted in the press and in academic writing that the "family" is in crisis. Colombian social analysts look with hope to the changes of the type I describe above, believing that a new kind of family must come into being to replace the old bonds de-stroyed by the upheavals of modernization. Cano (1981:12) says:

> The new family, less attached to the customs of their elders, with their own standards of how many children they will have—definitely fewer—with de-sires of improving themselves, will have to fight first and foremost against the biggest weight on the Colombian family: machismo, which is constantly present in the highest levels and the lowest, in the cultivated and in the illiterate.

It is intriguing that Cano identifies machismo as the stumbling block to upward mobility. Also, he sees it as a problem not for women or for men, but for the family as a unit. It is also sad and ironic that Cano, editor of the Bogotá newspaper *El Espectador*, was killed in 1986 by those icons of machismo—the *narco-traficantes* (drug traffickers).

What is critical here is the connection between upward mobility, forms of consumption, and sex role behavior. For many reasons, a move, or an attempt to move, into the "respectable middle class" entails an increase in sexual integration, a changeover from individualistic con-sumption patterns to household-based ones, and a corresponding align-ment of formerly contradictory male and female aspirations and values.

While this process is widespread in contemporary Colombia, and can also be said to break down along generational lines, it is of primary im-portance in understanding evangelical conversion. The intersection be-tween evangelical belief and the transformation of sex roles with upward mobility is discussed in the next chapter.

✠
CASE HISTORY: ROSALINDA

The following case study illustrates many of the central points raised in chapter 5. It is not a success story; Rosalinda has not experienced the changes in her life that she would like to have had as the result of her conversion. Although she is comparatively well off, many elements of her story are representative of the kind of response I received from women in a range of economic situations whose husbands had not converted with them. Rosalinda clearly articulates the links between her domestic problems and her conversion experience. Her impressions of the church of which she is a member and her description of her personal relationship with the pastoral couple also reveal a characteristically female and familial model. Rosalinda's story serves as a bridge between the discussion of Colombian sex roles and family roles outlined earlier and the explanation of the impact of conversion on the domestic realm, which follows in chapter 7.

Rosalinda is fifty-one years old. She is an active member of the Iglesia Cristiana Carismática (Charismatic Christian Church), more commonly known as "Los Juanitos," after the missionary couple, John and Jean Firth, who began the church. The Juanitos are at present missionaries of the Four-Square Gospel church, and have been for many years, since their charismatic "conversion" drove them out of the more theologically conservative Inter-American Mission, a branch of the Oriental Missionary Society.

The Juanitos church is one of the few charismatic or pentecostal churches that has been established among "professional"-class people in Colombia and is located in the prestigious northern sector of Bogotá. For the bulk of the forty-four years that the Firths have been in Colombia they, like other foreign missionaries, have directed their efforts toward the lower classes. According to the Reverend Firth, it was at the invitation of a cousin of former president Alfonso López that he and his wife moved to the north and began their work with the professional classes. He recounts how López's cousin and his wife converted after a visit from the Firths, and then challenged them saying "Why don't you do something for the professional people, too? Why do all you missionaries confine yourselves to the working-class people?" A Major Leal, who was the secretary of the DAS (Departmento Administrativo de Seguridad) at the time, said the same thing and promised to attend meetings and help if the Firths would come to the north. Starting with eight people in 1979, the church realized an annual growth rate of 100 percent to 130 percent each year, and in 1982 had five hundred members, with over six hundred people attending services on Sunday. In order not to discourage people from attending, the Four-Square Gospel affiliation is kept out of the name of this church because of its lower-class connotations.

The Juanitos have started holding special services devoted to the family, with the objective of pulling more men into the church. John Firth said, "One of the problems amongst the charismatics is we're getting a lot more women than men, and the men are coming along more slowly. The women seem to come first, in most cases. And then, the men sometimes they have another woman, they've got plenty of money, there's a lot of what we call machismo."

Rosalinda's story aptly illustrates the point that the problems that drive women to religion are not unique to the lower class. Rosalinda was born in Barranquilla, on Colombia's Caribbean coast. In terms of the regional stereotypes commonly applied in Colombia, costeños are livelier and more open than people from the highlands. In fact, as Rosalinda recounts her story, she is clearly saddened, but she does not have the usual somber reticence of highland women. Although we have met only once before, briefly, at the church, she talks very openly about the problems she has experienced in her marriage. She has five children, three boys and two girls, ranging in age from twenty-nine to sixteen, all of whom still live at home with her. Rosalinda and her husband, an executive, are separated. Her husband lives only a few blocks away, with another woman, with whom he also has children. Rosalinda is an attractive, well-groomed woman with short salt-and-pepper hair. She has a good figure for a Colombian woman of her age (or for any woman who has borne five children) and wears makeup and perfume. She lives in the far north of Bogotá, not far from Unicentro, the shopping mall that is the pride of modern Bogotá. Her house is a large, one-storey white structure of simple cinder block and cement construction, occupying a whole corner in the upper-middle-class neighborhood.

I was very much in love with my husband when we got married. I adored him, but now I realize that my adoration should be for God. My married life was a disaster—he was always drinking, he always had other women. Like all costeños, he liked to enjoy life. I was very proud and I fought with him a lot. There was no peace in the family. His other women would call me on the phone and insult me. I wanted to kill the woman who was going with my husband. If I had had a revolver I would have killed her. My husband was my God. I went to a psychiatrist, and he prescribed sleeping pills for me. Finally, a female dentist gave me a book by Norman Vincent Peale, as a present. I read it, and looked things up in the Bible. I was trying so hard to understand what the book said, but at first I didn't understand. I asked God to help me. I wanted to study the Bible even if I had to pay for it. I had taken courses in glamour, cooking, everything to please my husband, and at that point I thought I might as well pay for a course in Bible study. I told another friend of mine that I wanted to understand the Bible, and my friend, who is also a costeña, told me to go to this place, Alpha and Omega. I went there for five years, although all during that time I continued to go to the Catholic church. They do that at Alpha and Omega—they encourage you to continue going to your old church. All that time I was still with my husband. I took him to a meeting at the Alpha and Omega, but nothing came of it. He even knew the Bible well, because he had gone to the Colegio Americano [the Presbyterian high school] in Barranquilla. He was actually quite sympathetic to these ideas. He also has an aunt who is an evangelical—she's Baptist. His aunt, Tía Ramona, had a special affection for me. When I was first married, we were living in the same house as her, and she gave me Psalm 91, the psalm of protection, and told me "learn the psalm." In those days the Christians were being persecuted, and Ramona's family attacked and criticized her. But she prayed continually, and she was praying for me. In those days the Christians were without the power of the Holy Spirit. I learned the psalm by heart, but in those days it was to me like reciting the Ave Maria in the Catholic church—I said it without thinking about what the words meant. The Catholic priests were no help at all—they just told me to have patience, and that I had to put up with him. Before I came to know the Lord, all I used to ask for was peace. I never asked for riches. Sure, I like to be comfortable, but I've never been very materialistic. I would get down on my knees and pray for peace. Three years ago, when he finally left the house for good, part of me was relieved, because as long as he lived with me that way I felt that I was helping him in his life of sin.

That is a bad thing about this country, that divorce is not allowed. He gives us money for food, and he pays for tuition for the kids at the colegio and the university. But he doesn't give us money for anything else.

My father was also a drunk, but he never looked at other women. He was a very affectionate man, but I used to see that the peace in the household was shattered when my father drank. We were poor, we never had abundance, but my family is one of good name, at least on my father's side. My childhood was sad because of the lack of money, but my father and mother were always together. My father ran a business. My mother still lives in Barranquilla. She's very ill now, and trembles very badly. She got Parkinson's disease when my father died.

My parents were Catholic, but they didn't practice their religion. They were inconstant. My father didn't like priests. My mother used to go to

mass every day before she got married. From the time I was little I loved
God, but there is a lot of idolatry and error in the Catholic church. The
Catholic church doesn't really lead one to God. They don't have the power of
the Holy Spirit, so people don't change in that church. There's no love in the
Catholic church. The Juanitos church is full of love—they are like Corinthians 13. When you know the Holy Spirit, hate, pride, and jealousy fall away.
Because I know the Holy Spirit, I'm able to ask for forgiveness from my children, and from my husband, and even from the woman who lives with my
husband. I used to be violent with jealousy over my husband. I am by nature
melancholy and sensitive—that's just my personality.

I wouldn't change the Christian life for anything. God is a god of every
minute. I live in constant prayer, and I know that I'm not alone. When my
husband finally left me for good, I experienced much loneliness, but God
was my company. I felt *acompañada*. My husband didn't turn out to be the
kind of company I wanted.

There is work for everybody to do within the Christian life. God has
helped me so much, I must do as much as I can to help others. I see people
who are alone, and I feel drawn to help them, to make them feel less alone.
Unfortunately I don't have a *muchacha de servicio* [domestic servant]. If I
could take more time off from the family, that's what I would do, spend my
time helping others to feel less alone. Even after I have done a lot of house-
work, if I am able to help someone in the Lord I feel new—refreshed and full
of energy. The Lord gives me strength to do it.

My children aren't Christian. The second one and the youngest one believe a little bit, but they don't go to church. When my youngest son got
drunk for the first time, I had to be very tough with him, and that was hard.
After that I went to see Juanita, to cry on her shoulder. My children, especially the girls, are a little bad-tempered, because they feel the lack of their
father. The boys are better than the girls. The girls need a father for their
normal sexual development. The boys—they have their mother's love and so
they don't have as much of a problem. My oldest daughter [twenty-nine] is a
very frustrated person. At the University of the Andes, she studied economics for one year and then quit, then she studied biology, but she never finished that, even though she liked it a lot. She only had a year and a half
more to go to finish her degree. She's not married, she lives here with me.
She's a big help around the house, she does the marketing. Each person has a
function in the family. She loves the other kids a lot. Her bad temper is improving because I've been praying for her. I dedicated more time to her, because she was the first, so I protected her from things. Mothers here in Colombia have a tendency to overprotect their children. My second oldest, a
boy, is finishing his degree in economics at Los Andes. Another one studies
graphic design, and another one is studying public relations. Nowadays,

more than before, it's important to prepare oneself well for a career. A high school degree in business doesn't get you very far these days. The kids are able to get loans from ICETEX [Instituto de Crédito Educativo y Estudios Técnicos en el Exterior] to pay half of their university tuition, and their father pays the other half. The Juanitos are trying to win souls for Christ among the wealthier people. Their new church, which just opened, is in Chicó, which is the most elegant barrio in Bogotá. They are trying to make headway among people of that social level, but it's always been easier with the poor folk. The Juanitos started their church in Barranquilla in the Barrio del Chino, where the lowest people, the prostitutes, lived. The wealthier people are afraid of the tithing. The Catholic church doesn't ask for the 10 percent—they just ask for alms and for payments for marriages and burials. It's run like a business, so they don't have the power.

The Juanitos also have prayer meetings in people's houses. If you want to have a service in your home, they put your name on a list and it's announced in church. Sometimes it's just more convenient and comfortable to have the meeting in someone's house. The format for the service is basically the same as the *cultos* in church. At the moment there's no special instruction for the leaders of these home prayer groups, but that is something that is needed.

I preached in church once. In order to prepare a sermon you start by praying. Then you go to the Bible. You don't sit and write it all at once, the inspiration comes to you bit by bit, as you're cooking, doing things around the house and all. The Holy Spirit guides you in terms of what to write down. You have to have love and discipline. When I prepared the sermon for the service at the Juanitos I spent all week in prayer, and the Holy Spirit gave me the message little by little. Some people have a real calling to preach, like Rubi, who gave the sermon yesterday. At Alpha and Omega they teach you how to preach. You start in front of small groups. The Holy Spirit helps you get over your nervousness, helps you to forget the people in front of you. People from all different churches come to the Juanitos for the Liberation services, and from all different social classes. The Juanitos have started having services on Thursday nights, special services of intercession, to pray for the family. On Thursdays one of the things we have to do is to pray for more men, to pray that people's husbands will come to church. Men are very cold.

Religion is different from Christianity. Christianity is not religion, it's an entire change in one's life. In religion, one gets all hung up on the rites of the church, but if you're not fulfilling all of the things in the Bible, it's not Christianity. You have to experience the gifts of God. If there's not a change in your life, Christ hasn't entered.

God is always looking for man. It's not that man is looking for God. Before I became a Christian, I thought that everything came from the hand of my husband rather than from the hand of God.

I like stability. Even down to the arrangement of the living room furniture. My daughter and her friend changed the furniture around one afternoon when I was out, and when I came home I made them put it all back the way it had been. I feel well situated at the Juanitos, I don't feel like I have to look around for anything else.

I feel somewhat bitter toward the people at Alpha and Omega, because they were interested in selecting the people who had money, and I don't think that was very Christian. They demanded that the members tithe, and I felt they were robbing the food out of my children's mouths. One day I went to talk to one of the zone leaders, and he was having an elegant luncheon and wouldn't give me the time of day. If I had been a rich person they would have helped me more. I'm kind of slow to figure out when I'm being taken advantage of. Besides that, there was a woman who attended meetings there who was friendly with the woman whom my husband is living with, and so there was gossip. I finally left Alpha and Omega because they lacked love.

I am a very sincere person—to the point that sometimes I'm accused of being rude. My kind of sincerity doesn't have a place in society nor in the church. Juanita told me that she had noticed how sincere I was.

Juanita's special gift is teaching. She also preaches from time to time in the services. She has a very tranquil temperament. She is Juanito's helper, she's always ready to help him. Juanito is completely opposite from her. This is the ideal. Juanito is very sweet and affectionate. Sometimes after a day of fasting he will give me a plate of soup. He is a perfect pastor—exactly the way this is described in the book of Tito. He cares for his flock. They complement each other—he is good for some things, and she is good for others. They have the ideal marriage—he is sanguine and she is phlegmatic.

In my family, we were six children—three boys and three girls. All of my brothers and sisters are still alive. My oldest brother lives in Venezuela. Three are still in Barranquilla, and the sixth brother is here in Bogotá. I lived in Barranquilla throughout my childhood, until I was thirty-one. I studied business in the Colegio de Barranquilla, which is a state high school. I left twenty years ago. When I was eighteen I went to work in the Office of the Exchange Registry in the Bank of the Republic. My husband worked in another bank, an American bank. That's how we met. He used to bring his deposits to me—I was the teller who used to receive his deposits. When we met I was twenty and he was twenty-one. At that time I was making a good salary, quite a bit more than he was earning. We courted for about two years, and got married without really thinking. We were very crazy in love—and I was more in love than he. We were married in 1953 in the Catholic church. The first thirteen or fourteen years we lived in Barranquilla, and then he was transferred to Montería for one year and then to Tunja for two years. I went with him to help him succeed in his post. I had gotten him the job, at the Bank of the Republic. He is now the head of a branch office and has fifty employees under him. After we were married he wouldn't let me work—he was very jealous. I'd like to work now, but what could I do? Once I taught a street urchin to read and write, here in my house, and also a *muchacha de servicio*, and I liked that very much. But here a mother dedicates her life to her children, and that is a good thing, helping them in whatever she can. Now when I help them it is with the love of God rather than with human love.

I always consulted my husband about decisions that affected the household. We decided things together. That's basic. He is still the head of the house, even though he doesn't live here any more. I still consult with him when difficult things come up. He comes to visit on Sundays, eats lunch with us, and visits with the kids. Sometimes he sleeps over. I'm surprised he hasn't shown up today, since it's a holiday.

[When I asked her if she still held out hope that he'd come back to her, she said yes.] I hope he'll come to Christ. This would be the biggest thing that I could do in my Christian life. The maximum. I ask this of the Lord more than anything else. [She begins to cry.] I still believe what it said in the marriage ceremony—that we are one single flesh. I pray that I don't die without seeing my husband come to Christ and return to the family.

Rosalinda showed me around her house, which was quite large. Only about half of it was finished. There were several very pretty rooms that were completely bare, no glass in the windows, although there were bars covering them. She described to me her plans for the rooms—how she wanted to fix them up. The kitchen was very new and modern. The bedrooms that were finished had several beds crowded into each of them. There was a two-car garage, containing a smashed-up Renault-4. She told me that her daughter had had an accident but that God had spared her injury. As we stood in a front room with low windows overlooking the street, she told me that if the room were finished it would make a nice place for prayer meetings. The rain was dribbling in through the unglassed windows. She turned to me and said, "This is what happens in a broken home." The physical condition of the house was a visual illustration of all that she had told me. When the husband is absent, things stay incomplete, a mess. If her husband did not have another woman and another house, all of these rooms would be finished and the house would be whole and beautiful, instead of a shell.

Colombian Evangelicalism from the Household Out

✛

GENDER ROLES AND MARITAL ROLES IN THE CONVERSION PROCESS

The Dangers of Machismo

There are compelling reasons why men under certain circumstances would be open to an ideological system that would release them from the pressures of machismo. According to Pachón de Galán (1981:105), violence in Colombia causes more deaths than cancer and heart attacks, and the primary cause of death in the population between fifteen and forty-four years of age is homicide.[1] Although even long-term city dwellers are susceptible to violent incidents of all sorts, male migrants to urban areas are particularly vulnerable. Female migrants outnumber male, and in some respects the situation favors them. Very few, if any, women or girls would migrate to the city if they did not have family there to receive them, and hence they are enfolded in the protection of a household and its networks from the moment they arrive. Men, on the other hand, may also rely on kin for a place to stay and for help in locating a job, but it is unlikely that they will be satisfied with limiting their sphere of activities to the household. The public life they get involved in is geometrically more dangerous than the corner stores where they drank beer with their friends and neighbors (and enemies) in the small town they came from, and the complexities of urban living are not yet known to them. Stories abound about the many misadventures of sons, husbands, and nephews who have unwisely ventured off into the mysterious and dangerous world of the streets. This is not simply a case of the country boy being hoodwinked by sophisticated urbanites. The inexperience of the rural migrant in the ways of public urban life may have fatal consequences. Although women may repeat these stories as object lessons to impress upon their sons the advantages of staying close to home, they have an undeniable basis in reality. The culture of machismo, which is dangerous even in the relatively more regulated world of the small town, may not, in the urban area, carry along with it enough benefits to outweigh the proportional increase in its risks. As Ehrenreich

(1983:139) states somewhat facetiously, "machismo may be an asset on the dance floor, but it's a health hazard at high altitudes."

Moral Inequality and the Role of Women as Reformers of Men

According to Colombian sex-role stereotypes, women are generally considered to be the morally superior partners in a relationship. This is perhaps one of the few inherent "strengths" attributed to women within a gender system that is strongly prejudiced in favor of males in every other realm.[2] It could be argued that women's presumed moral edge functions as yet another burden, restricting as it does their behavior and keeping them "good," that is, submissive, long-suffering, and occupied with serving others rather than pursuing the gratification of their own needs and interests. However, there is also a more active aspect to the female role in this regard, and I think it is of much importance in considering the dynamic of evangelical conversion within the household context. I would argue that in a sex and gender system dominated by machismo, the woman's role as the defender of moral standards includes her responsibility continually to attempt to reform the male. She exerts moral pressure on others as well, including her children and other women, but for the moment I would like to consider male and female interaction in this regard.

The particular focus of a woman's reformist impulse will vary depending on the stage in the developmental cycle of the relationship, but I believe that it continues from the early stages of courtship throughout married life, and the only thing that can actually put a stop to it is success, when the male lives up to her standards. The playing out of this drama is especially vivid during courtship. During this period, if he is living up to machista standards, a man must try to conquer (i.e., commit an "immoral" act by having sex out of wedlock), and the woman for her part must resist (i.e., defend both her own and the man's moral standards).[3] Although other strategies may be involved and complicate the issue somewhat, in general a woman will hope that she is sufficiently attractive to her novio (sweetheart) that he will eventually choose her over his machista standards. Therefore, during this time she will try to utilize his desire for her to cut back on his involvement in the culture of machismo. Her primary concern will be that he has other women, and the amount of jealousy and competition that exists among women involved with the same man is, in part, related to the fact that as long as he has other women the fiancée's advantage in reforming him is undermined. Of course there are other reasons, including simple economic interest: a woman obviously prefers not to share a man's already limited resources with his other lovers or households. (See, e.g., Rubbo's excellent analysis [1975] of women's economic interest and the use of love magic against other women in Colombia.)

Here I would like to elaborate on the ideological system surrounding this harsh economic reality, taking women's economic dependence on men as a given for the moment. A woman's persuasiveness in controlling her *novio* is proportional to the intensity of his interest in her; hence, if his interests are divided (among several women), her leverage decreases. This issue is of paramount importance, as evidenced by the fact that, even if there is no real competition, a girl may indulge in rages over imagined or potential rivals. Such behavior might be viewed as a kind of test of her *novio*'s commitment.[4]

That this pattern during courtship extends beyond issues of mere sexual jealousy is evidenced by the fact that a man's involvement in the male world of public drinking, fighting, and so on, will also be subject to his *novia*'s censure. Although she obviously must be very delicate in her criticism, because to be too aggressive would not be in keeping with her role, the *novia* has more power in this regard during courtship than she will after she is married. She can make demands on his time and money, as a proof of his love, that will conflict with his investment in the *machista* lifestyle. A primary argument used in this respect will be the dangers of his activities (see the first section). She has a real interest in reforming him in this regard, because once she has committed herself to the relationship with him, should he be killed she would not only grieve, but be left in a difficult position in terms of starting up with someone else.

Within the gender ideology that prevails in popular music, the male looks to his sweetheart as his salvation from the trials of the life required by the standards of machismo. In a popular *vallenato* (from the coast) song, a man wants to speak to his sweetheart, to tell her all the things that she saved him from. In fact, a temporary or "pretend" reform by the male is often an element in the courtship pattern. It is not unusual for a man to mend his ways while he is courting in order to please his girl (young couples, both Catholic and evangelical, will attend church together), and then to continue with his former habits after he has her safely married to him. In this case her reformer role continues, and although she complains about many of the same things (other women, drinking, his failure to come home), the power she enjoyed during courtship may have diminished drastically. She hopes that bearing his children will give her some leverage over him, but having a wife and children at home does not usually inhibit the expression of *machista* impulses. Her criticism of him at this point may function to drive him away even more. Under what circumstances, then, would he be likely to reform? As long as his wife is maintaining moral standards at home, he is free to do as he likes.

A fruitful place to look for the answer to this question is in the testimonies of male converts to evangelical Protestantism. While religious conversion is by no means the only manner in which Colombian men "reform," and it is surely possible that Catholic women also experience success in their efforts toward this end, in keeping with the argument being developed here I would like to direct attention to the way in which evangelical conversion (for men) erodes the essential separation between male and female spheres.

Many factors may serve to predispose a man toward religious conversion, and my goal here is to elaborate on one of them that is clearly imbedded in the male-female dynamic. Men frequently state that they were led to convert as the result of having been healed of an illness. They describe a series of visits to doctors, expensive X-rays and treatments without result, and continuing affliction. When nothing else has seemed to work, they agree to attend an evangelical service, usually at the invitation of their wife or another relative. Two things usually happen: they are healed of their illness, and they convert out of gratitude. They report that that night "the Lord spoke to my heart," so they are open to the evangelical message and become curious about it. If we place this type of testimony in the context of the argument outlined earlier, the male-female dynamic inherent in it becomes clear. *Machista* culture, with its premium on individual independence and physical prowess, makes no provisions for illness, and in fact, physical disability is anathema to it. When a man gets sick he must withdraw from his usual activities and return home so that his wife can nurse him.[5] (Although in an urban area the service sector can replace many of a wife's functions, in Colombia, even a hospitalized person relies heavily on the family to bring food and see that the patient is cared for.) Because he is physically disabled, he becomes dependent on his wife and family in a way that would be unthinkable if he were well. He is also physically present in the home to a much greater extent than is usual. His suffering, his fear of what is going to happen to him, and his dependence on his wife and family combine to render him uncharacteristically receptive to their counsel. If his wife has already converted, she is armed with the logic of the church to argue that his illness is the result of his *vicios* (vices), and that only by giving them up will he be well again. A nonevangelical woman might apply a variant of this logic, but the evangelical wife will be better equipped with extensive ideological backing from other believers.

For some men, then, a debilitated state (brought about by illness or another sort of personal disaster) may be crucial to rendering them susceptible to evangelical conversion. Numerous writers on Pentecostalism and evangelical Protestantism in Latin America and elsewhere have noted the role of illness in the conversion process, but it has not been analyzed to reveal how it functions within the underlying male-female dynamic. In terms of this type of male testimony, it is the interplay of these two things, illness and the continual effort of women to reform men, that often results in a man's conversion.

It is interesting that the pattern of recruitment into Mexican Spiritualist groups described by Finkler (1983) corresponds in certain strategic ways to this variety of evangelical conversion experience. Although Spiritualists do not proselytize, "the most common route for which individuals are recruited into Spiritualism is through an 'illness network,' encountered during an episode of sickness. This network is composed of the friends, relatives, or neighbors who tell a sick person about Spiritualist therapy after treatment by a physician has proved unsuccessful" (Finkler 1983:289). It is also intriguing that, although men seek temple therapy as the result of a variety of disorders, "those who are recruited and choose to become adherents usually have a history of alcoholism" (p. 292). Spiritualist temples do not prohibit drinking as vigorously as do Pentecostal sects, but they do prohibit drunkenness; and Finkler notes that the change in drinking habits resulting from the man's becoming an adherent provides an economic advantage to the household.

Like Colombian evangelicalism, Mexican Spiritualism is a strongly female-dominated religion, and Finkler notes that a temple goal is to rid males of their machismo. The components of machismo that are cited by Spiritualists include not only drinking, but womanizing and "lack of submissiveness and obedience" (p. 291). Spiritualism, like evangelical Protestantism, "fosters positive male-female relationships within the family unit" (p. 300). The three elements of machismo—drinking, womanizing, and aggression—mentioned by the Spiritualists are those habits or characteristics that are most often the objects of ongoing female reform efforts within male-female relationships. This suggests that the pattern outlined for Colombian evangelicals may also be relevant to other dissident religious movements in mestizo Latin America.

The mention of lack of "submissiveness and obedience" is particularly interesting. These are classified as female traits in Colombia as well as in Mexico. Yet they are essential to the development of a true commitment to evangelicalism (as well as to Spiritualism). Referring to the testimonies cited earlier, the experience of healing and the gratitude resulting from it are only one component. The other, that "the Lord spoke to my heart," is in fact much more central to the individual's continuing commitment. This phrase refers to a deep emotional experience of contrition and a longing for personal change. It can occur only when the individual is in a submissive and obedient frame of mind, an attitude antithetical to the dominance and defiance revered as *machista* qualities. For the man who has been heavily involved in *machista* culture, then, the debilitation of illness will often serve to shatter certain emotional barriers that would preclude his receptivity to evangelical teaching.

Although illness figures prominently in many male testimonies, the situation outlined earlier is by no means the only way that men become involved in evangelical religion. Some men report that they converted "junto con la esposa" (along with their wives). Where the conjugal bond is stronger, in other words, where men are more involved in their marriages than in *machista* culture, women's role as reformer and moral superior is less significant. Also, some evangelical men never experienced conversion per se. At present, many men, among them many evangelical pastors, report that they were raised in the faith, or that they converted when they were very young and attended church with their mothers. These men, of course, fall outside of *machista* culture. Their personalities and aspirations have taken form within a value system that stands in opposition to much of the dominant culture, and to machismo in particular. Also, many testimonies reveal a curiosity about religion that stimulated an individually motivated "search for the truth" and do not seem to be tied specifically to gender issues. I believe that these men also fall outside of machismo culture, for a variety of reasons outlined below. These testimonies are important because they dovetail with the material on households and illustrate the transformative potential of evangelical conversion on Colombian society.

Finally, Finkler mentions that Mexican Spiritualism holds an attraction for some men because it allows them "to avoid drinking and sidestep the macho role, for which all men are obviously not cut out" (1983:293). I think this is also true in the case of Colombian evangelicalism, but it needs elaboration. Some of the literature on Pentecostal conversion has explained individual attraction to the movement in terms of psychological factors. In this view, "deviant" individuals may find a place in these religious movements that has been denied to them by the wider society. (For a review of this literature, see Hine [1974].)

Although this may be true to a minor degree, I think it is inadequate as an explanation of motivation for conversion to evangelicalism in Colombia for a number of reasons. In terms of the *machista* role, I believe that this complex must be considered as central to shaping male-female relations in Colombia, but not all Colombian men fulfill this role to the same degree, and failure to fulfill it does not necessarily make a man a "deviant" in the sense of a person whose psychological peculiarities make him a social outcast shunned by the rest of the community. Certainly, if a man refuses to establish himself as "*macho*" he is sacrificing a certain kind of social status within particular circles, but such a man would be more accurately called "unusual" rather than "deviant." Moreover, the full range of modern machismo characteristics is unevenly represented within the Colombian male population. Although the *machista* role as a sex-role stereotype is very much a part of Colombian society, the actual fulfillment of the role by individual men will depend on a number of factors, including the particular subcultural background of the individual, the amount of disposable income available to him, his own as well as his wife's class background, the degree of involvement in a "household mode of production," his integration into various family networks, and the size of the settlement he lives in. In terms of this last factor in particular, it is commonly believed that a man's potential for getting into trouble increases with his move to town from the countryside, and from the town to the city (see "The Dangers of Machismo"). Obviously, since much of machismo culture involves leisure time activities, his involvement in it will also depend on the amount of time he is freed from the grind of daily subsistence work. In Colombia, machismo is, over the long run, very demanding and difficult for all under its sway, including the males who must perform this role. The sacrifices a man makes for opting out of the system may be outweighed by the benefits.

Conjugal Sexuality before and after Conversion

When machismo is replaced by evangelical belief as the main standard for male behavior, conjugal relations are also affected in terms of the role of sexuality in marriage. Masculine sexuality is clearly subjected to constraints that are unheard of and would be intolerable to machismo thinking, but conjugal sexuality is redefined to accommodate the element of desire now unsatisfied by outside expression. For Catholics, conjugal sexuality is overwhelmingly defined in terms of its procreative function. The good wife is not supposed to enjoy sex—she submits to it as her "sacred duty." In 1979 María Ladi Londoño, a Colombian clinical psychologist and president of the Colombian Society of Sexology, conducted a study in Cali, Colombia, on female sexual pleasure. She interviewed 264 women living in stable unions, most of whom were between the ages of twenty-five and thirty-five. Most of the women had more than two children. Only 15 percent of the women in the group claimed to enjoy sex—the remaining 85 percent said they experienced only a minimum of pleasure. The women spoke openly of various ploys they used to get out of having sex with their partners, an event that they commonly referred to as "the cross" and "the heaviest burden of matrimony." Londoño points out that the striking lack of sexual pleasure in the experience of these women contrasts sharply with a study done with Ecuadorian women, 80 percent of whom reported that they were greatly satisfied in their sexual relations.

It is interesting that the Colombian women interviewed were originally contacted at a "Profamilia" clinic, a private organization started with foreign funding and the compliance of the national government. Its main function is the distribution of birth control at low fees. Unfortunately, Londoño did not question the women regarding their feelings about the reproductive role of sex, which is probably a primary issue for them and bound up with their experience of sexual pleasure in a central way.

For whatever reasons, pleasure and procreative purpose are at odds in Colombian Catholic conjugal sexuality. A man's indulgence of his desire outside of marriage in a way collaborates in protecting his wife's "chaste" image, and her lack of enjoyment in sex reinforces the idea that the union between husband and wife is primarily for procreative purposes.

Most evangelical churches in Colombia hold special classes and "campaigns" on family relations and deal with the topic frequently in sermons and Bible study during regular services. A basic text for evangelicals with reference to marital relations is found in Paul's First Letter to the Corinthians, which is commonly a central focus. Implicit in the teaching of this text is that sex is pleasurable and that it is human nature to desire it. Although Paul wishes that everybody could be like him— that is, celibate and dedicated only to the Lord—he concedes that it is better for people to marry if they cannot exercise such self-control. "For it is better to marry than to be aflame with passion" (1 Corinthians 7:9). The reproductive role of marriage is barely mentioned in this passage, probably because to Paul, reproduction of the world was the last of his worries; what difference would it make when "the appointed time has grown very short" (7:29) and "the form of this world is passing away" (7:31). He suggests that husband and wife should not refuse one another his or her conjugal rights, except perhaps by agreement for a short time to devote themselves to prayer, "but then come together again, lest Satan tempt you through lack of self-control" (7:5). Marriage, then, is the holy outlet for sexual desire.

The positive emphasis on sexuality in marriage, rather than solely on procreation, marks a significant change from the Catholic ideal. One outcome of the acceptance of this teaching is that, for evangelicals, male sexuality becomes defined in terms of and expressed within the role of husband. Although there is considerable variation in terms of evangelical teaching about birth control and abortion, in general the churches take a noninterventionist stand on the topic.

Changing Sex Roles with Conversion

With conversion, machismo is replaced by evangelical belief as the main determinant of husband-wife relations. The boundaries of public (male) life and private (female) life are redrawn and redefined. The relative power positions of the spouses change. This is not to say that women now have power over their husbands. In evangelical households the husband may be the powerful one, but his "relative aspirations" have changed to coincide with those of his wife. Oppong (1974:115) has provided some of the parameters that must be considered in a discussion of conjugal power relations:

> The process of decision-making in the home, how domestic tasks and re-
> sources should be allocated, is an admittedly complex sequence of events,
> taking place between spouses and between them and their kin, affines, col-
> leagues and other significant sets of associates and reference groups, with
> and about whom they exchange goods, services, and communications. It de-
> pends to a great extent upon the *relative power position of the spouses and
> their respective aspirations.* A spouse's power position may be thought of as
> consisting in his or her ability to alter the partner's behavior to conform to
> that desired, even in spite of counter demands and pressures from outsiders,
> especially in terms of the use of money and time upon objects persons and
> interests valued by the spouse. (Emphasis added)

The evangelical husband will be more likely to confer with his wife when making decisions that affect the household, but more important, the way he disposes of his income and his concerns regarding his family are probably going to be consistent with his wife's desires anyway. This is why the evangelical response is so powerful and successful: instead of trying to revolutionize the public realm, which is what would be necessary for women to be allowed greater direct access to regular public sector jobs and "male" income, it reorders the relative participation of men and women in the private realm, enhancing the value of family and household so that they are in the ascendance. Thus issues about public sector success take on a different meaning—they are subsidiary to and contingent on a private valuation (or meaningful in terms of private realm values rather than in their own right). A transformed domestic realm becomes the center of life for both women and men.

✛

THE ECONOMIC EFFECTS
OF GENDER ROLE TRANSFORMATION

The Family Economy of Evangelical Households

Although conversion may not return the production capacity to households, it does reinstate the household's role as the locus of consumption. Insofar as consumption as investment is a form of production, and pooling of resources and other financial strategies generate income, evangelical households do often have the look of family corporations. In this they resemble much more the peasant families that Rothstein discusses (see chapter 6, "Sex Roles and Familial Roles") than the individualistic, dependent households of nonconverts.

In Weber's interpretation (1905), the Calvinist doctrine of asceticism allowed for the amassing of capital because of reduced expenditures on vices and luxuries. Because of ascetic standards the Protestant did not have much else to do with profits but reinvest them. Asceticism is a key issue for Protestants in Colombian society, the one that at first blush most dramatically sets them off from nonconverts. However, the way it operates in the Colombian economic situation is distinctly different from what Weber described. While conversion affects consumption patterns, investment patterns in these cases are fundamentally different from the situation with which Weber is concerned. What generates money in this case is not profit per se, but rather the transformed consumption pattern itself.

In one sense of the word, asceticism is about consumption patterns. Ascetic codes designate proper and improper (or moral and immoral) types of consumption. In the Colombian case, and I think this is true for Protestantism more generally, asceticism does not mean rejection of the world—it is not a withdrawal from material reality in the manner of Hindu ascetics. Instead of being monastic, Protestant belief is profoundly social, although the nature of the Protestant social world, especially for men who convert in Colombia, is dramatically altered so that the family is placed at the center. "Otherworldliness" has a meaning beyond the dichotomy between the spiritual and the material. For Colombian evangelicals, "*cosas del mundo*" (things of the world) commonly denotes sinful conduct outside of the bounds of the family, in other words, "improper" or "immoral" types of consumption that are pervasive in the male (public) world.

In a way, then, the "other world" that the male convert enters is the feminine world. He eschews male values and conforms to a value system and to behavioral norms that are consistent with women's aspirations. In this light, asceticism actually entails a shift from male consumption patterns to female ones. In other words, in Colombia, women, Catholic as well as evangelical, are already ascetic. Willems notes that "most Latin American males would probably agree that the Protestant model of asceticism admirably fits their concept of correct female behavior" (1967:49).

Much of Weber's discussion of asceticism does not apply to the present discussion, but he does mention the home orientation in connection with Calvinist asceticism: "Over against the glitter and ostentation of feudal magnificence which, resting on an unsound economic basis, prefers a sordid elegance to a sober simplicity, they set the clean and solid comfort of the middle-class home as an ideal" (1905:171).

Flora (1976) surveyed current possessions and acquisition patterns among samples of Colombian Pentecostal and Catholic households. She found that the first item bought by Catholics is a radio (97 percent of Catholics as opposed to 66 percent of Pentecostals have a radio), while the first item bought by Pentecostals is a dining room table (82.5 percent of Pentecostals contrasted with 47.5 percent of Catholics own a dining room table). This consumer pattern indicates something about family relations. Flora interprets the importance of the radio to the Catholic households as an outreach for identification outside the home, while the centrality of the dining room table indicates a higher family solidarity among Pentecostals:

> The typical eating pattern in lower-class Colombia, which Willems (1967: 172) substantiates for Brazil, is for the meal to be served directly from the stove to each individual separately when he is ready. He then takes his meal to some quiet corner to consume alone in silence. This contrasts with the Pentecostal experience, where the family tends to eat together more, and the women, particularly, benefit from this increase in status through inclusion. (1976:221)

In terms of investment, money that would otherwise have been spent on "vices" by men in the public realm is reoriented back into the house-hold budget. Asceticism and a family orientation go hand-in-hand for most Colombian evangelicals. One of the striking features of evangelical Protestantism in Colombia is a pervasive concern with the quality of family life. Such things as a husband's responsibility to his wife and children, marital fidelity, and the mother's role in the raising of her chil-dren are common themes in sermons and Bible study. More than in any other area of life, conversion, especially of both husband and wife, will have a profound impact on the family. Ascetic codes forbid much of the behavior associated with the machismo complex: men can no longer drink, smoke, or have women outside of their marriage. A man's social world becomes transformed also, from the male public world to a re-defined private world where the family is the central focus.

Although asceticism does not specifically lead to capital accumula-tion, the transformation of consumption patterns can be linked to up-ward mobility. Household consumption can include income-generating purchases, such as real estate (houses or land, urban and rural), live-stock, a car or truck, and of course education for children. It is important to note that such investment is distinct from individual entrepreneur-ship because it is strategically linked to consumption and it is house-hold-based. The household is acting as a corporation, and although a profit motive may operate in any particular case of investment, the form that investment takes is influenced by the consumption orientation (i.e., houses, land, cars, and livestock all have use value for household mem-bers as well as market value as commodities). It might be said that this kind of consumption pattern is traditional, that it does not create new economic opportunities (i.e., it does not have a transformative effect on the economy). But it does frequently lead to upward mobility, or at least to greater financial security, for the family involved. I will consider this last point in more detail later.

Colombian Evangelical Women and the Transition
from Peasant to "Professional" Class

A striking process of upward mobility for certain evangelical families is based on the education of children for professional careers. Whitten (1969) has noted that capital spent on children's education in the Colombian-Ecuadorian littoral is related to the desire of rising groups to enhance their social prestige. A common pattern in Colombia is for a family to experience financial success through entrepreneurial activities and then to spend money on educating its children in order to bring its social status into line with its increased economic status. Here I would like to suggest that for evangelical families (and possibly for many non-evangelical ones) education plays a very different role in terms of upward mobility. Education is the primary means by which families, and extended kin groups, are realizing a dramatic upward mobility specifically in terms of professional-class status. The celebration of Martin Luther's five-hundredth birthday described in chapter 2 was a dramatic illustration of the changing status of many converts. Women as mothers are playing a strategic role in this process, and for evangelicals church membership provides institutional and ideological support, which facilitates mobility.

The evangelical movement in Colombia, since its very beginnings in the nineteenth century, has always had at its core a concern with education. The first missionaries, who were Presbyterians and came to Colombia in 1856, almost immediately set up a school for working-class people in Bogotá. The Colombian Bible Society quite appropriately views its major enemy in Colombia to be illiteracy and encourages literacy programs. Small evangelical churches in rural areas will often start their own primary schools, sometimes just the first three grades. These schools fill up with the children of nonevangelicals, who, despite their lack of interest in converting or sometimes open hostility to evangelicals, believe that their children will be better educated in the evangelical school than in public schools and often report that there they will learn discipline and respect. The *colegios americanos*, which evolved out of the early Presbyterian schools, are now established and quite prestigious high schools where only a small fraction of the students are actually from evangelical families. There are several of these schools located in major cities in Colombia, and they are considered to be a sort of factory for future professionals. Many evangelical denominations have established Bible institutes, which train pastors and train teachers for the primary schools. These Bible institutes continue to provide an opportunity for education for the poorest classes. Many evangelicals who are now professionals began their advanced education in Bible institutes, and entering a religious career is sometimes the first step toward secular professional-class status.

Evangelical groups also provide some scholarships for members' children through the university level. The Colombian Lutheran Synod has been particularly active in this regard since its beginnings in the 1930s; and in conjunction with the Lutheran World Federation in Geneva, it also offers numerous opportunities for young Colombian evangelicals to study or to attend conferences abroad.

In addition to these institutional arrangements, there also exists a pervasive attitude within evangelical families that lays the groundwork for the high valuation placed on learning. The major focus for this attitude is Bible reading and a contemplative attitude toward religious and moral issues. In the countryside, where the never-ending routine of rural tasks consumes the energies of all family members, time is specifically set aside for family Bible reading, discussion, and prayer. From the time they are very young, evangelical children are expected to read or recite from memory in church services, and to be able eventually to lead Bible study or to preach a sermon. Even the manner in which prayer is conducted is conducive to a certain kind of creativity. For Catholics, to pray is "rezar," which means to recite by rote, whereas for evangelicals to pray is "orar," which evangelicals describe as a spontaneous outpouring from the heart that is different for each individual and different for every prayer that is said. All of these skills distinguish Colombian evangelicals from their Catholic counterparts, among whom Bible reading, until very recently, was considered to be an activity fit only for the priesthood. As noted earlier, the Catholic hierarchy actively discouraged members from owning or reading the Bible, maintaining that such activity could only lead to a proliferation of misinterpretations of the sacred text. Among evangelicals, then, the "priesthood of all believers" exists not only on a doctrinal level but also is put into extensive practice and establishes an ethic of reading, contemplation, and analysis that is clearly useful in orienting young members toward higher education.

The growth of the professional class in Colombia has the dimensions of a major social phenomenon. This development is affecting large segments of the Colombian population, regardless of religion. However, because of the factors outlined above, many evangelical families have been particularly successful at making this class transition. An examination of some of the dynamics involved in these cases might prove to be suggestive for subsequent studies of women and class mobility. The growth of the professional class and the mobility of families from peasant or

poor backgrounds to urban professional status are often the direct result
of women's activities. The education of their children is an area in which
Colombian women can exert real influence. Whereas a woman has some
hope of her child's training for a career, and in fact this is the stated
hope of most mothers for their children, it would be less possible for her
to contribute to a child's success in business, for example, which is a
domain controlled by men and also much more class-bound than the
professions. For evangelicals, success in business is particularly difficult
because the ascetic codes of behavior prohibit much of the social behavior that is critical in Colombian business dealings, in particular, drinking with business associates.

This quandary is vividly illustrated by the testimony of Gilberto, a
member of the Charismatic Christian church in Bogotá. He had been a
very talented architect, but acute alcoholism had brought him to the
brink of financial disaster. As the result of his conversion he was able to
give up drinking, but had been suffering financially because he could
not play according to the social rules required by the men who might
offer him contracts. In his testimony, he praised the Lord because he
had finally been able to land a contract even though he was drinking
Coca-Cola.

Similarly, evangelicals are also notably absent from the legal profession, which has traditionally occupied a position of importance and
prestige in Colombian society (Goode 1970). This may be traced to the
close connection between law and politics in Colombia and to the fact
that the same kind of sociability is required of men in political activities
as is required for making business deals. Also, success in law and politics requires a kind of social visibility and approval that would not be
forthcoming for non-Catholics in Colombia. Extensive social networks
and "*palanca*" (influence or "pull") are strategic to any endeavor in Colombian society, including education and the professions.

By contrast, the people who constitute the clientele of physicians
and dentists (often women and children) do not require the same kind
of sociability on the part of the professional whose services they are
utilizing. A reasonable amount of success in one's profession can be
achieved as the result of diligence in one's studies and expertise in a
particular area (such as medicine or agronomy). A far smaller degree of
favoritism and pull is necessary than one would need in any sort of
business dealings. Also, investment in education takes the form of relatively small outlays of money over an extended period of time. A rural
woman might pay school fees for her children out of money earned selling milk from her cows or eggs from her chickens.[6]

The point to be made here is that the ostensibly "private" concerns of women receive institutional and ideological support from membership in the evangelical churches. When their husbands share their values and aspirations, for example, educational opportunities for their children, the success of their strategies is further guaranteed and can have profound transformative potential in terms of the social mobility of the family over the generations.

✛

THE FEMININE ETHOS
OF EVANGELICAL RELIGION

The discussion that follows aims to tie the points made above about gender and household to a more general understanding of the character of Colombian evangelical churches. I argue that the predominance of women in Colombian evangelical churches determines, to a very great extent, both the form or organization of the churches and the content of their religious teaching and expression.

The numerical preponderance of women in evangelicalism in both the United States and Latin America has been widely documented (see, for example, Argyle and Beit-Hallahmi 1975; Blanchard 1975; Flora 1976; Garrison 1974; Harrison 1974; Sexton 1978). To a much greater extent than in other Christian denominations, women occupy significant positions within the formal organization of these churches. They also gain prominence through the less institutionalized "authority of personal charisma" (Clark 1937; Flora 1976; Hardesty 1979; Hollenweger 1972; LaRuffa 1971; Ruether 1979; Samarin 1972). Where Pentecostalism is the result of missionary activity or develops out of (and often in opposition to) an established religion, women are often the first to convert to the new religion; their husbands may or may not be persuaded to join them later (Goodman 1972, 1973; LaRuffa 1971; Mintz 1960).

My data from Colombia support the findings of other researchers with regard to women's prominence in the churches. Furthermore, women's participation has given Colombian evangelicalism a "tone" or "flavor" that is distinctly consistent with Colombian femininity: what we might call a "feminine ethos." Bateson defines ethos as "the expression of a culturally standardized system of organization of the instincts and emotions of the individuals" (1936:118). Ethos sets a definite tone of appropriate behavior and a standardized system of emotional attitudes: "ethos constitutes a factor in the determination of the needs and desires of individuals. [It is] the system of emotional attitudes which governs what value a community shall set upon the various satisfactions or dissatisfactions which the contexts of life may offer" (p. 220). As a determinative factor, then, the concept of ethos is useful to the present discussion because it allows us to move beyond the level of individual strategizing.

What I call a "feminine ethos" is represented in the nature of evangelical religion in Colombia in various ways. In numerous cases, the merger of church and household exists in concrete spatial terms as well as on the more abstract level. The temple, or meeting place for evangelical services, is very frequently a large room in the pastor's house. This arrangement is facilitated by Colombian architectural style. When the house has more than one door facing the street, a front room can be opened up to admit people directly into the house, without disturbing the family's residential space. The room utilized for this purpose is usually the *sala*, or living room, where guests would normally be received. The integration of the temple in the *casa pastoral* (pastor's house) is true of even quite large churches. The Charismatic Christian church in the prosperous north of Bogotá conducted services in the home of the pastoral couple. On Sundays, some six hundred people would attend services, which were conducted in three shifts because the large downstairs room could squeeze in only two hundred at a time. The couple was blessed with a very good cook, and during the morning services as people sang and prayed, the room was often filled with enticing smells wafting from the kitchen. In El Cocuy, the little Lutheran church and the Lutheran primary school are located in the *casa evangélica*, which is a large old house in town. Both the director of the day school and her brother, the pastor of the church, live in this house. When their brother comes down from the mountains on horseback, clad in *alpargartes* (rope sandals) and *ruana*, to attend a meeting of the Municipal Council, of which he is a member, they sometimes roll out a mattress for him on the altar, which is carpeted and slightly raised and hence not as cold as the bare floor.

This spatial arrangement of evangelical churches in Colombia is much more than simply a matter of poverty or convenience. It is an outgrowth of the continuing household basis of evangelical religion in Colombia. The movement experienced its most dramatic growth during the period when it was driven behind closed doors by persecution during La Violencia (see chapter 3).

Up to the present, the core of evangelizing efforts is the *cultos a domicilio* (services in the home). Every church, in addition to frequent services and special meetings held in the *templo*, has a list of these

home services, which are held at varying times and in a range of loca-
tions during the week. It is usually the case that members (almost always
women) volunteer their homes for these meetings and take on the responsibility of leading the prayer, Bible reading, and hymn singing. This
technique of evangelization is a brilliant use of the primary resources
available to the church—the commitment of female members, their interpersonal skills in a traditional context, and their personal networks
of kin and friends. A female preacher stresses the compatibility of evangelization with the Colombian woman's traditional role: "The Bible says
to go out to the whole world and preach the gospel. Those of us who
have homes and children, it's very difficult for us to go all over the world.
But we can give the message to our neighbors, to our families, to our
friends, our block—we have a lot of people to give it to."

Testimonies of conversion experiences reveal that quite often a potential convert will attend home services for some time before ever ventur-
ing into the main *templo*. There are a variety of reasons for this. If a man
opposes his wife's involvement with the evangelical group, her visits to
a neighbor's or a relative's house are less visible and hence less likely to
be a provocation. A similar rationale applies for some men also, who
would be embarrassed to be seen publicly attending an evangelical service, but are open enough to the idea that they would go along to a relative's house (or stay in their own home if their wife was conducting the
service, assuming they are not openly opposed to her involvement).

There is also evidence that other kinds of proselytizing activities are
far less productive than the home services. The "soapbox" approach,
where a preacher takes his place on a street corner or, more often, near
the marketplace, and proceeds to declaim to any listeners about the Gospel, has been used since the early days of missionization with mixed
results. It has many drawbacks. First, nothing ties the preacher to his
audience. Since he is addressing a group of strangers he must depend
exclusively on their curiosity about what he has to say and has no other
hope of holding their interest. Second, especially in the smaller towns
where this is practiced, he is likely to provoke a considerable amount of
animosity from a crowd that believes, as the result of the teaching of the
Catholic clergy, that he is a heretic (and possibly also a Communist). In
the past, even outside of the epoch of La Violencia, he risked being
thrown into jail for his efforts. It would be fairly certain that his activities
would be reported to the local Catholic priest, who would respond with
a sermon lambasting the intrusion of heretics into the town. Even recently, evangelical groups that have attempted this type of public evangelizing have been attacked by angry mobs. The Assemblies of God, during a campaign they ran in 1980, sent a group of evangelists to the small

town of Villapinzón in the Department of Boyacá. The group attempted to begin open-air evangelization but was thwarted by a mob of angry men who attacked them and destroyed valuable sound equipment. It probably does not help that on market day most men will be engaged in endless rounds of reciprocal drinking, and as a consequence are going to be less than enthusiastic about a preacher's denunciation of their activities. Finally, even when a preacher manages to overcome these considerable obstacles and his message reaches the heart of a listener, little will come of it unless "the seeds are cultivated," that is, unless there is a continuing effort made by believers to draw the neophyte into an ongoing set of religious activities. It is this continuing availability and reinforcement that the *cultos a domicilio* supply to the potential convert, and when an evangelical mentions public preaching as a factor in bringing about his or her conversion, it is usually the case that he or she already had friends, relatives, or neighbors who were involved with the evangelical church.

Another type of activity associated with evangelization in many parts of the world, but which is peculiarly unsuccessful in Colombia, is the giant "crusade," an open-air rally, usually held in a stadium, where a famous preacher such as Billy Graham addresses a huge crowd and at the end of the service invites people to come down to the front to commit their lives to Christ. Apparently in the past, evangelists such as Billy Graham have visited Colombia, but the outcome of their crusades was never considered as successful as in other countries, so they have not returned. Evangelicals attribute the failure of these rallies to difficulties in transportation and communication in Colombia, but these difficulties do not seem to stop people from hearing about and attending soccer games. I would suggest instead that the failure of the open-air rallies is tied to the fact that they are inherently inconsistent with the feminine ethos of evangelical religion in Colombia. It is understandable that the technique that is the farthest from the *cultos a domicilio* should be the least successful. Whereas the home services are personal, intimate, and private, the open-air rallies are impersonal, anonymous, and public. There is no basis for a Colombian woman's involvement in such an activity, and the concept is likely to seem foreign to her.

Most successful evangelical churches in Colombia have active women's organizations. Flora (1976) found that eight of thirteen Pentecostal churches in the area she studied had "active and aggressive" women's organizations, the leaders of which were often the wives of the pastors. All of the evangelical churches I studied had women's organizations, and although their degree of activity as groups relatively independent of the rest of the church varied, it was often the case that the *confraternidad de damas* (brotherhood of ladies) took on the lion's share of responsibility for the church.

These organizations carry out a number of primary functions, foremost among which are evangelization campaigns, but they also include such things as fund-raising activities, social welfare work, and furnishing, maintaining, and decorating the church. Special weekly services for women are held by many churches, sometimes as part of the activities of the women's society and sometimes independent of them. In both the Canaan church (an independent working-class church in the south of Bogotá), and the Charismatic Christian church in the affluent north, the women's midweek services were extremely popular and as well attended as the Sunday services.

The imagery used by women in their sermons is very specifically and compellingly female: images of cleanliness and images of food—tied to two of the central activities Colombian women engage in. The following examples are from a sermon given by a woman at the Charismatic Christian church. The major theme of her sermon was spiritual sustenance, and the metaphor that she used repeatedly was the word of God as food:

> We as Christians have to feed ourselves, sisters, because, some time ago (and I am still a bit thin), I was completely malnourished. When I traveled to the United States, and the first doctor that I saw said to me, "Señora, I've never seen a person as thin as you—I think you must have tuberculosis." And I thought to myself, if that's what it's like for the body to be malnourished, what must the person be like who is malnourished spiritually? We are nourished—body, soul, and spirit. And our spirit must be completely nourished, fat, but if we don't eat of the word of the Lord, if we don't nourish ourselves with it, we are going to be more malnourished than I was when I was sick.
>
> Some people say, my Bible is very pretty. I keep it as an adornment. Well, we may have a fine, clean Bible, but our life is not going to be as clean as the Bible, it will more likely be dirty. What is clean is the Lord's word.
>
> Really, speaking is an art. What we have to tell the world is short, small, but substantial. It's like food; it might just be a little bit, but it should be nutritious.

The *hogar* (home) is the perennial topic for special weeklong or monthlong "campaigns" held at regular intervals during the year. A great deal of teaching is done on the topic of home and family. This is an example of how the content of evangelical religion appeals to Colombian women. The churches pay much attention to a topic that is close to their hearts and that is in many cases their primary frame of reference. In El Cocuy, the Lutheran church sponsored a class on the family that met weekly over several months, covering such topics as courtship, marriage, sexuality, and family roles. During the annual convention of the Four-Square Gospel church, the guest pastor delivered a series of sermons over the course of five days on the topic of the Christian husband and father. A sign announcing the *semana del hogar* in the United Pentecostal church listed a full week of activities, with different meetings for wives, husbands, parents, and children, the whole family together, with an emphasis on family unity. The sign encouraged people to attend, claiming, "Ud. puede tener un hogar feliz—asista!" (You can have a happy home—attend!)

Rather than viewing this emphasis as a ploy on the part of the church to draw women in (in which case we would be preconceiving the church as male-dominated), I think that the heavy emphasis on the family in Colombian evangelical religion might have to do with the fact that women were allowed a say in the church, as preachers and teachers, from the early days, and hence their concerns went into the shaping of Colombian evangelicalism when it became Colombianized. As a consequence, it had a great appeal to other women, and for that reason the church grew.

✚ 8 ✚
Conclusion

In this final chapter, I propose that Colombian evangelicalism can be seen, in one regard, as a "strategic" women's movement, aimed at fundamentally altering sex role behavior. I expand on this point to suggest that notions of "progress" held by converts reveal a "prosperity ethic" that is consistent with a female view of family well-being. I contrast this idea with the Marxist and Weberian views of Latin American conversion, in which Western notions of "progress" (whether agreed with or not) are uncritically applied to social and historically distinct situations.

✚
COLOMBIAN EVANGELICALISM
AS A "STRATEGIC" FORM OF
FEMALE COLLECTIVE ACTION

A feminist interested in discussing the experience of women in contemporary Christian fundamentalism might be inclined to quote some particularly imposing ancestors: Elizabeth Cady Stanton, for example, said that "the Bible and the Church have been the biggest stumbling blocks in the way of women's emancipation." More recently but no less forcefully, Mary Daly has stated that "a woman's asking for equality in the church would be comparable to a black person's demanding equality in the Ku Klux Klan" (1973:6).

On the other hand, an anthropologist commenting on the explosive growth of evangelicalism in Latin America might conclude that conversion is a counterrevolutionary act that produces a docile labor force (or, in Weberian terms, progress-minded entrepreneurs), thereby indicating that the movement is best interpreted as an ideological servant of capitalist interests penetrating their world market.

Putting the two approaches together, an anthropologist who considered herself a Marxist-feminist might regard the whole situation of women in Christian fundamentalism in Latin America as too gloomy even to consider. She might readily concede that evangelicalism serves women's psychological needs by promising them that their earthly suffering will be compensated with rich rewards in the hereafter. But it is unlikely that she would feel any philosophical affinity to Latin American female evangelicals, or believe that they are involved in an intensely pragmatic movement aimed at reforming those aspects of society that most affect their lives.

I have argued here for a quite different point of entry into the debate about the role of evangelicalism in modern Latin America. This point of entry, based on an analysis of social process within households, reveals both the revolutionary nature of the evangelical movement as a challenge to the prevailing form of gender subordination and its capacity as an especially powerful ideological tool that radically alters sex role behavior, promotes female interests, and raises the status of women.

Fundamentalist and revolutionary movements share certain features: they stress collective interests over individual ones and they make goals and values explicit in a way that is unusual in everyday life. To some extent, also, both fundamentalism and revolutionary programs can entail a fusion of male and female values. For example, in the context of nationalist liberation movements in Africa (Angola, Mozambique, Guinea-Bissau, Zimbabwe, and Namibia; see Urdang 1984), women in the military and in decision-making bodies were united with men in their goal of establishing a new and just society that would end all forms of exploitation. A similar unity of purpose characterized the sexes during the Cuban Revolution. However, the prominence of women in revolutionary movements is often eroded after the battle has been won and the new structure established.

One problem is that, although they look good on the books, even the most well intentioned and vigorous legislative reforms aimed at promoting gender equality often fail to bring about real changes in male and female status and role behavior, particularly within the context of the family and household. Although many would argue that the "private" world of the family is ultimately shaped by wider political forces, the intimate world of courtship patterns, marital roles, and who washes the dishes seems to be one of the most conservative areas of life, or at least one of the areas that is the most difficult to police.

The comparison of fundamentalism and revolutionary movements highlights the remarkable success of a movement such as Colombian evangelicalism in radically altering the most resistant roles. That it has had no effect on legislation concerning women's rights and that at first glance it bears little resemblance to what we would consider a feminist movement might lead us to the conclusion that, insofar as evangelicalism in Colombia enhances the quality of women's lives, it accomplishes this only within the bounds of traditional structures and is in no way revolutionary. Such movements are quite commonly noted in the literature on women's collective action across cultures. Molyneux (1986:284) has provided a useful distinction between two kinds of women's movements: those that are based on women's "practical interests," such as consumer movements, which are generally formed around some encroachment on women's ability to fulfill their traditional obligations; and those based on women's "strategic interests," which, like Western feminism, are aimed at revising the sex-gender system. I believe that Colombian evangelicalism in certain respects resembles the latter type of women's movement.

The appeal of evangelicalism in serving women's practical interests is very clear. Many writers have been content to note this and then move on to what they consider a more encompassing explanation of the movement, an explanation that, for some reason, often ignores their observations about women's interests.

The tangible changes and improvement in the standard of living of women and children in dependent households is only a symptom or an indicator of something much more remarkable that is happening. With conversion, machismo is replaced by evangelical belief as the main determinant of husband-wife relations. The machismo role and the male role defined by evangelicalism are almost diametrical opposites. Aggression, violence, pride, self-indulgence, and an individualistic orientation in the public sphere are replaced by peace seeking, humility, self-restraint, and a collective orientation and identity with the church and the home.

One outcome of conversion, then, is that the boundaries of public (male) life and private (female) life are redrawn and the spheres themselves are redefined. The relative power positions of the spouses change. This is not to say that women now have power over their husbands. In evangelical households the husband may still occupy the position of head, but his relative aspirations have changed to coincide with those of his wife. I believe that this last fact constitutes a change of revolutionary proportions, and is the key to the analysis of Colombian evangelicalism.

The numerical preponderance of women in evangelical churches and

the fact that they frequently occupy leadership positions has not pre-
vented some writers from concluding that women's place is still struc-
tured to be behind that of men (see Cucchiari 1990; Gill 1990). These
writers argue that the organizational structure of the evangelical church
does not include women in the higher leadership roles. For one thing,
this position ignores the parallel nature of male and female organizations within the church, and the fact that women do lead their own organizations. It is simply automatically assumed that the women's organizations will be less important than the male-controlled ones, despite
the fact that they are sometimes equal to if not more powerful than their
male counterparts. But even more important, when they share the same
values and aspirations as women, most men in positions of leadership
are not operating at odds with female members. This is what makes the
evangelical response so powerful and successful: instead of trying to
revolutionize the public realm, which is what would be necessary for
women to be allowed greater direct access to jobs and male income and
to have their interests taken seriously by male power holders, it reorders
the relative participation of men and women in the private realm. Part of
this process entails the revaluation of the private realm of home and
family, placing it at the center of both women's and men's lives.

Here I would like to refer to some of the work on the topic of resistance. Scott (1985) has argued that we need to broaden our notion of
resistance to include acts and beliefs that challenge the structures of
inequality in a more covert and less risky fashion than open confrontation. Martin (1987) leads us in a similar direction by enumerating some
of the many forms that consciousness and resistance may take, along a
continuum from acceptance to rebellion. In terms of the argument I am
developing here, it is abundantly clear that the success of the evangelical
movement in reforming gender roles derives from its not being perceived
as a way women are gaining supremacy and control over men. Hence,
searching for overt evidence of female dominance within the movement
misses the point.[1]

I would like to return to the consideration of evangelical Protestantism in Colombia as a form of female collective action. One of the biggest
problems faced by feminist reformers in the United States and elsewhere
is that, while woman's role is redefined to allow her greater "freedom"
(in terms of jobs, education, political participation, etc.), man's roles do
not automatically transform themselves to accommodate this changed
situation. The result of the expansion of woman's role is that women end
up working a double day. But imagine if male and female values were
the same.

While it is hard for us to see the changes that result from evangelical conversion in Colombia as involving anything that from our perspective could be called "liberation," one of the hard-won lessons of contemporary feminist anthropologists is that "woman" is not a universal category, nor are women's problems and interests likely to be uniform across cultures. Western feminism has been true to its cultural origins in that it has tended to reflect an emphasis on individual freedom. Kaplan (1982) reveals this bias in her evaluation of types of female collective action. She labels certain movements as emerging from what she calls "female consciousness" and claims that these differ from true feminism in that female consciousness values social cohesion over individual rights, and quality of life over access to institutional power. I prefer Molyneux's distinction (1986) because it tends not to be as culture bound.

Antagonism toward the family has been a frequent bone of contention between Western feminists and Third World feminists, who are also interested in ameliorating structures of sexual subordination but who see the family as their main source of security. Like other institutions within society, the sex-gender system must be seen as culturally specific, and also functionally integrated with other aspects of society. Whether the family, then, is either woman's primary oppressor or her special source of power and security, is not a philosophical debate but a question that must be answered empirically. At this point in Colombia, changes in the family that work to the advantage of women are a most desirable reform.

Many women's collective movements have been organized around regaining basic rights that are being infringed on by modernization, social change, and so on (see, for example, Molnar 1982, discussed below). They may seem reactionary, because they do not challenge the traditional sex-gender system, but in fact they are challenging a prevailing situation, which neither provides them with the basic rights they are accustomed to nor replaces them with new rights.

The basic premise here is that traditional systems may be more effective in providing for the fulfillment of women's basic needs and goals and allocating status to their activities, even when they remain separate from the activities of men. Male and female activities complement each other within a basically shared system of values. This is not to say that male and female perceptions of the universe are congruent in traditional societies. This can often entail a good deal of antagonism between the sexes, but the antagonism itself is regulated by implicit cultural rules. In general, however, I think that there is a more humane and effective articulation of the two worldviews (within systems that contain a much more limited range of possibilities in any case).[2]

The Colombian situation provides a particularly powerful example of a disruption of the traditional mode of articulation of the two world-views, resulting in a disjuncture between male and female value systems. In a historical context where women's access to resources becomes increasingly tenuous, women become dependent on what portion of male salaries they are able to extract on the basis of personal persuasion rather than through formally recognized rights, and the economy is strongly prejudiced against female laborers.

This conflict between the value systems has many negative results. Abandonment of a woman and children by a male wage earner is a manifestation of the disjuncture of the articulation between female and male values and has devastating economic consequences for those who remain behind. The high frequency of abandonment in Colombia would be unthinkable in a society where a man's values and goals were realized through his attachment to a family. Another indicator is that when women work, a larger portion of their earnings are spent on the family, whereas a much larger part of a man's income is spent on his personal consumption (Benería and Roldán [1987:120] describe a similar situation among Mexican workers). Severe competition among women for men and a great deal of mystification of each sex by the other and of the male-female relationship in general is another symptom. And finally, the commoditization of sex, which is manifest on both sides, is one of the major indicators of a severe disruption of the male-female relationship. This runs a continuum from married women who reward their husband's contributions to the household with sexual favors and punish his failure to provide by withholding them, to women who enter into a series of relationships with men that depend on the men's ability to provide income, to actual prostitution.

In such a context, then, a template such as evangelicalism for re-articulating men and women is as desirable to women in terms of improving their condition (and surely to some men) as any feminist reform movements I know of. It is not simply practical but also strategic, in that it challenges and seeks redress for gender inequalities. That it accomplishes this through the transformation of male as well as female roles is the key to its effectiveness, and something that Western feminism, despite having labored mightily, cannot claim to have achieved to the same degree.

I am not arguing that this type of religious movement in all places and at all times serves the same function. Where there is less sex segregation, less female dependency, and a more individualistic orientation for both men and women, I could imagine that such a movement would not be viable in terms of improving women's status but it would also probably never get off the ground anyway. Perhaps this interpretation is relevant only to situations where conversion challenges the specific male role defined as "machismo." However, there is compelling case material from areas far removed from Latin America that indicates that the evangelical ideology serves this function in situations of culture change that have disrupted the articulation of male and female worlds.

Not too long ago, among the Telefolmin people of Papua, New Guinea, a revival movement that took on the ecstatic features of evangelicalism occurred after the establishment of a large Baptist Bible school. Among the Christian converts who led the revival, women played a key role, often manifesting shaking seizures that were attributed to possession by the Holy Spirit. During these trances, the Holy Spirit made known his wishes that all Telefolmin convert to Christianity and that the old Telefol religion be abandoned (this includes the esoteric men's cult practices). The Holy Spirit also demanded, through a female trance victim, that egalitarian relations between men and women be established and that conjugal ties and nuclear family obligations take priority over men's duties in the men's cult. As a result of this revival, over a dozen men's houses were destroyed or desecrated (Jorgensen 1980). The report indicates that the Telefolmin were being affected by the transition to a cash economy. This transition may have included an increase in female dependency on male wage labor.

In the final section I will briefly address the question: What do these observations about the role of evangelical conversion in changing gender roles and domestic organization mean in terms of current interpretations of Latin American conversion and social change?

✛

PROGRESS, MODERNIZATION, AND CULTURE CHANGE

Notions of social change implicit in writings about evangelical conversion in Latin America fall into roughly two categories: (1) the Marxist, or dependency, perspective, and (2) the neo-Weberian, or development, perspective.

In the first of these, conversion is viewed as a conservative force, retarding change by orienting people away from the political and hence away from involvement in the future of their country. In the strongest version of this view, religion serves as an "opiate," which makes people placid and inured to the status quo. Lalive d'Epinay (1976) observes that for evangelicals, politics is an evil to be avoided. He believes that the insurrectionary potential built up over centuries is neutralized by their prescribing noninvolvement. It is axiomatic to this approach that *all* religion is bad because it rationalizes or mystifies oppression. It follows that evangelicals, as fervent converts, would be particular obstacles to change, since the more involved people are in religion the more drugged they are. Conversely, the least devout are the most likely sources of culture change. Furthermore, evangelicalism, as in an import, must be considered as an aspect of ideological imperialism. Implicit in this evaluation are ideas about what constitutes the proper direction of social change.

The development, or neo-Weberian, approaches to Protestant conversion in Latin America usually ignore the issues of imperialism and mystification that engage the Marxists and focus on the transformative role of Protestant belief in the process of modernization. In this approach, conversion brings about a rationalization of activity that is useful for upward mobility and hence for development. Development and modernization are both synonymous with capitalism. In a prescriptive sense, the modernization and development of a country depend on its citizens acquiring habits and attitudes that are consistent with capitalist economic behavior. Generally, "traditional" patterns of thought and behavior, including Catholicism, are considered to contain "irrational" elements, which inhibit the development process.[3] This approach also clearly contains implicit ideas about the proper (or at least *inevitable*) direction of social change.

It would appear that we are still under the influence of the nineteenth-century notion that "progress" is a teleological process, unfolding inevitably and leading to an eventual amalgamation of the world's cultures into one depressing uniformity. Most anthropologists have come to recognize that what we view as "traditional" was itself arrived at through a creative process of change. Yet, founded as it was on the study of the "exotic," it is often the case that within anthropology there exists an understandable romanticization of the "traditional" and the diverse. "Progress," then, is anathema in that it leads to "modernization," which entails a rejection of the indigenous, the traditional, and the diverse in favor of the imported, the contemporary, and the uniform.

Since the days of the early diffusionists, we have been aware that the process of cultural borrowing is characterized by two important features: (1) cultures are selective about what they adopt from outside and are unlikely to accept something that they do not need or that contradicts basic premises of the society; and (2) a borrowed culture trait will be tailored to fit the setting into which it is adopted. The acculturation process that operates within arenas of gross inequalities in power allows for a great deal less freedom of choice in this regard than the simpler process of borrowing between relatively equal neighboring groups. Nevertheless, these basic observations about the process of diffusion have generally been disregarded entirely when it comes to discussions of the "modernization" process. Modernization is not considered to entail selection and adaptation as identified in the diffusion process, but rather is seen as a wholesale "conversion" of all aspects of society.

Notions of "progress," "development," and indeed the inference that there is any particular directionality in social change must be analyzed to reveal their hidden meaning and the values of those using these terms. It is clear that all societies do not share the Western notion of progress, which has been implicit in social science models for a century. For example, Mead reported that the Chambri of the Sepik River area of New Guinea have no idea of "unilateral development." They have "no goal beyond the attainment of the status—artistic, economic, or technical— of some neighboring tribe" (1938:37). Yet among the Chambri, the importation of culture traits and the social change that results are common features.

Importation and change must be separated from our notion of progress, and local attitudes toward particular changes must be assessed. It is by no means inevitable that the importation and acceptance of a particular "modern" trait is equivalent with "progress." Stoll has remarked on a tendency to blame evangelical growth in Latin America on external agents and financing from the United States. Such an attitude, he says, "suggests a deep distrust of the poor, an unwillingness to accept the possibility that they could turn an imported religion to their own purposes" (1990:xvi). In Colombia, the long history of cooperation between the government and the Roman Catholic church has meant that evangelicals have been notably absent from political office beyond the local level. However, even where Latin American evangelicalism has figured into national and international power struggles, the potential of the movement at the local level to affect the changes I have outlined here is not nullified. The schismatic nature of the evangelical movement may protect it from becoming exclusively a vehicle for male political interest. The movement works best through small groups that are based on personalistic ties, and its tendency to keep reproducing such groups through schisms when a church gets too large is highly functional in terms of women's involvement.

✢

WOMEN, THE PROSPERITY ETHIC,
AND THE HOUSEHOLD WRIT LARGE

I would like to utilize a modified version of Scott's (1976) "subsistence ethic" to elaborate on the notion of progress held by Colombian evangelicals (see especially the end of chapter 4) and relate this to the household base of Colombian evangelicalism and women's special contribution to the movement.

In her paper on the political action of Kham Magar women in western Nepal, Molnar (1982) applies Scott's (1976) concept of the subsistence ethic in evaluating whether the women's collective action she observed constitutes a change in traditional female roles and attitudes, or is simply an extension of women's traditional political roles. She outlines Scott's definition of the subsistence ethic: "that an individual or community has a right to subsistence; that the ability to survive crises and maintain minimum subsistence should not be jeopardized by laws or economic relations imposed on an individual or community" (Molnar 1982:497). Scott concludes that the peasant revolts in Southeast Asia resulted from the violation of this ethic by colonial rulers: "He contends that their revolt was not to stop exploitation or to achieve equality but to protect their right to minimum subsistence, which they felt was jeopardized by colonially imposed laws" (Molnar 1982:497). Molnar cites several cases in which women's protests (utilizing traditional forms of female militancy) have resulted from a similar breach of expectations.

In this concluding section, I would like to propose that Colombian women's involvement in evangelicalism emerges from a similar kind of disappointment of expectations. Unlike the situation of Scott's peasants, however, something more than the individual's right to minimum subsistence is involved. A commitment to well-being, which in its application at the household level is synonymous with "prosperity," is at the core of this attitude.

An attitude or belief characteristic among Colombian women is that the conjugal unit should cooperate to promote the well-being of "the family," which I will leave loosely defined as an important residential or kin unit. What I am calling the "prosperity ethic" constitutes an affective component of the conjugal bond in many places, for both men and women, particularly when the household is a cooperative productive and consumption unit (for instance, in the peasant family economy, see discussion of Rothstein, chapter 5). It is the assumption that, on marrying, spouses enter into a partnership committed to the well-being of the conjugal pair (i.e., each other), to a more widely construed unit that usually roughly coincides with the household, and most important, to the children who result from their union. It is manifest in the cooperative enterprise of husband and wife, pooling of resources between them (the "conjugal fund" is one example, but other sorts of economic arrangements whose primary reference is the sustenance of the household unit, such as budgets, also illustrate the operation of this ethic), and most broadly, a sense of responsibility for others, including the material world (i.e., objects that constitute the immediate environment).

Given the relations of exploitation, poverty, and scarcity that characterize most peasant societies at present, hardship (as opposed to prosperity) is a great likelihood, no matter what intentions or aspirations a husband and wife might have. The same situation applies to the rural proletariat and the urban poor. Whether or not the couple succeeds in their joint aspirations of providing for the well-being of the family will depend to a large extent on the realities of gaining a livelihood. What is at issue here is whether or not this is a shared goal of the conjugal unit.[4]

It is important to note, however, that the opposite of prosperity is hardship. Progress in the sense of modernization is not implicit in the attitude of Colombian evangelicals, nor is its antithesis "backwardness" or "traditionalism." The notion of progress as improvement is present, in part as a reflection of the centrality of the parent-child relationship, in defining expectations. Parents expect to be able to maintain their children, but in addition, a child's development is inevitable; one stage supersedes another and growth is equated with progress.

The prosperity ethic, applied to conjugal or intrahousehold relations, describes a fundamental expectation of one individual about another. A central premise, therefore, is that aspirations are shared: The goal of both individuals is the well-being of the household. The individual strategies of maximization described by Browner and Lewin (1982) contrast markedly with this situation. In this case (discussed in chapter 5) women emphasize either their role as mothers or their role as wives, depending on which role promises the greatest return. Machismo undermines the prosperity ethic as a component of conjugal mutuality, erodes the male's role as husband, and results in the divergence of male and female aspirations. I would propose here that such individualized strategies result from the disjuncture of male and female aspirations as outlined earlier. When these aspirations are no longer aligned, the expectations characteristic of the prosperity ethic are shattered.

It is a mistake to assume that evangelical emphasis on progress constitutes a "Protestant ethic" consistent with capitalist development.

Because conversion revives the prosperity ethic as a feature of the conjugal bond, the economic situation of evangelical families does often improve. But the main point to be made from introducing this concept into the discussion is that it is not "progress" per se in our Western sense that evangelical conversion in Colombia brings about, but rather a re-institution of the prosperity ethic in the conjugal relationship. By distinguishing between progress and prosperity, the way in which evangelical conversion is embedded in gender relations and domestic organization remains visible.

✢ Appendix ✢
Fieldwork with Colombian Evangelicals

The core of my sample consists of two large *gran familias*. These resemble what Nutini recognized as significant kinship groupings in Mesoamerica and called "non-residential extended families" or "limited kindreds" (1967:385). In the literature on Latin American social organization, such groupings have been variously called simply "families," "extended families," or "great families." It has been widely acknowledged that, despite the prevalence of nuclear family households as a residential form in mestizo Latin America, individuals situate themselves within the context of a much wider range of relatives. This network provides a vital form of support for its participants.[1]

The first family I lived with, the Melados, is based in Bogotá; and the second, the Azucena-Ortegas, in El Cocuy.

✢
THE MELADO FAMILY

Composition

This family includes about forty-five members, residing in nine households in Bogotá. It consists of three generations: the grandparents (*los abuelitos*); their children (*los hermanos*, what I am calling "the sibling set"); and their grandchildren (*los nietos*). At the time of my field stay, the family was just starting to extend into four generations of depth, with the birth of the first great-grandchild to the oldest grandson.

Both of the founding grandparents of the group are still alive and recently celebrated their fiftieth wedding anniversary with a big party and special communion service in the Lutheran church attended by the whole family. Cenobio Melado is in his eighties, and his wife, Olivia Flores de Melado, is in her mid-seventies. Both grandparents, but especially Olivia, continue to exert a strong influence over the whole group. The family resembles a clan in that group membership is determined through relation to these founding ancestors, ambilineally.

Of their nine adult children, ranging in age from twenty-nine to forty-five (four women and five men), seven are married and live with their spouses and children in separate nuclear family households. The two youngest children of this generation, a man aged thirty-one and a woman aged twenty-nine, continue to live with their elderly parents. There are twenty-five children in the grandchild generation, ranging in age from two to twenty-six. With only a few exceptions, the entire family is actively involved in the Lutheran church in Bogotá. (One daughter-in-law is a Jehovah's Witness, another is Mennonite, and one or two of the male members are not devout.)

Brief History of the Melado Family

Cenobio and Olivia are from campesino backgrounds: Cenobio moved to Bogotá from rural Boyacá, and Olivia grew up in the small town of La Calera, Cundinamarca. Always a thoughtful man with a great interest in reading, Cenobio converted to evangelicalism during the early years of their marriage, in the 1930s, and became a traveling evangelist with the "Cruzada" church. (Formerly the World Evangelical Crusade, the church is at present divided into a national and a foreign-based branch, and in terms of style of worship can be considered one of the "radical," Pentecostal-style sects.) The family was very poor as it was growing during the 1930s and the 1940s. Olivia started a bakery to help support the household, and the business thrived. Then a conflict erupted with the church because the bakery was open on Sundays, and some of the members accused the Melados of selling beer. As a result, Cenobio left the Cruzada and joined the Lutheran church, which had recently been established in Bogotá as the result of people's fleeing the countryside to escape La Violencia.

Around that time he enrolled in a correspondence course in homeopathic medicine and began to develop a medical practice in connection with his evangelist circuit. At first he treated people for free as an adjunct of his ministry to their souls, but as he gained more confidence in his healing abilities, and as the result of several spectacular cures, he began to charge a small fee, and his reputation and his practice grew. He worked hard, and Olivia invested the profits in real estate. The family prospered, and the four eldest sons were all sent to university. The oldest son, Carlos, is an economist, the next son, Bartolomé, studied business administration, Pablo was sent to study medicine in Mexico, and Juan Edgar is a dentist. The youngest son, Deno, is something of a black sheep, and although the family constantly encourages him to take up a gainful profession, his projects consistently founder and he seems content for the moment to serve as his parents' driver.

Of the five daughters, only the youngest was sent to university, but she lacked motivation to commit herself to a career and failed to complete her degree. The older daughters did not finish high school, but attended the Lutheran Bible Institute, which functioned in Bogotá in the 1950s and the 1960s. Of the three married daughters, two have successful marriages. The eldest, Magdalena, married a mild-mannered man who complied with her wishes and converted to Lutheranism and is now active in the church (he is an accountant). Liduvina married a black man from the coast who is a pediatrician and comes from a devout evangelical background. The middle daughter, Adela, married an evangelical from Soata, Boyacá, and her marriage has been beset with problems. Her husband, César, left home several years ago to work in Venezuela. He continues to visit his family at least once a year at Christmas, but his relationship with Adela is problematic. He seems overwhelmed by his wife's close-knit family. César contributes little or nothing to the support of his family, and Adela and the children rely on her parents and other members of the family for support.

The Melados have frequent family gatherings: Christmas Eve, Christmas Day, New Year's Day, January 6 (Epiphany), anniversaries, birthdays, and graduations are all marked by celebrations attended by most of the sibling set and their families. In addition, the sons and daughters frequently visit their parents' house, usually at lunchtime. Several of the daughters and their children regularly eat lunch at the grandparents' house. In Colombia, the midday meal is the major one of the day, the time when the family congregates. There is frequent visiting among the sisters. Until recently the family had devotionals at the grandparents' house every week. Most of the family attends weekly church services, and several sing in the choir, participate in youth groups or women's groups, and serve on the church council. Every member of the family attends communion at the Lutheran church on the first Sunday after the New Year.

Family members are very affectionate with one another. At lunchtime at the grandmother's house, the grandchildren always kiss their mothers and their grandparents when they come in from school. There is a great deal of affectionate physical contact, hugging and kissing, and also a lot of horseplay among the sisters, between uncles and aunts and nieces and nephews.

Generally, however, the day-to-day attitudes and behavior of the Melado family is accurately glossed by the commonly used Colombian term "*formal.*" This is not well translated literally as the English word "formal," because while it does connote something about good manners it has none of the stuffiness associated with the English term. It is also much more pervasive as an ideal model of behavior—it is something that all Colombians strive to be. A way of saying "thank you" to someone is to say "*muy formal.*" It suggests both respectability and kindness. The person who is *muy formal* is fulfilling customary obligations, being responsible toward others with whom he or she shares a relationship. This element of responsibility (and concern) toward other family members and toward people in general is very strong among the Melados.

The family also manifests a distinctly puritanical streak, which in some ways can be viewed as an appendage of this "formal-ity." A vivid illustration of this occurred when the Colombian author Gabriel García Márquez won the Nobel Prize for Literature in 1982. There had been a tremendous clamor in the media over the success of this native son. Colombia very rarely receives anything but bad press in the international media, most of which focuses on the drug trade, emerald smuggling, violence, and poverty. The Melados, like other Colombians, would complain to me that most foreigners thought that *all* Colombians were violent drug dealers or thieves or beggars, and that this was an unfair stereotype. Colombians generally were ecstatic to receive outside recognition of (what they viewed as) their widely unappreciated creative and literary side. In Bogotá, whose elite at one time called their city "the Athens of the Americas," even illiterate cigarette vendors in the streets posted the front-page photographs of the Nobel Laureate with the legend "Tenemos premio Nobel" (We have the Nobel prize). Given this state of affairs, I was very puzzled by the reaction of the Melado family to the news. The house of Cenobio and Olivia is one of the few I visited in Colombia that contained books. In fact, the house has a separate small room, the *biblioteca*, lined with bookshelves. Given the emphasis on learning that pervades the family, and Cenobio's much-discussed fondness for books, I thought that the family would be particularly proud about García Márquez. But instead there was very little mention of the event, and when I tried to bring up the topic for discussion, several of the Melado brothers and sisters admitted that they had never read his work. Most of the family, outside of the grandfather and a couple of the brothers, are not avid readers, but I thought that surely they had been exposed to this famous author during their school years. Finally one of the sisters explained that García Márquez is "muy grosero"; that is, he uses vulgar words. Their objection to his books, which should have occurred to me early on, was that they were too "steamy."

Given the dramatic degree of upward mobility that the Melado family has experienced in the past fifty years, it is quite interesting that almost all of the nine households are located in the south of Bogotá. The city of Bogotá is spatially divided along class lines in terms of a north-south division. As Tadeo, my fifteen-year-old "little brother" (Adela's son) described it to me, "People look down on you for living in the south." It always made him nervous to visit his aunt's neighborhood in the northern part of the city, because the other boys loved to make fun of him for living in the south. The poorest barrios, the squatter settlements, and industrial zones are located in the south. But vast expanses of the southern part of the city are working-class neighborhoods, ranging from fairly poor to quite respectably middle class.

In the north, on the other hand, live the *ricos*, rich people with connections who have been among the urban elite for several generations. (This is in many ways more of a fantasy than a reality. To the uneducated eye many of the neighborhoods of the north would be indistinguishable from some in the south, and the occupations of their residents in many cases would likewise be indistinguishable. I think one of the factors here is length of residence in Bogotá. "Recent" migrants, that is, families that came from elsewhere during La Violencia in the 1950s, generally have lower status than Bogotanos who can claim to have been urbanized for generations.) Although the major government buildings are located in the Centro, the center of town, which has a different status altogether (see below), the fancier restaurants, the embassies, elite schools, clubs, and the fanciest barrios are all located in the north.

Four of the nine Melado households are located within a block or two of each other in the barrio Ciudad Jardín Sur (Garden City South). A fifth is only a short walk away, in an adjacent barrio. On several occasions, people who made my acquaintance when I was living with Adela in Ciudad Jardín refused to visit me at home when they heard the "Sur" in my address. Even long-term Bogotanos were under the impression that if they ventured into a southern neighborhood by cab they would no doubt be robbed and beaten and left for dead. In actuality, Ciudad Jardín is a respectable, residential barrio. Most of the houses are two-storey cinder block constructions, inevitably surrounded by high railings and with bars on all of the windows. There is nothing "pretty" about the barrio; the architecture is a bland, boxy, modern style that suggests rapid

development. But the streets are paved, and people generally fastidi-
ously keep up the little postage stamp of lawn within the front patio.

A number of the residents own cars. Pablo, Adela's brother who lived
across the street from us but worked as a physician in a town some two
hours from Bogotá, owned a 1956 Pontiac in immaculate condition.
Many other people owned versions of el carro Colombia (the Colombian
car), which is the least expensive car available in the country, manufactured by Renault.

The primary and secondary school in the barrio run in two shifts.
The neighborhood is purely residential, the only businesses within its
boundaries being a variety of small stores that provide groceries or
dry cleaning or home repair services. Several Protestant groups have
churches in the barrio: the Baptists, Assemblies of God, and the Mormons have thriving congregations. The barrio is also distinguished by
having a Carulla supermarket. Supermarkets are just starting to catch on
in the urban areas of Colombia, and it is usually an indication of middle-
class (or better) status when a woman shops in one.

Across the wide Avenida Caracas is the commercial barrio of El Restrepo. The Melado women do most of their shopping in El Restrepo, and
although they travel out of the barrio of Ciudad Jardín to attend church
and choir practice, and occasionally to visit the sisters and brothers who
have moved to other parts of the city, they never go into the center of the
city, which is only about ten or fifteen minutes away by bus. In their
minds it is a dangerous and frightening place. Except when they can get
one of their brothers to provide car service, the Melado ladies usually
travel by buseta (the half-size buses that clog the streets of Bogotá, and
are slightly more comfortable than the regular-sized buses.) The fare was
9.50 pesos in 1982 and went up to 11 pesos in 1983. (The exchange rate
for the Colombian peso was 62 to the U.S. dollar when I arrived in 1982;
when I left in December 1983, it was closer to 100 to the dollar.) They
never take the buses, which are much cheaper (3 pesos), because they
believe the buses are full of thieves, although the busetas are not safe
either.

The Melados are difficult to categorize in terms of their class position.
Although I would like to call them middle class, they manifest certain
characteristics that distinguish them from other middle-class Bogotanos.
None of the households has a live-in muchacha de servicio, although a
woman was hired to come in once a week to the grandmother's house to
clean. The sisters are all hard workers—they and their daughters do the
cooking and cleaning. Like other city women in Colombia, the Melado
women pay compulsive attention to their fingernails and their manicures. Like the symbolic message of long fingernails elsewhere in the

world, a perfect manicure in Colombia conveys that the person is not engaged in physical labor. For the Melado women, who frequently wash clothes on the cement scrubboard of the *lavadero* (washtub), maintaining this illusion is time-consuming.

The grandparents own a *finca* (farm) in a temperate zone about an hour from Bogotá near Fusagasuga. Owning a *finca* in the hot lands is a goal for all upwardly mobile Bogotanos, and although the name indicates a link with an old concept of the rural "estate," much of the time such *fincas* are simply vacation homes. For the Melados, the *finca* provides an opportunity for a kind of indulgence in the old ways of the *campo*. The house and property are cared for by a campesino couple, but when the family visits, the sisters do the cooking and cleaning. When the grandparents return to Bogotá from a weekend trip they bring fresh fruit and vegetables produced on the farm.

It was striking to me that the caretaker's children in Fusagasuga referred to the Melado children with the honorific titles "El Niño" (for boys) or "La Señorita" (for girls) before their names, rather than by their name alone. When I asked about this it seemed to make the Melados uncomfortable. I was told by Magdalena that they did not like it, but it was a term of respect and a holdover from the ways of the upper class that the peasants were accustomed to.

On several occasions I heard various members of the Melado family identify themselves (and the family as a whole) as "*clase profesional*" (professional class). In chapter 7 I discuss the implications of this class status in contemporary Colombia and for evangelical families in particular.

My Relationship with the Melados

I lived with the Melado family (in Adela's house) from July 1982 to April 1983. In April I moved to El Cocuy to complete the rural part of my study, but I continued to maintain my room at Adela's and returned there during my visits to Bogotá. My relationship with the family was very close throughout my field stay, and I am still corresponding with them.

My original contact with the family came about through a friend of a friend, an architect and contractor who had been hired by Doña Olivia at one time to remodel the third floor of one of her houses as an apartment. During my first few weeks in Colombia I described my proposed research to this man, who told me that he knew some Protestants and would introduce me to them. He arranged for me to meet Pablo, Adela's brother. When I mentioned to Pablo that I was looking for a room to rent, preferably with an evangelical family, he told me that his sister Adela had a place and that she could use the extra income because her husband had left her. In short order I was installed in the maid's room of Adela's house, a room that came to be referred to as *"el barco"* (the boat), because I complained that it was so tiny that it was like being in a berth on a ship. Adela had inherited this house from her parents, and she lived there with her three children: Amanda (nineteen), Patricia (seventeen), and Tadeo (fourteen). Adela supported her family with what she earned working for her father in the *consultorio* (medical office), a job that often included preparing lunch for the ten to twenty people who showed up at noon each day. Tadeo and Patricia were still in secondary school when I arrived and Amanda was attending a technical college, studying for a degree in special education.

Despite the drawbacks of living in the bosom of this straightlaced family, my connection with them was a very fortunate one. As a long-term evangelical family they had extensive contacts with the evangelical community of Bogotá. Through them I made the acquaintance of the Colombian Bible Society representative who in turn introduced me to the width and breadth of the evangelical clergy in the city, and later in scores of towns on his bimonthly circuit.

Adela's fourteen-year-old son, Tadeo, volunteered to escort me on my numerous trips to churches and interviews around the city, amusing himself with my camera and tape recorder to make up for the tedium of the trips for a boy his age.

But most valuable of all was being allowed the insider's view of a Colombian evangelical family. For the kind of data I was interested in, this experience was invaluable. I found that, perhaps due to the desire most Colombians have to appear *formal* to outsiders, the interviews I conducted with people I had met only once or twice often lacked substance. People very much tended to keep their answers polite and vague. Also, the kind of information I wanted was of a nature not often articulated by Colombians—how people fulfill their various roles and how their attitudes about the family change. It was difficult for people to put into words in the context of an interview what seemed self-evident to them.

Sharing day-to-day life with the Melados, I came to know firsthand the concerns of family members. I was also a privileged witness to their dialogues with one another, which provided fine detail on how they perceive themselves and others in the context of the family and the wider Colombian society. In Adela's house, the five of us gathered around the dining room table every night, to eat our bread and cheese and chocolate, and I listened as they reported to each other on the day's events. Lunch was almost always eaten two blocks away at *la casa* (the house), which was what everyone called the grandparents' home. I was often frustrated by the lack of modifiers in much of their speech. For example, if I asked one of the kids where they had been, they might reply "donde mi tío" (at my uncle's house), never indicating which of the five possibilities this referred to. It was assumed that I would know by the context which one they meant. It required a great deal of this intimate kind of fieldwork to easily understand the informal discourse of the family. Lunchtime was an opportunity for me to observe and listen to the extended family and their frequent visitors. Often the banter was rapid-fire, and filled with inside references that at first slipped past me. But over the months I was able to put together profiles of the various players in this lunchtime "circus."

My original plan for the study had been to spend a few months in Bogotá collecting overview information on the evangelical movement in Colombia and establishing contacts that would facilitate my move to a small town. My reasoning behind the plan to conduct the bulk of the data collection in a small town was that such a community would have a more stable and homogeneous population, which would lessen the difficulty of isolating the relationships among different variables. Also, as a single investigator, a small town would be more manageable for data collection purposes.

As the months passed and I became increasingly enmeshed in the Melado family, I began to feel frustrated by my inability to locate an appropriate town. I had visited scores of small towns on my travels with Roberto, the Colombian Bible Society field representative, and through him met and conducted interviews with the evangelical pastors we visited. By December, I was strongly considering Armero in the Department of Caldas (which was destroyed by a volcano eruption in November 1985). Armero had a range of well-established evangelical churches, it was a busy market town of medium size, and the people I spoke with had been relatively open and friendly. But when I brought up the topic of Armero to the Melados, they would react politely but seemed uncharacteristically uninterested in using their extensive contacts to help me get established in the town. Although they did not openly refuse to allow me to move, I understood that if I were to go off to Armero on my own they would consider this unwise, impolite, and a breach of the trust that had been established between us. To their way of thinking, if I insisted on removing myself from the bosom of the family, they should at least have a say in where I went. As I had been "adopted" into their family, they took very seriously their responsibility toward their "daughter." Their peace of mind would be ensured only if I were handed over directly to people with whom they had a relationship of *confianza* (trust, confidence). Armero was situated in the Magdalena Valley, and hence viewed as an alien place by these highlanders. There one could contract malaria and Chagas' disease and be kidnapped or killed by guerrillas. Besides which, they did not know anyone there very well.

The process of deciding on a town where I would be "allowed" to go seemed so slow that at times I considered cutting my losses and exerting my will. But several considerations led me to have patience. First, I did not want to jeopardize my extremely valuable relationship with the Melado family; second, I was truly grateful to them for all they had done for me and I felt I owed them my allegiance; and finally, and perhaps most important, after six months of living with this family I was beginning to think like a "dutiful daughter," and such behavior would have been truly inconsistent with that role.

Fortunately, around Christmas of 1982, I began to develop a relationship with the pastor of El Redentor, the Melados' church, and his wife, Doña Clara, and their daughters. Doña Clara's family, the Azucenas, came from the remote highland town of El Cocuy. In January 1983, the pastor's family spent a week or so with the Melados at their *finca* in Fusagasuga.

For the women, most of this "vacation" was spent preparing food and caring for the hordes of children. In the kitchen, as she prepared *arepas boyacenses* (a cross between a pancake and pita bread), Doña Clara talked about the beauty of her native town, and about her childhood experiences there. Plans were made (jokingly) for a mass trip of the Melado clan to visit the beautiful snow-capped peaks surrounding the town. I was very intrigued, even more so when I learned from the pastor that this was the region of the earliest evangelical missionary activity in the 1930s.

When I returned to Bogotá after a brief trip to the United States in March 1983, I came armed with the news that I had been "ordered" by my professors to move to my rural site immediately. I am grateful to Jane Schneider for the "order." When I discussed my plight with her she quite insightfully suggested that this phrasing might make my mission clearer and more legitimate to the Melados. By saying this, my removal from the bosom of the family seemed less like a personal rejection and more like an odious task imposed by a higher authority. It worked wonderfully. In short order, calls were made, and I was on my way to El Cocuy, escorted by the pastor's wife herself.

My removal from the Melados was not completely without trauma, and they perpetually made slightly bitter jokes about my "abandonment" of them and my "ingratitude." This seems to be a highly stylized form of female discourse in Colombia (although Melado men used it, too, I think it is more characteristically female and that they were mostly imitating their mothers and sisters). I received the same treatment from the other end when I would leave Cocuy for a visit to the Melados in Bogotá. I learned from this experience that, from the female point of view, having more than one family is considered betrayal. This is probably linked to the traditional double standard, where women have one family and men have two or more, and the assumption that divided loyalties inevitably lead to disloyalty. It is not only husbands that provoke this jealous response, but sons and daughters also. The natal family should always be more important than the conjugal one, and the son or daughter who shows more interest in the spouse (and by extension, possibly, the spouse's family) is a potential stray from the fold.

On arriving in El Cocuy, I was handed over immediately to the care of Clara's sisters, Ursula, Lucía, and Marta. Thus began my association with the Azucena-Ortegas, whose composition and history I will describe first before going on to detail my relationship with them.

✠

THE AZUCENA-ORTEGA FAMILY

Composition

In terms of composition and residence the Azucena-Ortega family is quite a bit more complicated than the Melado. For one thing, it is split residentially between Bogotá and El Cocuy. Its approximately seventy living members reside in some sixteen households. Eight of these I would call "dominant" households, in that they are focal points for activities, exchange, and communication for the entire nonresidential extended family group. Of these eight, six are located in El Cocuy and two in Bogotá. Members whose actual residence is elsewhere (in other words, outside of the eight dominant households) often participate in one or more of these households, both in terms of important domestic activities, such as taking meals, or frequent visiting, which includes the exchange of goods and information. Household composition is much more fluid than within the Melado family, with frequent shifts of residence within the town or the city, or between the two. Extended visits to the urban households are often precipitated by the need for medical care, educational resources, or simply for vacations. The urban-centered members return to El Cocuy for vacations, which are sometimes construed as being beneficial for the health (particularly for children), and are also the occasion for the transaction of business. The Bogotá-based residential groups still own land and livestock in El Cocuy, and hence arrangements for the rental of land or pasturage rights, and the care, buying, and selling of livestock often take up a good portion of the visit. Among the El Cocuy–based households, nieces and nephews change residence frequently, residing in town-based households in order to attend school and to assist with chores. Personal animosities are another important factor in determining residence.

The original conversion of the family is recounted in chapter 3, and its early history was described in chapter 4. Lucía and Graciliano Ortega-Azucena, whose roles in the community were described in that chapter, are two members of the "sibling set," equivalent to the generation referred to as *los hermanos* within the Melado family. This generation, among both the Azucena-Ortegas and the Melados, is the first generation born to parents who themselves converted. Although some of the children of this generation, in both groups, were born before their parents converted and thus were baptized as Catholics, most of their lives (and for the younger siblings, all of their lives) they have been evangelical.

In terms of the developmental cycle of the extended kin group, the Azucena-Ortega group is older. The grandparent generation (who were the first converts) is dead, and the oldest sibling (Ursula) is approximately the same age as Doña Olivia Melado. Certain members of the family, both of the sibling set and among their children, have achieved a significant degree of upward mobility, but this has not been as uniform as among the Melados.

At the time of my fieldwork, the oldest sibling, Ursula Azucena de Ortega, served as a focal point for the larger kin grouping in that its members, to a certain degree, include themselves in the family on the basis of their ties to her. The matrifocality of the Latin American family becomes clear when kin groups beyond the nuclear family are considered. Bryce-Laporte (1970:90) reported that, while the father figure may have considerable authority within the nuclear family household, it is rare to find men of the grandparent generation who wield the kind of power or influence over a wider circle of kin that women of the same generation do. My data on these two *gran familias* certainly support the latter half of his assertion. Both Ursula and Doña Olivia Melado were predominant in terms of authority and influence within the wider kin group. They also represented, as symbolic figures, idealized reference points for determining and demonstrating inclusion in the kin grouping and stood as constant reminders, above all, of the value of family unity.

My Relationship with the Azucena-Ortegas

I first met Ursula one very rainy, cold, foggy day, a few days after I arrived in El Cocuy. I had gone into the mountains outside of town with Clara to visit some of her relatives. Clara is Ursula's youngest sister, in her late fifties. She is one of the Cocuyanas who has made the transition from her peasant background to a more or less middle-class existence in Bogotá. Although she suffers from arthritis, she had been kind enough to make the arduous fourteen-hour bus trip from Bogotá with me, to introduce me to her family in El Cocuy and help me get established. That day we borrowed her brother Graciliano's jeep and drove up into the hills to visit her brother Israel and her sister-in-law Zaida. They live in an idyllic spot, next to a rushing river, in a highland valley. After we had been fed *onces*, or elevenses (coffee with milk and home-baked bread), we went for a walk. I understood we were going off to see Ursula. Climbing up the side of a mountain at a forty-five-degree angle, struggling up a practically vertical, rocky path in the dripping rain, sloshing through a very wet pasture, we slowly approached a little, crumbling hut, made out of stone and mud, with a corrugated metal roof partly covering it.

Ursula loved this spot; she spent as much time as she could up there with her cows. Standing in the door to the hut one could look down over the sloping hillside to the rushing river that cuts through the valley from the snowcapped peaks down into the town of El Cocuy. In the distance the mountains rise consecutively, the tallest one the peak of Maoma, which is where the "Mohan" lives, stealing the most beautiful women and children and turning them into forlorn zombies like himself. The air smelled like wood smoke and eucalyptus; huge trees lined the paths and the borders between people's farms. That day her daughter, Luisa, her son Francisco, and Luisa's daughter Neftali had come up from town to visit her for the day. Inside the hut, which was tiny, about ten feet by ten feet, there was an open wood fire, over which a blackened pot full of potatoes boiled propped up on three large stones. The hut had a deeply rutted dirt floor, and a bed made out of saplings tied together on top of which Ursula threw her mattress. They were getting lunch ready, which consisted of heaping plates of boiled potatoes with a sauce made out of onions, tomatoes, and milk curd. In keeping with the standard etiquette of the *campo*, even though we had just eaten, they insisted that we join them.

There was a great deal of laughter and joking about the "elegance" of Ursula's estate because they were all slightly embarrassed about my first impression of Ursula. She had on a dirty, worn dress that looked like it dated from the early fifties, old beat-up shoes, and a straw hat that was falling apart. Underneath the bed was strewn a large assortment of wrecked shoes and slippers, which I came to learn were a standing joke in the family. Ursula's children try to keep her from spending so much time up at the *rancho*; they say she is old, she could become ill, it is so cold and damp up there, and it certainly is not a seemly thing for her to be doing. But she is tied to the old ways and is really happiest in the *campo*. She spends her time caring for the cows, milking, and making the *cuajada*, or milk curd, that she sends down to the market once a week to sell. There is no running water or toilet or electricity there, and she makes do like the other poor people of the *campo*, using the woods or the hillside as her toilet, and taking water from a little stream that runs across the pasture up from the house. There is also no chimney in the house, and it fills with smoke when she is cooking. There is an old wood stove standing in the corner of the hut, a relic of a missionary family that had transported it all the way from the United States in the 1930s, but this is used as a table and to store the few things she needs to cook with. Many people still prefer to use the *fogón*, or open fire, rather than a wood stove because it is more economical in terms of the amount of firewood needed. The cows graze all around the house, which is in the middle of the pasture.

A few days after this visit, I was invited to Ursula's house in town for lunch. Later I came to understand that this had been a ceremonial lunch, planned to impress on me that I was not really dealing with a little, poor old campesina, as I had at first assumed. She served three kinds of meat and vast quantities of potatoes and noodles. Her house in town is rather nice by Cocuy standards, although like all houses in the center it was built a long time ago and is falling to pieces. She is not a fastidious housekeeper; the city standards of housekeeping are for the most part unknown in Cocuy, where processing and preparing food, washing clothes, and caring for the animals is all done with very rudimentary technology, and hence is very time-consuming. Ursula had spruced herself up for the occasion. She had on a clean dress, although it looked like it was of the same vintage as the one she had worn in the highland pasture. Her long black hair was pulled back in a ponytail. When Ursula's children and grandchildren make fun of her they like to say that the reason her hair has not turned white with age is because she never washes it. All of these habits they associate with how peasants behave.

During the months that I stayed in Cocuy Ursula adopted me. There was a period after I had established myself in my own house, with one of her daughters as my companion and caretaker, that she kept flooding my rooms with roses. My house was always filled with roses: vases, glasses, pails of them all over the place. Ursula would send me huge bouquets every four or five days, via her daughter or grandson. The roses did not have time to die before I would get replacements. Other people would often say, casually, "Here, I make you a present of this rose," in the midst of an otherwise homely chat. As a city dweller, I was astounded to have such an abundance at hand. Lilies also grow in great abundance in El Cocuy. The chapel of the little Lutheran church was always decorated with floral bouquets that would shame New York City's great gothic cathedral of St. John the Divine. Many women have gardens in the central patios of their houses, and they can (and do) talk endlessly about flowering plants. The tone of voice is almost identical as when talking about children—pride in the beautiful, flourishing ones, vexation with the scrawny ones that do not progress no matter what you do, mournfulness for the ones that inexplicably die. It seemed amazing to me that women with so much drudge work to do in what remains partially a peasant family economy could find the time and energy for tending these gardens. You cannot eat these plants, but they serve the perhaps almost as important function of adorning social relations that are otherwise very stark. Ursula's patio garden was particularly luxurious. Her children would often bring her a special plant when they came to visit from Bogotá. She never empties a can or any other container without observing to herself that it would serve nicely as a flower pot.

In 1933, at the age of twenty-two, Ursula married Amadeo Ortega in the Catholic church in El Cocuy. Amadeo is her first cousin, and of their ten children, four are deaf. As she points out in the interview, and as is corroborated by the records of the Catholic church register, in earlier times people commonly selected their mates from those close at hand, and over a period of several centuries this practice has resulted in much close intermarriage. Ursula's relationship with Amadeo was the source of great unhappiness for her. His affairs with other women, his drunkenness, and his opposition to her wishes in practically every matter made her life a perpetual struggle. It is only because of her tremendous tenacity that she has managed to create a family and to see several of her children achieve a social and economic status that she would never have even dreamed of. At the time of my fieldwork her husband was still alive, but he lived permanently up in the *campo*, taken care of by a *campesina* woman. He was eighty-four years old. In September they had their fiftieth wedding anniversary, which her most successful daughter, who lives in Bogotá, insisted on celebrating with a big party in Bogotá. The party was almost canceled several times, because Ursula does not speak to her husband. She always mentions him with rage, recounting times when he used to hit her across the face with the horse's reins, or flip hot soup into her face with a spoon because she did not let it cool a bit before serving it to him. He is notorious in town as a drunken, brutal man. Ursula's daughters told me how their mother would get up in the morning covered with black and blue marks and explain that witches, sent by Amadeo's "*indias*," had attacked her while she slept.

Within the family they commonly refer to the fact that he never has contributed economically to the support of the family. Miraculously, not having the strength to work them any longer himself, he divided his lands among his children a few years ago, and all of them, the sons and the daughters alike, received their inheritance. There continues to be a problem with the lands that he held jointly with Ursula, for example, the pasture with the hut on it where I first met her. This was given to one of her younger daughters, Liliana, but she really cannot use it because her mother is constantly moving her cows up there and staying in the rancho. Liliana was thirty-seven at the time, and was frustrated because her siblings were all able to derive a small amount of income off their lands, mostly by selling pasture rights on a monthly basis, and she had to resort to working as a maid for her better-off sisters in Bogotá if she wanted to have any cash of her own. When she brings this issue up to her mother it inevitably ends up in a tearful fight, with Ursula saying, "You might as well just go ahead and bury me while I'm still living and breathing." Liliana is soft-hearted and certainly a faithful daughter, so she is not pushing her case. Ursula has always seen her cows as her main source of economic security, and even though this is really no longer necessary because she has children who are making money and who would gladly see that she had enough to live on, she refuses to give up her cows. And as long as she has her cows she has to have pasture for them. Her most successful daughter, Amarilis, is constantly trying to lure her mother to come live with her and her husband, Paco, in Bogotá, which Ursula does from time to time, but after a few weeks she is bored with being a captive in the house and wants to return to Cocuy.

Amarilis is Ursula's second-oldest daughter, and the one who has done best for herself. Ursula's rendition of Amarilis's courtship and eventual marriage to Paco provides an excellent illustration of the family dynamics within both her own nuclear family and the larger kin grouping. Ursula recounts:

Amarilis had a sweetheart, but then this guy took a shot at his brother-in-law and wounded him in the head. And the whole family at that point, Graciliano, all of us, said to her, "Don't marry him, you see what kind of a guy he is?" the same as they had said to me with regard to Amadeo. But she didn't pay any attention to us. At that time she was teaching at the Lutheran school in the *vereda* of El Carrizal. And the very same night that he shot his brother-in-law, he went up into the mountains to visit her and tell her what he had done. And I thought to myself, I hope now she'll recognize what he's really like, and she'll hate him for it and break up with him. But as for that, it was as if she liked him even better for what he had done! The guy fled to Bogotá, so they wouldn't put him in jail here in El Cocuy, but they managed to find him there and arrested him and brought him back a prisoner. After they put him in jail here, Amarilis used to go on the sly to visit him. Around that same time, my daughter Luisa had a sweetheart who was a captain in the army. That's when Paco came on the scene. I had a little store, here in the house, and the captain and some of the other soldiers used to come and drink in my store. That's how Paco met Amarilis. It wasn't long after that that he asked her to marry him. And she hesitated, but he told her to go ask her mother. So she came to talk to me, and I told her, "These things shouldn't be decided from one moment to the next, after all, you haven't known him that long, and you need to know your feelings before you take such a big step. You can't just rush ahead and say, 'Yes, let's do it.' Get to know each other first." They were so impulsive. Besides which, she was still interested in the other guy, she still loved him and kept going to see him in jail. Then Paco left with the army, he was stationed in Sogamoso and after that in Soatá, but he kept on writing to her. I'd always manage to find the letters she'd received from him, and I'd read them. And from those letters I discovered that he was a guy who had very fine sentiments, he was a very good person. And he was clearly making an effort to win Amarilis. And he came back to visit, and he tried to talk to Amarilis's father, but Amadeo always gave him the cold shoulder. Amadeo never wanted him to be Amarilis's husband. But nevertheless, little by little we were coming to an agreement about the marriage. And all this time Amarilis continued to visit the other guy in jail! That Salazar had some relatives who were very good people, they were university educated, and they always held us in very high esteem. And finally one day they came and paid us a visit, and one of them said to Amarilis, "It's true that Salazar is a member of my family, but it upsets me that you would consider marrying him, because he's so reckless, and he's a drunkard. It pains me to see you acting the way you do with him." And they all agreed. They said that Salazar had something like four girls on the string, and all of them were going to visit him in jail. So finally, one day it resolved itself. I don't know what else happened between them, but the guy said something to Amarilis that was the straw that broke the camel's back. He said, "All right, I'll marry you, but I won't let you go to Protestant services any more." And at those words she finally woke up, and she answered him, "By God, then neither will you be the husband of Amarilis! Goodbye!" And she finally left him for good. So then we arranged for her marriage to Paco, who was stationed in Sogamoso at the time. And the wedding was held on January 1, 1966, and all of us went from here in El Cocuy, my brothers and sisters and all of my kids. I hired a truck to take us directly, because we also had to take some chickens and a potato or two. And they were married in the Catholic church, because Paco used to be a very devout Catholic. But he was very open to advice, and he listened carefully to everything that Amarilis said to him. Even up to today he accepts everything that Amarilis says to him! He used to drink and smoke a lot, whole bottles of *aguardiente* and whole packages of cigarettes. But Amarilis slowly proceeded to rid him of these vices, and now he doesn't smoke anymore, and he doesn't drink. Well, he'll take an occasional drink from time to time, but not because he has that vice. Just to be sociable. The wedding was very beautiful. Thank God that Amadeo stayed away. He was so angry about it, that from the day we left to go to the wedding he spent the whole time drinking. He drank and drank, with a compadre, and one day my oldest daughter, Blanca, looked out of her window and spotted him heading for the *campo* without his pants on! He was so drunk he was unaware of what he was doing. He refused to go to the wedding because Amarilis had ignored his wishes in the matter. He had wanted her to marry Salazar, the guy who was in jail, not Paco.

Paco and Amarilis live in Bogotá now, in a quite comfortable large house shared with Amarilis's sister Stella, who is single. Paco has been a member of the Lutheran church for some time, and occupied the position of administrator of the Colombian Lutheran Synod during the time I was there. They are very upwardly mobile, striving to achieve a professional-class lifestyle, which includes cars, a comfortable house, and much conspicuous consumption. Their connection with the little old lady in the shepherd's hut is quite remarkable, and that relationship and the history of Ursula's life and her goals for her children represent on a small scale the vast social changes that have occurred in Colombia during this century.

✣
THE CHURCH SERVICES

It is difficult to study evangelicals at close range without spending a great deal of time in church. A colleague who was doing her fieldwork in Belize at the same time I was in Colombia wrote to me that she envied my research because it was so easy to meet people in the church. This was certainly true, and I could depend on frequent meetings of my database.

Many researchers on Pentecostalism and other proselytizing religious groups have expounded on the hazards associated with this kind of fieldwork. Flora, who also worked with Colombian Pentecostals, described the obstacles to her research presented by members' constant demands that she and her husband convert.

In my experience with the Pentecostals, while it is possible to do short-term work without being foiled by their interest in one's soul, there is a definite time limit to it, after which the pace of confrontation increases and further questioning is hampered. Questions will be turned back on the interviewer and the focus of the interview switched from the informant onto the condition of the fieldworker's immortal soul. The nature of this interaction may in itself be interesting, but it can also be extremely trying and for my purposes was tangential to the topic of the study. An example of the kind of exchange I am speaking about may be helpful.

I had been working for several months with a thirty-year-old man who was a very active member of the Assemblies of God. He was something of a free-lance journalist, and when he heard about my study from a friend whom I had interviewed after a service, he called me to express interest in my study. His aim, as I understood it, was to write a history of the evangelical movement in Colombia, from the point of view of how great is the love of God in working miracles for his people.

He was organized and knowledgeable, and we collaborated on constructing a questionnaire to be administered in a wide range of evangelical churches in Bogotá. We would both have access to the data collected to use as we saw fit. I was grateful for his help in phrasing questions in a way that would seem meaningful to evangelicals, and he benefited from my willingness to take on the burden of production of the questionnaire. Over the course of three months we met many times, and he told me much about himself.

For Colombian evangelicals, the first order of business when meeting a new person is to find out if he or she is a *creyente* (believer). I had two factors working in my favor in terms of my acceptability to the evangelical community. First because I was a *gringa*, people did not always know how to categorize me. For many people, the only *gringos* they had ever met had been evangelical missionaries, and they assumed that a North American, especially one who was spending a great deal of time with the *creyentes*, was probably a missionary. Second, I had been raised in a Lutheran family, and when more detail on my religious beliefs was solicited, I told people that I was Lutheran. This explanation satisfied many people, who knew that *luteranos* were *evangélicos*, and hence I was one of them. Only the more theologically sophisticated tried to push it beyond that. My collaborator and I would begin and end each of our meetings with a prayer, and at first he seemed quite content when I would demur to him to proceed when he asked me if I would like to lead us. Once, when I was suffering from a cold (and also anger at his having been two hours late for our last several meetings), he interrupted our conversation to pray for my healing and laid hands on me. By this time I was used to this kind of behavior, and felt reasonably comfortable going along with it as long as I could assume a passive role. But as our acquaintance went on, more time was spent on prayer and less on work. Finally he asked if I had accepted the Holy Spirit as my guide, and when I tried to evade the issue by saying, of course, I had been baptized and confirmed in the Lutheran church, he refused to accept this and kept pressuring me to accept and experience the work of the Spirit in my life. I told him that for me the most important order of business at the moment was completing my study, and that if I lost my objectivity I would be unable to complete it. For him this was no answer, and he responded that the Holy Spirit knew all, and that if I trusted in the Spirit, the Spirit would lead me to the truth. This sort of impasse began to characterize all of our meetings, and he seemed to lose interest in our collaboration on the questionnaire. After I left for El Cocuy, our relationship ended.

Notes

2. THE EVANGELICAL MOVEMENT IN COLUMBIA

1. The dates of the arrival of various missions in Colombia during the 1930s and the 1940s are as follows: 1932, Assemblies of God; 1933, World Evangelization Crusade; 1934, United Brothers; 1934, American Indian Mission; 1937, Calvary Holiness Mission; 1937, Evangelical Lutheran Mission; 1937, Latin American Mission; 1941, Southern Baptist Mission; 1942, Wesleyan Methodist Mission; 1942, Evangelical Union of South America; 1942, Church of the Four-Square Gospel; 1943, Interamerican Mission; 1945, Mennonite Mission of Colombia; 1945, Mennonite Brothers Mission (SEPAL 1981).

2. In Colombia the total number of communicants reported for 1967 was over seventy thousand—seven times the total for 1950 (Read et al. 1969). One could argue that the evangelical movement has experienced a geometrical growth rate (this would be logical, since each new member becomes an evangelist and converts new people), and that the rate has been steady all along. The important point, however, is that it was during La Violencia that the movement really took off; before then growth was small. Of course, after 1967 and until the present growth has been the most spectacular in terms of numbers (see SEPAL 1981 for details of this expansion).

3. In Colombia the current Catholic attitude toward Bible reading is somewhat equivocal and varies from priest to priest. In a Catholic publication (Salesman 1982) that criticizes the evangelicals strongly and enumerates the "errors" in their doctrine, the author gives definite if somewhat grudging recognition that evangelicals tend to have excellent knowledge of the Bible, and that this lack among Catholics is something that needs to be remedied. It is also recognized that one of the attractions that the evangelicals hold out to potential converts is the accessibility of the Bible to individual members. The Catholic hierarchy seems to recognize that if they are to compete successfully with the evangelicals, they must be willing to relinquish exclusive control by the clergy over the sacred text and make it accessible to the laity.

4. The Apocrypha consists of fourteen books that are not regarded by

Protestants to be canonical: they are not found in Hebrew and are entirely rejected in Judaism, but eleven of them are fully accepted in the Roman Catholic canon. The accusation against the Protestants by the Colombian Catholic hierarchy has been that they were teaching heresies. The omission of the eleven books from the Protestant Bible does not seem to impress the potential convert as much as the fact that, phrase by phrase, the books that are included in the Protestant version in no way differ from the ones in the Catholic Bible. Because of the long-standing reluctance on the part of the Catholic hierarchy to allow the laity access to any of the Bible, it is doubtful that potential Protestant converts would interpret the omission of the books of the Apocrypha as meaning that the evangelicals are trying to sell them an incomplete truth. In part, the absence of these books was not a concern because relatively few people, especially before they began to think about converting, had ever seen a Catholic version of the Bible.

5. The least expensive paperback editions of the New Testament could be obtained for between 50 and 100 pesos ($.77 and $1.53) in 1982. The least expensive complete Bible—including both Old and New Testaments—could be purchased in either hardback or paperback for between 200 and 250 pesos ($3.07–$3.85) at that time. Although spending this much money at once might represent a hardship for the poorest sectors, these prices would be within the reach of most lower-class people. To give some sense of how the purchase of a Bible relates to the cost of some commonly used goods, the prices for comestibles around that time were as follows: rice and sugar, 25 pesos ($.38) per pound; coffee, 50 pesos ($.77) per pound; chocolate, in bars, for making hot chocolate, 70 pesos ($1.08) a pound. The cheapest brand of cigarettes, Piel Rojas, cost 18 pesos ($.27) a pack, while Marlboros were available for 80 pesos ($1.23) a pack. A bottle of beer cost 17 pesos ($.26), and aguardiente, the anise-flavored national liquor of Colombia, sold for 340 pesos ($5.23) for a liter bottle.

6. The Roman Catholic policy that the Bible should be read and interpreted by the church hierarchy and kept out of the hands of the laity, lest it lead to erroneous interpretations, apparently dates from the Council of Trent, in 1545. This edict was reformed by the Council of Vatican II.

7. "Folk" Catholic beliefs are quite pervasive in both rural and urban Colombia. This is a different dimension of religious practice, at times only tenuously attached to institutionalized Roman Catholic belief and at times independent from it (or condemned by it). Men who rarely attend Catholic mass can still be quite involved in folk aspects of Catholicism, especially in terms of special claims and prayers to specific saints for protection. Other belief systems, such as santería, have a good number of adherents in Colombia, and the use of indigenous healers is quite widespread. The noninstitutionalized belief systems are frequently condemned by evangelicals (as well as by the Catholic clergy) as heretical or satanic.

8. When I discussed the nature of my fieldwork with a Colombian colleague, especially the amount of time I spent in church services, he commented that I must be spending a great deal of time "rezando." I looked at

him blankly, not understanding the meaning of the word. This moment brought home to me the disparity between evangelical and Catholic vocabulary. I also realize that the perception of the difference between *orar* and *rezar* is that of my evangelical informants; the contrast mentioned here thus does not imply a judgment.

9. Pentecostal prayer style in Colombia is quite uniform throughout the various denominations. When the pastor or leader of the worship service begins to pray, each individual in the congregation begins his or her own prayer, out loud. The individual prayers may be actual supplications (e.g., "Please, dearest Lord, heal my daughter of her illness") or, more often, simply words of praise repeated over and over again (e.g., "Lord, Lord, we praise your name, Glory to God"), which sometimes spills over into glossolalia. With everybody talking at once, the prayers can be quite clamorous. The emotional pitch of the prayers tends to follow the pace set by the leader of the service (although the actual words he [or she] is saying seem to be ignored). The leader usually builds to a crescendo, the congregation following along, and then slowly tapers off in a soothing voice to a closing amen. The physical posture is standing with the arms raised and the palms up. That this prayer style is distinct from that of Pentecostal churches in the United States is evidenced by the irritation of a Four-Square Gospel missionary who had come to Colombia from the United States to attend their annual convention. He complained that the congregation was not listening to his prayer and, after a few times, instructed them to keep silent and to pray to themselves while he led the prayer. John Firth, a Four-Square missionary who has served in Colombia since 1938, acknowledges that this was a problem. He finds it necessary to instruct his congregation before some prayers, "Let us pray, now, with your heads down, and your eyes closed." When he instructs them this way, they will often keep quiet while he prays out loud, perhaps murmuring "Amén" or "Sí, Señor." If he does not give this instruction but launches into a prayer spontaneously, the congregation will participate in the manner just described.

10. Evangelicals were included, along with many other formerly disenfranchised groups, in the drafting of the new Colombian constitution in 1991.

11. While it is clearly useful and desirable to have some numerical estimate of the size of different churches, it is with certain reservations that I commit these numbers to paper. The Assemblies of God will claim that they are the largest single evangelical denomination in Colombia, but the figures cited to me were substantially lower than the IPU count. There is a great deal of flexibility in terms of the way the counting is done: some denominations count as churches places that are actually *lugares de predicación* (preaching locales), which are considered by other churches to be satellites of one local church. One of the reasons for the apparently greater size of the United Pentecostals is that, since they do not send their pastors to Bible school, they can count many more "pastors" than other denominations with stricter requirements.

3. RELIGION AND POLITICS

1. This quote is taken from a small book entitled *"Cuidado: Llegaron los protestantes"* (Watch Out: The Protestants Have Arrived), which was selling in the Catholic bookstore in Bogotá in 1983. The book's stated aim is to provide the faithful believer (Roman Catholic) with a way to "defend himself" against the onslaught of the Protestants. In includes an outline of the ten Christian truths that are denied by Protestants: (1) that there are seven sacraments; (2) that there are seventy-two books in the Bible; (3) the veneration of sacred images; (4) the cult of the Virgin and the saints; (5) the presence of Jesus Christ in the Eucharist; (6) the forgiveness of sins by means of confession to a priest; (7) that the Bible must be interpreted according to the doctrine and explanations of the church hierarchy, who are guided by the Holy Spirit, and not by each believer, for fear of falling into error; (8) that faith is not sufficient for salvation, but good works are also necessary; (9) the authority of the pope, the bishops, and the priests; and (10) appreciation of Holy Mass. The author states, in at least two places, that there are "more than 666" Protestant sects. Although he does not make the connection explicit, the number 666 in the Bible is significant as the number of the Antichrist.

2. For this information I am indebted to the scholarship of Daniel Levine (1981).

3. Levine (1981) maintains that Colombia has experienced an altogether slower rate of change than Venezuela, in the structural as well as in the symbolic realms. The continuing prominence of the Catholic church in Colombia is consistent, in his analysis, with a relatively slow rate of economic change, including the fact that the Colombian economy is still basically tied to agriculture. In Venezuela, the civil wars of the nineteenth century were won by the Liberals, who stripped the church of its property and social functions, while in Colombia the Conservatives emerged victorious. Traditional ideologies and legitimations of power and privilege survived in Colombia, where a unified social and economic elite has been carried over into the twentieth century. In contrast, after 1920 the impact of oil on the Venezuelan economy propelled it toward becoming "a fundamentally different kind of society from Colombia . . . in Colombia, the basic problem for elites has been to preserve existing structures and retain old loyalties. In Venezuela, the problem has been to create new institutions, to reach and engage the loyalties of a mobile population in new and fast-changing circumstances" (Levine 1981:59, 61–62).

4. The preamble to the old Constitution clearly makes Roman Catholicism the official religion of Colombia. It reads: "In the name of God, supreme source of all authority, and for the purpose of strengthening national unity, one of whose bases is the recognition by the political parties that the Apostolic and Roman Catholic religion is that of the nation, and that as such the public powers shall protect it and see that it is respected as an essential element of the social order." While the new preamble does invoke the

protection of God, any reference to the Roman Catholic church has been dropped (Morgan and Alzate 1992:384).

5. The argument being developed here has to do with the relative positions of the Liberal and Conservative parties with regard to religious plurality. It should also be noted, however, that the Catholic hierarchy's hatred of the Liberals can also be connected historically to the expropriation of church lands by Liberal reformers following the civil wars of the mid-nineteenth century. Oquist has pointed out that "the church, deprived by the Liberals of its lands and aggrieved by the separation of church and state, launched a holy war against the Liberals . . . The Church from 1863 onward . . . advised that 'Liberalism was sin'" (1980:68).

6. The expanded dates for La Violencia, predating the assassination of Gaitán, are used by many historians. For example, Sánchez (1985:792) includes the twenty-year period from 1945 to 1965. This lack of clarity in the dates parallels the confusion over the causes of La Violencia: it is hard to pinpoint with precision the starting point for the "conglomeration of processes that characterized this struggle—that mixture of anarchy, peasant insurgency, and official terror" (Sánchez 1985:792).

7. Oquist (1980) has analyzed the multitude of factors contributing to La Violencia. He concludes that a partial collapse of the state and the erosion of centralized authority due to interparty conflict allowed traditional rivalries on the local level to be settled by violence. Although a range of motivations led to hostility, conflict over land was a major problem. The fighting took place both within class groups and between classes, but interclass conflict was more characteristic during the later years of La Violencia (1955–1966).

8. As Stoll (1990) has so effectively pointed out, Latin American Protestants run the gamut of political inclinations from left to right; hence, it is erroneous to make simple generalizations about their political beliefs. Moreover, because of the "world-rejecting" nature of many evangelical groups, secular politics are often not a primary concern. Among the evangelicals who provided information for this study, most were either not interested in politics or relatively conservative. Several, however, were markedly leftist in their political views.

9. The names of evangelicals in this book are pseudonyms unless otherwise noted.

4. EL COCUY: COLOMBIAN EVANGELICALISM ON THE COMMUNITY LEVEL

1. My first trip to Colombia, in the fall of 1973, came about as the result of my participation in a program for undergraduate majors in anthropology sponsored by the School for International Training of the Experiment in International Living. The small group of students traveled from the United States directly to the small town of Silvia, Cauca, where we resided for the first few months in the homes of local families. During our five-month stay

in Colombia, I spent a few weeks traveling around the country and visited the cities of Cali, Bogotá, and Pasto. The bulk of the time, however, was spent in the rural areas, including one month of independent field research I conducted with return migrants in the extreme southern part of the country, in Funes, Nariño.

2. The classification "urban" is slightly misleading in this generalization, because "percent urban" includes all people living in a county seat (*cabecera municipal*). *Cabeceras* may in fact be tiny towns with fewer than 1,500 people (and there may be other settlements with larger populations that are not classified as *cabeceras* and hence are not considered urban). In terms of everyday life, these small *cabeceras* (including the town of El Cocuy), appear much more rural than urban. Perhaps a better indicator of the rate of urbanization is the percentage of the entire population living in the major cities, which has also increased markedly over the past fifty years. In 1938 Bogotá claimed only 3.8 percent of the Colombian population (numbering 8,702,000 in that year), while in 1973, 12.7 percent of the 22,500,000 Colombians lived in that city (Mohan 1980:13).

3. I also collected data on births, deaths, and marriages during this century from the Catholic church parochial office in El Cocuy. There are many difficulties with these figures, but the one clear pattern that they reveal is the decrease in population. Since there is now also a secular registry, it is possible that the decreasing figures after the 1950s reveal a switchover to the government registry. The government registry was started around 1900, however, and I believe that births are now recorded in both places.

4. There is a hierarchy of footwear among Cocuyanos. The poorest peasants wear rope-soled *alpargates*, which provide a little protection from the sharp rocks but function much as bare feet would—they get wet, but then they dry. More successful peasants and middle-class people who must spend time in their fields checking on lifestock or irrigation hoses, etc., wear rubber boots, which keep feet dry but are hazardous when negotiating the steep paths strewn with slippery rocks. Next on the scale, younger people and town folk favor running shoes, which can be scrubbed clean after each muddy outing. Appearing in town in muddy shoes is unthinkable, and the time and energy spent trying to maintain the illusion that mud does not exist in El Cocuy or that, if it does, one does not go anywhere near it, adds to the burden of social reproduction on women, especially status-conscious ones. In town, the people with highest status, professionals and other town folk, wear normal "city" shoes. For women, this often means spike heels. Presumably for appearance's sake such things are important enough that one is willing to risk the dangers of teetering around on the rough, acutely inclined cobblestone streets and negotiating the irregularities of terrain and mud patches that characterize the streets even in town.

5. This custom seems to be rather prevalent in small towns in Colombia, and control of the loudspeaker (either by secular or clerical authorities) is a source of considerable political power. Jorge Velosa Ruiz, a university stu-

dent of rural Boyacense origin, is a songwriter who has composed a number of verses celebrating rural life in Boyacá. One of his songs, "El parlante de mi pueblo" (my town's loudspeaker), is dedicated to this phenomenon. The refrain characterizes the ambivalence of public attitude toward the constant noise.

6. There is evidence of the predominance of Spanish settlers and the domination of the indigenous population in El Cocuy from the seventeenth and eighteenth centuries. Molino García (1976) reports the following figures for the municipality. The total number of Indians in 1635–1636 was 748, while in 1755–1756 this number had fallen to 634, constituting a 15 percent reduction in the indigenous population during the 120 years of colonial settlement. In 1755–1756 vecinos españoles already substantially outnumbered the Indians, the Spanish population being reported as 1,648. The relatively small reduction in the Indian population during this time (compared to other towns in the region, where the figure was as high as 85 percent), along with what seems to be a surprisingly small number of Indians in 1635 in an extensive and fertile area, might indicate that displacement of the indigenous population (including wars of extermination) had occurred much earlier, during the period of conquest in the sixteenth century.

7. The actual fate of these elite families is something of a mystery. I have searched through the Colombian Who's Who (Perry et al. 1952; Quién es quién 1978) for the surnames my informants mentioned, in order to determine what happened to these families. In 1952 one individual with the surname Gallo was listed. This lawyer living in Bogotá was born in El Cocuy in 1911. By 1978 there were no listings for the three major families mentioned by my informants: Gallo, Saravia, and Santos Gutiérrez, nor was there any indication that other individuals included in the directory had been born in El Cocuy. It is possible that the families have either died out or left Colombia, but more intensive research is clearly necessary.

8. In 1983 the monthly tuition for a child attending the Colegio CELCO in El Cocuy was 250 pesos ($3.13). In that year, there were fifty-two children enrolled, and the income from the tuition was not sufficient to cover the salaries of the two teachers. In earlier times, there were as many as eighty students in the CELCO, and all five primary grades were offered. During my field stay, the school was informed by the national administration of the Lutheran church that within the next year or two it would stop providing even the minimal subsidy that the school had been receiving in the past. The rector was instructed to draw up a plan to make the school self-supporting, but was encountering a great deal of difficulty. She refused to raise the tuition, stating that parents would not be able to pay a higher fee and would send their children to the public school. The parents' association, most of whom were nonevangelicals, was attempting to raise funds through various methods, including sponsoring dances. Their methods were not always consistent with the standards of the Lutherans involved.

9. It is unlikely that an evangelical pastor would have been appointed

to such an office in a community that was dominated by the Conservative party. In addition to being well known as an evangelical, in El Cocuy Graciliano was respected as a staunch Liberal.

5. DOMESTIC ABDICATION, INDIVIDUALISM, AND MACHISMO

1. Ethnic, regional, and class differences complicate generalizations about the Colombian domestic group. At the same time, rapid culture change within the context of neocolonial dependency, the prevalence of migration, and the relative scarcity of unassimilated Indian groups make for a degree of similarity among Colombians of different ethnic, regional, rural, and urban backgrounds. The ethnic breakdown of the Colombian population is estimated to be mestizos and mulattoes, 75 percent; whites, 20 percent; blacks, 4 percent; and Indians, 1 percent (Blutstein et al. 1983:viii).

2. Both the Gilmores (1979) and Brandes (1981) believe that the term "machismo" is an English neologism based on the Spanish word for male (*macho*) and state that the term "machismo" is not used by their Spanish informants. Kutsche (1984:6) notes the native use of the term in New Mexico and Costa Rica and states that there is little evidence that it is an importation. In Colombia, the term is definitely in use, although it was characteristically employed in the context of social analysis offered to me by teachers and others with more than the average level of formal education. The form of the word is pertinent here, because I often heard women label particular men or categories of men (e.g., those from Boyacá or the coast) as "*machista*," and whether the adjective or the noun form is employed seems to reflect differing levels of abstraction from personal experience. Interesting also is the fact that the Spanish word *macho* as used in Colombia has to do with biological sex and, like its female counterpart, *hembra*, is used to refer to the sex of animals and not, in polite speaking, to that of humans. When asked about the sex of their children, people will describe a child as *varón* (a boy) or *mujer* (a girl).

3. Arrom (1985) traces the development of *marianismo* in Mexico City during the first half of the nineteenth century. Rejecting the notion that *marianismo* is a characteristically Latin American phenomenon, she notes similarities between it and the Victorian "cult of true womanhood," which has been of great interest to feminist historians of Europe and the United States. She notes, however, that this model of femininity had a substantially different outcome in terms of women's status in the Hispanic context.

4. A third arena within which machismo has been treated (in addition to the psychological and the anthropological) is in the work of Latin American writers. Not all have followed Octavio Paz's grim view, put forth in his classic *The Labyrinth of Solitude* (1961). For some writers, machismo is seen as a positive and vital national characteristic. This is clear in a statement made by the Puerto Rican writer René Marqués: "Apparently, the writers are the only ones in Puerto Rican society who have rebelled against the disappearance of the last cultural bulwark from which one could still com-

bat the collective docility: machismo" (quoted in Barradas 1977). See also Mollinger's (1984) psychoanalytic treatment of machismo in the works of Paz and Carlos Fuentes.

5. Hunt describes the Mexican domestic patriarch whose claim to his familial authority is earned by his fulfillment of his responsibilities, and whose identity is intimately connected to the well-being of his family: "Many of them are highly puritanical, and often deeply committed to what they call progress, honesty, and justice. They are the pluperfect example of what by their culture norms the perfect father ought to be: tolerant, wise, just, honest, and very effective in coping with all aspects of the world . . . It is our supposition that these men realize the best parts of the ideal male identity" (Hunt 1971:116).

6. "It is the fruitful cooperation of man and woman as a unity that produces culture" (Harris 1978:280).

7. The ambivalence of many mestizo Colombians toward their indigenous heritage is quite clear from the popular usage of the word indio. "La malicia india" translates as something like "Indian shrewdness," but with an overtone of wickedness or malice. People will refer to this as the quality, in themselves or others, that inspired a clever but not altogether legitimate deal. A mother will refer to her children as "indios" when they look particularly scruffy or are ill-behaved. And in terms of Ramos's analysis of Mexican sex roles, "india" is often used to refer to a prostitute or to a man's "outside" woman. That a husband has gone off "con una india" is said with great contempt by his legitimate wife, who may in fact share an identical ethnic heritage with the other woman.

8. An additional factor cited by Kutsche and others is a national sense of inferiority in the face of overwhelming power, a situation true of Mexico in its relation to the United States. Kutsche further suggests that Spanish machismo resulted from the loss of national prestige after the empire fell apart during the eighteenth century.

6. COLOMBIAN SEX AND GENDER ROLES AND THE FAMILY

1. An earlier study that documents the disparity and conflict between male and female experiences within the household and attitudes with regard to domestic life is Reichel-Dolmatoff and Reichel-Dolmatoff (1961). In general, the wealth of detail provided in this study is impressive, and it is one of the few earlier works in which women's roles are given full recognition (Lewis in Mexico might be another). The culture and personality approach that the authors utilize leads to some questionable interpretations on their part, but it seems also to have directed them toward an inclusion of women's reality.

2. Mohan (1981:82) elaborates on why employers discriminate against women, citing the interruption in careers necessitated by child bearing and child care. He believes that these factors provide employers with "objective" reasons for discriminating against women. A further consideration in com-

paring male and female income in Colombia is the fact that most women work part-time, informal sector jobs. The disparity may be even worse than Mohan has estimated, since such jobs are not reflected in aggregate statistics on employment, and in general the more formal jobs are likely to pay better or at least to provide more steady income.

3. The degree to which Payne believes these traits also pertain to Colombian *women* is unclear in his study. In Payne's article, the Colombian is "he," and in general his examples seem to apply more to Colombian men than to Colombian women. As I will point out later, men and women in Colombia have different experiences with regard to enhancing or maintaining status.

4. Fals-Borda (1962) records the household budgets of several families in Saucio. He reports that about 20 percent of earnings were spent on beer; during holidays this increased 100 percent (representing 42.1 percent of the household budget).

5. A World Bank study (Mohan and Hartline 1984) shows that women are in control of savings, in most cases, in Bogotano households. It would be very interesting to consider how males and females are likely to invest resources they control in terms of the patterns of status acquisition outlined here.

7. COLOMBIAN EVANGELICALISM FROM THE HOUSEHOLD OUT

1. Other sources have mentioned the extremely high homicide rate in Colombia. An article in *The Economist* (Anonymous 1985:45) cites a Gallup survey allocating to Colombia the status of "the most violent country in the world" and claiming that ordinary crime in Colombia is more widespread and violent than in most parts of Latin America. In the same article, Colombian police records of violent crimes for 1984 are given: "299 kidnappings (three times as many as in 1981), about 10,000 murders and 25,000 armed robberies." Jimeno and Volk, quoting a Bogotá weekly magazine (*Semana*), give an even higher figure for the homicide rate in recent years: "In the late 1970s and early 1980s, there was an average of 36,000 murders and 83,000 attempted murders each year" (1983:20). The anonymous correspondent in Bogotá responsible for *The Economist* article states that "critics of the government's inability to limit the violence blame a shortage of police, too many corrupt judges and increasing poverty and unemployment."

2. This situation differs markedly from the sexual ideology of Spanish men in Andalusia, described by Brandes (1981). Brandes points out that, despite the fact that women are restrained by society, men feel severely threatened by them. He states that the essential moral dichotomy within this system is that men believe themselves to be inherently more virtuous than women, an opinion that they justify primarily on religious grounds. Women are considered to be sexually voracious, and for men sex is debilitating. Brandes makes no mention of the "Virgin Mother" ideal of femininity within this ideological system, although Kenny (1962:79), who worked in Castile,

states that the "cult of the Virgin Mother" is fervent throughout Spain. Kenny sees the pervasiveness of this cult as indicating that "the picture of the ideal woman lies in the dual ideas of immaculateness and virginity." This apparent contradiction in the reports may be related to the duality of the female role as wife and as mother.

3. This discussion primarily refers to courtship ending in church (or civil) marriage. There is a high rate of consensual union in Colombia, and both courtship and conjugal relations within the consensual union pattern can be expected to differ in many details from the situation being outlined here. I think it could be argued, however, that women's interests (in courtship and marriage) are quite consistent across class lines and in cases of both church marriage and consensual unions.

4. Much has been written about male sexual jealousy of women in Latin culture. Given the pervasiveness of the "double standard" for male and female sexual behavior in Colombia, I do not think that the kind of female sexual jealousy I am describing here can in any way be considered a similar attitude. For one thing, while men try to enforce the double standard (through jealous rages), women are trying to erode it (establish a single standard for themselves and their men).

5. If it is not his wife, it will be his mother, sister, or another woman. Although the preceding argument is phrased in terms of husband-wife interaction, it should be widened to include other female kin, because often a woman who is not successful in converting her own husband may alternatively benefit from the conversion of any male within her kin network.

6. The position of the newly emergent and quite numerous professional class in Colombia, and elsewhere in Latin America, I expect, is quite interesting and has only been touched on briefly here. This particular class status is a relatively tenuous one, since it does not normally entail much in the way of capital accumulation. In fact, the professional is still a sort of high-grade worker, whose livelihood is solely dependent on the sale of labor. Because the rise of this new professional class in Colombia is a relatively recent phenomenon, further research is needed to determine how effective this strategy of upward mobility actually is.

8. CONCLUSION

1. Lewis has interpreted women's possession cults such as the Egyptian *zar* as "thinly disguised protest movements directed against the dominant sex" (1971:130). Insofar as they protect women from the exactions of men and are useful in manipulating husbands and male relatives, he believes they "play a significant part in the sex-war in traditional societies and cultures where women lack more obvious and direct means for forwarding their aims." Lewis sees the same process occurring in Christian contexts and quotes Ronald Knox, who said, "from the Montanist movement onwards, the history of enthusiasm is largely a history of female emancipation, and it is not a reassuring one."

2. A somewhat similar situation seems to hold true for newly Orthodox Jewish women in the United States. Kaufman (1989) reports on the disillusionment of these women with social movements that value self-fulfillment and personal autonomy over family and community. Like Colombian evangelicalism, Jewish Orthodoxy provides for the "positive and sacred use of the symbols and structure associated with the female and the feminine" (p. 309). Kaufman's informants claim that through this system of meaning "they hold men and the community accountable to them."

3. As Vallier put it: "Catholicism, and Roman Catholicism more specifically, emerges as a religious system that blocks, restrains, and otherwise handicaps a country's capacities to generate and institutionalize modernizing forces" (1970:156).

4. I would like to stress that I do not mean to suggest a kind of cognitive determinism after the fashion of Banfield's "amoral familism" (1958) or Foster's "image of limited good" (1965). Although the prosperity ethic is an attitude that may have material consequences, it cannot be said to determine in the last instance the nature of Colombian households. Clearly, the material constraints within which these households variously operate will set the outside limits for their relative prosperity or hardship.

APPENDIX: FIELDWORK WITH COLOMBIAN EVANGELICALS

1. I would strongly agree with Carlos and Sellers (1972) who argue that the importance of kinship ties in Latin America is not being eroded by modernization. They suggest that quite the opposite process is taking place: the modernization process is being molded to existing family and kinship institutions.

"The importance of familial networks of nuclear and extended kin in providing support to the individual's adaptation to socio-economic and cultural environments, regardless of his community of residence or his class standing, has long been recognized. Perhaps the classic statement of this point of view was made by Gillin concerning the Latin American family: 'A man without a family of this sort (i.e., extensive and functioning as a unit) is almost helpless in Mestizo America' (1949:171)" (Carlos and Sellers 1972:95).

When Carlos and Sellers state that "the family is the critical social institution in Latin America," it is evident that they are referring to the wider range of relatives that Nutini (1967) specifies, rather than to the simple nuclear family households. This is an important distinction because, despite the prevalence of nuclear households as the common residential unit, in Colombia the kinship roles within such units are relatively less elaborated compared to those that organize behavior among other kin. This point is important to the argument presented in chapter 5, on the "attenuation of conjugal roles".

In an intriguing link between the "public" and the "private" realms in Latin America, Carlos and Sellers quote a political scientist who has recognized that the family in Latin America is a key institution in understanding much larger social and political forces: "The family is easily one of the most important institutions in Latin America. As the primary group in society it exerts a greater influence on the individual than does any other group . . . the family and its role is of interest to us not only as a key social unit but also as one of the major influences shaping the nation's political and economic development" (Edelmann 1965:85, quoted by Carlos and Sellers, p. 95).

Bibliography

Adamoli, Ambrosio
    1973   *La realidad sagrada en una comunidad pentecostal del César*. Bogotá: Universidad de los Andes, Cuadernos de Antropología.

Anonymous
    1985   "Drugs and Thugs." *The Economist* 295, no. 7393 (May 11): p. 45.
    1991a   "Old Wars, New Constitution." *The Economist* 320, no. 7718 (August 3): 40.
    1991b   "Colombia: Family Planning Rights." *The Lancet* 338, no. 8771 (October 5): 676.
    1992a   "Colombia Moves to End the Privileged Position of the Vatican." *New York Times*, September 9.
    1992b   "Colombia, Vatican Sign Revised Treaty." *Facts on File* 52, no. 2718 (December 31): 997–998.

Arendt, Hannah
    1958   *The Private Realm*. Chicago: University of Chicago Press.

Argyle, Michael, and Benjamin Beit-Hallahmi
    1975   *The Social Psychology of Religion*. London: Routledge & Kegan Paul.

Arrom, Silvia Marina
    1985   *The Women of Mexico City, 1790–1857*. Stanford: Stanford University Press.

Banfield, Edward C.
    1958   *The Moral Basis of a Backward Society*. New York: The Free Press.

Barradas, Efrain
    1977   "El machismo existencialista de René Marqués." *Sin Nombre* 8, no. 3 (October–December): 69–81.

Bateson, Gregory
    1936   *Naven*. Cambridge: Cambridge University Press.

Beals, Ralph
    1946   *Cheran: A Sierra Tarascan Village*. Washington, D.C.: Smithsonian Institution, Institute of Social Anthropology, Publication No. 2.

Bellah, Robert N.

1964   "Religious Evolution." *American Sociological Review* 29:358–374.

Bender, Donald

1967   "A Refinement of the Concept Household: Families, Coresidence, and Domestic Functions." *American Anthropologist* 69:493–504.

Benería, L., and M. Roldán

1987   *The Crossroads of Class and Gender: Industrial Homework, Subcontracting, and Household Dynamics in Mexico City.* Chicago: University of Chicago Press.

Bird, Hector R., and Glorisa Canino

1982   "The Puerto Rican Family: Cultural Factors and Family Intervention Strategies." *Journal of the American Academy of Psychoanalysis* 10, no. 2:257–268.

Blanchard, Kendall

1975   "Changing Sex Roles and Protestantism among the Navajo Women in Ramah." *Journal for the Scientific Study of Religion* 14: 43–50.

Blutstein, Howard, et al.

1983   *Colombia: A Country Study (Area Handbook for Colombia).* Washington, D.C.: American University Foreign Area Studies.

Bohannan, Paul

1963   *Social Anthropology.* New York: Holt, Rinehart and Winston.

Bohman, Kristina

1984   *Women of the Barrio: Class and Gender in a Colombian City.* Stockholm Studies in Social Anthropology, no. 13. Stockholm: Department of Social Anthropology, University of Stockholm.

Bolton, Ralph

1979   "Machismo in Motion: The Ethos of Peruvian Truckers." *Ethos* 7, no. 4:312–342.

Boserup, Ester

1970   *Woman's Role in Economic Development.* New York: St. Martin's Press.

Bourque, Susan C., and Kay B. Warren

1981   *Women of the Andes: Patriarchy and Social Change in Two Peruvian Towns.* Ann Arbor: University of Michigan Press.

Brandes, Stanley

1981   "Like Wounded Stags: Male Sexual Ideology in an Andalusian Town." In *Sexual Meanings*, S. Ortner and H. Whitehead (eds.), pp. 216–239. Cambridge: Cambridge University Press.

Brown, Susan

1975   "Love Unites Them and Hunger Separates Them: Poor Women in the Dominican Republic." In *Toward an Anthropology of Women*, Rayna Reiter (ed.). New York: Monthly Review Press.

Browner, Carole

1983   "Male Pregnancy Symptoms in Urban Colombia." *American Ethnologist* 10, no. 3:494–510.

Browner, Carole, and Ellen Lewin
   1982   "Female Altruism Reconsidered: The Virgin Mary As Economic
           Woman." *American Ethnologist* 9, no. 1:61–75.
Bryce-Laporte, Roy Simón
   1970   "Urban Relocation and Family Adaptation in Puerto Rico: A Case
           Study in Urban Ethnography." In *Peasants in Cities*, William Man-
           gin (ed.), pp. 85–97. Boston: Houghton Mifflin Company.
Bushnell, David
   1954   *The Santander Regime in Gran Colombia*. Westport, Conn.: Green-
           wood Press.
Cano, Guillermo
   1981   "Prólogo." In *Se acaba la familia: investigación sobre la sociedad
           colombiana*, by Gloria Pachón de Galán, pp. 9–13. Bogotá: Editorial
           Pluma.
Cárdenas de Santamaría, María Consuelo
   1982   "El aborto y la mujer." In *La realidad colombiana*, Magdalena León
           (ed.), pp. 138–151. Bogotá: ACEP.
Carlos, Manuel L., and Lois Sellers
   1972   "Family, Kinship Structure, and Modernization in Latin America."
           Latin American Research Review 7, no. 2:95–124.
Clark, Elmer T.
   1937   *The Small Sects in America*. New York: Abingdon Press.
Clavijo, Hernando
   1982   *El machismo en los dos sexos*. Bogotá: Cenpafal.
Cucchiari, Salvatore
   1990   "Between Shame and Sanctification: Patriarchy and Its Transforma-
           tion in Sicilian Pentecostalism." *American Ethnologist* 17, no. 4
           (November): 687–707.
Daly, Mary
   1968   *The Church and the Second Sex*. New York: Harper and Row.
   1973   *Beyond God the Father: Toward a Philosophy of Women's Libera-
           tion*. Boston: Beacon Press.
Damboriena, Prudencio
   1969   *Tongues As of Fire: Pentecostalism in Contemporary Christianity*.
           Cleveland, Ohio: Corpus Books.
de la Cancela, Victor
   1986   "A Critical Analysis of Puerto Rican Machismo: Implications for
           Clinical Practice." *Psychotherapy* 23, no. 2 (Summer): 291–296.
Díaz, M. N.
   1966   *Tonalá: Conservatism, Responsibility, and Authority in a Mexican
           Town*, Berkeley and Los Angeles: University of California Press.
Dix, Robert H.
   1967   *Colombia: The Political Dimensions of Change*. New Haven: Yale
           University Press.
Edelman, Alexander T.
   1965   *Latin American Government and Politics*. Homewood, Ill.: Dorsey.

Ehlers, Tracy Bachrach
    1991   "Debunking Marianismo: Economic Vulnerability and Survival Strategies among Guatemalan Wives." *Ethnology* 30, no. 1 (January): 1–16.
Ehrenreich, Barbara
    1983   *The Hearts of Men: American Dreams and the Flight from Commitment.* Garden City, N.Y.: Anchor Press.
Eisenstein, Zillah (ed.)
    1978   *Capitalist Patriarchy and the Case for Socialist Feminism.* New York: Monthly Review Press.
Epstein, Barbara Leslie
    1981   *The Politics of Domesticity: Women, Evangelism, and Temperance in Nineteenth-Century America.* Middletown, Conn.: Wesleyan University Press.
Fals-Borda, Orlando
    1962   *Peasant Society in the Colombian Andes: A Sociological Study of Saucio.* Gainesville: University of Florida Press.
Finkler, Kaja
    1981   "Dissident Religious Movements in the Service of Women's Power." *Sex Roles* 7, no. 5:481–495.
    1983   "Dissident Sectarian Movements, the Catholic Church, and Social Class in Mexico." *Comparative Studies in Society and History* 25, no. 2:277–305.
Flora, Cornelia Butler
    1973   "The Passive Female and Social Change: A Cross-Cultural Comparison of Women's Magazine Fiction." In *Female and Male in Latin America*, A. Pescatello (ed.), pp. 59–85. Pittsburgh: University of Pittsburgh Press.
    1975   "Pentecostal Women in Colombia: Religious Change and the Status of Working-Class Women." *Journal of Interamerican Studies and World Affairs* 17, no. 4:411–425.
    1976   *Pentecostalism in Colombia: Baptism by Fire and Spirit.* Cranbury, N.J.: Associated University Presses.
Fluharty, Vernon Lee
    1957   *Dance of the Millions: Military Rule and the Social Revolution in Colombia, 1930–1956.* Pittsburgh: University of Pittsburgh Press.
Foster, George
    1965   "Peasant Society and the Image of Limited Good." *American Anthropologist* 67:293–315.
Friedl, Ernestine
    1967   "The Position of Women: Appearance and Reality." *Anthropological Quarterly* 40, no. 3:97–108.
Fromm, E., and M. Maccoby
    1970   *Social Character in a Mexican Village: A Sociopsychoanalytic Study.* Englewood Cliffs, N.J.: Prentice-Hall.

Garrison, Vivian
  1974   "Sectarianism and Psychosocial Adjustment: A Controlled Compari-
          son of Puerto Rican Pentecostals and Catholics." In *Religious Move-
          ments in Contemporary America*, Irving Zaretsky and Mark Leone
          (eds.), pp. 298–329. Princeton: Princeton University Press.
Gill, Lesley
  1990   "Like a Veil to Cover Them: Women and the Pentecostal Movement
          in La Paz." *American Ethnologist* 17, no. 4 (November): 708–721.
Gillin, John
  1949   "Mestizo America." In *Most of the World*, R. Linton (ed.), pp. 171–
          172. New York: Columbia University Press.
Gilmore, David
  1987   *Aggression and Community: Paradoxes of Andalusian Culture.* New
          Haven: Yale University Press.
Gilmore, Margaret M., and David D. Gilmore
  1979   "Machismo: A Psychodynamic Approach (Spain)." *Journal of Psy-
          chological Anthropology* 2&3:281–299.
Gissi, Jorge
  1982   "El machismo en los dos sexos." In *Primer concurso CENPAFAL
          acerca de la situación de la familia latinoamericana*, pp. 63–98.
          Bogotá: CENPAFAL.
Goldwert, Marvin
  1985   "Mexican Machismo: The Flight from Femininity." *Psychoanalytic
          Review* 72, no. 1:161–169.
Goode, Judith Granich
  1970   "Responses of a Traditional Elite to Modernization: Lawyers in Co-
          lombia." *Human Organization* 29:70–80.
Goodman, Felicitas D.
  1972   *Speaking in Tongues: A Cross-Cultural Study of Glossolalia.* Chi-
          cago: University of Chicago Press.
  1973   "Apostolics of Yucatán: A Case Study of a Religious Movement." In
          Religion, Altered States of Consciousness and Social Change, Erika
          Bourguignon (ed.), pp. 178–218. Columbus: Ohio State University
          Press.
Gough, Kathleen
  1959   "The Nayars and the Definition of Marriage." *Journal of the Royal
          Anthropological Institute* 89:23–24.
Gutiérrez de Pineda, Virginia
  1975   *Estructura, función y cambio de la familia en Colombia.* Bogotá:
          Asociación Colombiana de Facultades de Medicina, División de
          Medicina Social y Población.
Hagen, Everett Einar
  1971   "Need Aggression in Colombia." In *Conflict and Violence in Latin
          American Politics*, Francisco Moreno and Barbara Mitrani (eds.),
          pp. 92–95. New York: Thomas Y. Crowell.

Hardesty, Nancy; Lucille S. Dayton; and Donald W. Dayton
  1979   "Women in the Holiness Movement: Feminism in the Evangelical
          Tradition." In Women of Spirit, R. Ruether and E. McLaughlin (eds.),
          pp. 225–254. New York: Simon and Schuster.
Harding, Susan
  1981   "Family Reform Movements: Recent Feminism and Its Opposition."
          Feminist Studies 7, no. 1:57–75.
Harkess, Shirley J.
  1973   "The Pursuit of an Ideal: Migration, Social Class, and Women's
          Roles in Bogotá, Colombia." In Female and Male in Latin America,
          A. Pescatello (ed.), pp. 231–254. Pittsburgh: University of Pittsburgh
          Press.
Harris, Olivia
  1978   "Complementarity and Conflict: An Andean View of Women and
          Men." In Sex and Age As Principles of Social Differentiation, J. S.
          LaFontaine (ed.), pp. 21–40. New York: Academic Press.
Harrison, Michael J.
  1974   "Sources of Recruitment to Catholic Pentecostalism." Journal for the
          Scientific Study of Religion 13:49–74.
Hartlyn, Jonathan
  1988   The Politics of Coalition Rule in Colombia. Cambridge: Cambridge
          University Press.
Hine, Virginia H.
  1974   "The Deprivation and Disorganization Theories of Social Move-
          ments." In Religious Movements in Contemporary America, Irving
          Zaretsky and Mark Leone (eds.), pp. 646–661. Princeton: Princeton
          University Press.
Hollenweger, Walter J.
  1972   The Pentecostals. Minneapolis: Augsburg.
Holt, Pat M.
  1964   Colombia Today—and Tomorrow. New York: Praeger.
Hooks, Bell
  1984   Feminist Theory: From Margin to Center. Boston: South End
          Press.
Hunt, Robert C.
  1971   "Components of Relationship in the Family: A Mexican Village." In
          Kinship and Culture, F. L. K. Hsu (ed.), pp. 106–143. Chicago: Al-
          dine Publishing Co.
Jaquette, Jane
  1973   "Literary Archetypes and Female Role Alternatives: The Woman and
          the Novel in Latin America." In Female and Male in Latin America,
          A. Pescatello (ed.), pp. 3–27. Pittsburgh: University of Pittsburgh
          Press.
Jelín, Elizabeth
  1977   "Migration and Labor Force Participation of Latin American Women:
          The Domestic Servants in the Cities." Signs 3:129–141.

Jimeno, Ramón, and Steven Volk
1983   "Colombia: Whose Country Is This, Anyway?" *NACLA: Report on the Americas* 17, no. 3:2–35.
Jopling, Carol
1974   "Women's Work: A Mexican Case Study of Low Status As a Tactical Advantage." *Ethnology* 13:187–195.
Jorgensen, Dan
1980   "Telefolmin Follow-up." *Newsletter, Cultural Survival Inc.* 4, no. 2 (Spring): 7–8.
Kaplan, Temma
1982   "Female Consciousness and Collective Action: The Case of Barcelona 1910–1918." *Signs* 7, no. 3:545–566.
Kaufman, Debra Renee
1989   "Patriarchal Women: A Case Study of Newly Orthodox Jewish Women." *Symbolic Interaction* 12, no. 2:299–314.
Keesing, Felix
1958   *Cultural Anthropology.* New York: Rinehart and Co.
Kelly, Joan
1984   "The Doubled Vision of Feminist Theory." In *Women, History and Theory: The Essays of Joan Kelly,* pp. 51–64. Chicago: University of Chicago Press.
Kenny, Michael
1962   *A Spanish Tapestry: Town and Country in Castile.* Bloomington: Indiana University Press.
Kutsche, Paul
1984   "On the Lack of Machismo in Costa Rica and New Mexico." Paper presented at the AAA Meetings in Denver, Colorado.
Lalive d'Epinay, Christian
1969   *Haven of the Masses: A Study of the Pentecostal Movement in Chile.* London: Lutterworth.
1976   "Religion, spiritualité et société: De l'étude sociologique du pentecostisme latino-américain." *Dialectica* 30, no. 4:305–313.
Lamphere, Louise
1974   "Strategies, Cooperation, and Conflict among Women in Domestic Groups." In *Women, Culture, and Society,* Michelle Rosaldo and Louise Lamphere (eds.), pp. 97–112. Stanford: Stanford University Press.
LaRuffa, Anthony L.
1971   *San Cipriano: Life in a Puerto Rican Community.* New York: Gordon & Breach.
Latin American and Caribbean Women's Collective
1980   *Slaves of Slaves: The Challenge of Latin American Women.* London: Zed Press.
Levine, Daniel
1981   *Religion and Politics in Latin America: The Catholic Church in Venezuela and Colombia.* Princeton: Princeton University Press.

Levine, S. E.; C. S. Correa; and F. Uribe
  1986   "The Marital Morality of Mexican Women: An Urban Study." *Journal of Anthropological Research* 42, no. 2:183–202.
Lewis, Oscar
  1953   "Husbands and Wives in a Mexican Village: A Study of Role Conflict." In *Readings in Latin American Social Organization and Institutions*, O. Leonard and C. Loomis (eds.), pp. 23–28. East Lansing: Michigan State College Press.
  1961   *The Children of Sanchez*. New York: Random House.
Lewis, I. M.
  1971   *Ecstatic Religion*. Middlesex, England: Penguin Books.
Londoño E., María Ladi
  1982   "Sexualidad y placer de la mujer: Un estudio de caso." In *La realidad colombiana*, Magdalena León (ed.), pp. 152–162. Bogotá: ACEP.
Lynch, Dennis O.
  1981   *Legal Roles in Colombia*. New York: International Center for Law in Development.
Martin, David
  1990   *Tongues of Fire: The Explosion of Protestantism in Latin America*. Oxford: Basil Blackwell.
Martin, Emily
  1987   *The Woman in the Body: A Cultural Analysis of Reproduction*. Boston: Beacon Press.
Mead, Margaret
  1938   *The Mountain Arapesh: Part I: An Importing Culture*. New York: American Museum of Natural History.
Meyer, John
  1986   "Myths of Socialization and of Personality." In *Reconstructing Individualism: Autonomy, Individuality, and the Self in Western Thought*, Thomas C. Heller, Morton Sosna, and David Wellbery (eds.), pp. 208–221. Stanford: Stanford University Press.
Michaelson, Evalyn, and Walter Goldschmidt
  1971   "Female Roles and Male Dominance among Peasants." *Southwestern Journal of Anthropology* 27:330–352.
Mintz, Sidney W.
  1960   *Worker in the Cane: A Puerto Rican Life History*. New Haven: Yale University Press.
Mohan, Rakesh
  1980   "The People of Bogotá: Who They Are, What They Earn, Where They Live." Washington, D.C.: World Bank Staff Working Paper, no. 390.
  1981   "The Determinants of Labour Earnings in Developing Metropoli: Estimates from Bogotá and Cali, Colombia." Washington, D.C.: World Bank Working Paper, no. 498.
Mohan, Rakesh, and Nancy Hartline
  1984   "The Poor of Bogotá: Who They Are, What They Do, and Where They Live." Washington, D.C.: World Bank Staff Working Papers, no. 635.

Molino García, María Teresa
1976   La encomienda en el nuevo reino de Granada durante el siglo XVIII.
        Seville: Escuela de Estudios Hispanoamericanos de Sevilla.
Mollinger, Robert
1984   "Creative Writers on Personality: Octavio Paz and Carlos Fuentes on
        the Mexican National Character." Psychoanalytic Review 71, no. 2:
        305–317.
Molnar, Augusta
1982   "Women and Politics: Case of the Kham Magar of Western Nepal."
        American Ethnologist 9, no. 3:485–502.
Molyneux, Maxine
1986   "Mobilization without Emancipation? Women's Interests, State, and
        Revolution." In Transition and Development, Richard Fagen, Car-
        men Diana Deere, and José Luis Coraggio (eds.), pp. 280–302. New
        York: Monthly Review Press.
Morgan, Martha I., and Mónica María Alzate Buitrago
1992   "Constitution-Making in a Time of Cholera: Women and the 1991
        Colombian Constitution." Yale Journal of Law and Feminism 4,
        no. 2 (Spring): 353–413.
Nash, June
1960   "Protestantism in an Indian Village in the Western Highlands of
        Guatemala." Alpha Kappa Deltan (Winter): 49–53.
Nash, June, and Helen Safa
1976   Sex and Class in Latin America. New York: Praeger.
Nutini, Hugo G.
1967   "A Synoptic Comparison of MesoAmerican Marriage and Family
        Structure." Southwestern Journal of Anthropology 23, no. 4 (Win-
        ter): 383–404.
Oppong, Christine
1974   Marriage among a Matrilineal Elite: A Family Study of Ghanaian
        Senior Civil Servants. Cambridge: Cambridge University Press.
Oquist, Paul
1980   Violence, Conflict and Politics in Colombia. New York: Academic
        Press.
Ordóñez, Francisco
N.d.   Historia del cristianismo evangélico en Colombia, Cali. Colombia:
        La Alianza Cristiana y Misionera.
Pachón de Galán, Gloria
1981   Se acaba la familia: Investigación sobre la sociedad colombiana.
        Bogotá: Editorial Pluma.
Paredes, Américo
1971   "The United States, Mexico, and Machismo." Journal of the Folklore
        Institute 8:17–37.
Payne, James L.
1968   Patterns of Conflict in Colombia. New Haven: Yale University
        Press.

Paz, Octavio
1961   The Labyrinth of Solitude. New York: Grove Press.
Peñalosa, Fernando
1968   "Mexican Family Roles." Journal of Marriage and the Family (November): 680–689.
Perry, Oliverio, y Compañía
1952   Quién es quién en Venezuela, Panamá, Ecuador y Colombia. Bogotá.
Quién es quién
1978   Quién es quién en Colombia, 1978: Biografías contemporáneas. Bogotá: Editorial Temis Librería.
Ramos, Samuel
1962   Profile of Man and Culture in Mexico. Austin: University of Texas Press.
Read, William R.; Victor Monterroso; and Harmon Johnson
1969   Latin American Church Growth. Grand Rapids, Mich.: William B. Erdmans.
Reichel-Dolmatoff, Gerardo, and Alicia Reichel-Dolmatoff
1961   The People of Aritama. Chicago: University of Chicago Press.
Reiter, Rayna R.
1975   "Men and Women in the South of France: Public and Private Domains." In Toward an Anthropology of Women, Rayna Reiter (ed.), pp. 252–283. New York: Monthly Review Press.
Renner, Richard
1971   Education for a New Colombia. Washington: U.S. Department of Health, Education and Welfare.
Riches, David
1986   "The Phenomenon of Violence." In The Anthropology of Violence, D. Riches (ed.). Oxford: Basil Blackwell.
Riegelhaupt, Joyce F.
1967   "Saloio Women: An Analysis of Informal and Formal Political and Economic Roles of Portuguese Peasant Women." Anthropological Quarterly 40, no. 3:109–126.
Rogers, Susan Carol
1975   "Female Forms of Power and the Myth of Male Dominance: A Model of Female/Male Interaction in Peasant Society." American Ethnologist 2, no. 4 (November): 727–756.
1978   "Woman's Place: A Critical Review of Anthropological Theory." Comparative Studies in Society and History 20:123–162.
Rothstein, Frances
1983   "Women and Men in the Family Economy: An Analysis of the Relations between the Sexes in Three Peasant Communities." Anthropological Quarterly 56:1–23.
Rubbo, Anna
1975   "The Spread of Capitalism in Rural Colombia: Effects on Poor

Women." In *Toward an Anthropology of Women*, Rayna Reiter (ed.), pp. 333–357. New York: Monthly Review Press.

Ruether, Rosemary
1979   "Introduction: Women's Leadership in the Jewish and Christian Traditions: Continuity and Change." In *Women of Spirit*, R. Ruether and E. McLaughlin (eds.), pp. 15–28. New York: Simon and Schuster.

Ruisque-Alcaino, Juan, and Ray Bromley
1982   "Autobiography of an Urban 'Marginal': Miguel Durán." In *Third World Lives of Struggle*, Hazel Johnson and Henry Bernstein (eds.), pp. 111–125. London: Heinemann.

Ryan, Mary P.
1980   "A Women's Awakening: Evangelical Religion and the Families of Utica, New York, 1800–1840." In *Women in American Religion*, J. James (ed.), pp. 89–110. University of Pennsylvania Press.

Sabogal, Hugo
1983   "Colombia, tierra fértil para el protestantismo." *Lecturas Dominicales* (November 6): 3.

Salesman, P. Eliecer
1982   *Cuidado: Llegaron los protestantes*. Bogotá: Librería Salesiana.

Samarian, William J.
1972   *Tongues of Men and Angels: The Religious Language of Pentecostalism*. New York: Macmillan.

Sánchez, Gonzalo
1985   "*La Violencia* in Colombia: New Research, New Questions." *Hispanic American Historical Review* 65, no. 4 (November): 789–807.

Schneider, D. M., and R. T. Smith
1973   *Class Differences and Sex Roles in American Kinship and Family Structure*. Englewood Cliffs, N.J.: Prentice-Hall.

Scott, James C.
1976   *The Moral Economy of the Peasant: Rebellion and Subsistence in Southeast Asia*. New Haven: Yale University Press.
1985   *Weapons of the Weak: Everyday Forms of Peasant Resistance*. New Haven: Yale University Press.

Secretariado Nacional de Pastoral Social
1981   *Aproximación a la realidad colombiana*. Bogotá.

SEPAL (Servicio Evangelizador para América Latina)
1981   "El avance de la iglesia evangélica en Colombia." Bogotá: SEPAL.

Sexton, James
1978   "Protestantism and Modernization in Two Guatemalan Towns." *American Ethnologist* 5, no. 2:280–302.

Shanin, Teodor
1971   "A Russian Peasant Household at the Turn of the Century." In *Peasants and Peasant Societies*, T. Shanin, (ed.), pp. 30–36. Baltimore: Penguin.

Silverblatt, Irene
    1987   Moon, Sun, and Witches. Princeton: Princeton University Press.
Stack, Carol
    1974   All Our Kin: Strategies for Survival in a Black Community. New
            York: Harper and Row.
Steinmann, Anne, and David J. Fox
    1969   "Specific Areas of Agreement and Conflict in Women's Self-Percep-
            tion and Their Perception of Men's Ideal Woman in Two South
            American Urban Communities and an Urban Community in the
            United States." Journal of Marriage and the Family 31, no. 2 (May):
            281–289.
Stevens, Evelyn
    1973   "Marianismo: The Other Face of Machismo in Latin America." In
            Female and Male in Latin America, A. Pescatello (ed.), pp. 89–101.
            Pittsburgh: University of Pittsburgh Press.
Stoll, David
    1990   Is Latin America Turning Protestant? The Politics of Evangelical
            Growth. Berkeley and Los Angeles: University of California Press.
Stycos, J.
    1955   Family and Fertility in Puerto Rico. New York: Columbia University
            Press.
Sywulka, Steve, and John Maust
    1991   "Evangelicals Win in Latin Elections." Christianity Today 35, no. 2
            (February 11): 61–62.
Thornton, W. Philip
    1984   "Resocialization: Roman Catholics Becoming Protestants in Colom-
            bia, South America." Anthropological Quarterly 57:1.
Ulrich, Laurel Thatcher
    1980   "Vertuous Women Found: New England Ministerial Literature,
            1668–1735." In Women in American Religion, J. James (ed.),
            pp. 67–87. University of Pennsylvania Press.
Urdang, Stephanie
    1984   "Women in National Liberation Movements." In African Women
            South of the Sahara, M. Hay and S. Stichter (eds.), pp. 156–169.
            London: Longman.
Vallier, Ivan
    1970   Catholicism, Social Control and Modernization in Latin America.
            Englewood Cliffs, N.J.: Prentice-Hall.
Weber, Max
    1905   The Protestant Ethic and the Spirit of Capitalism. New York: Charles
            Scribner's Sons.
Weinert, Richard S.
    1971   "Violence in Pre-Modern Societies: Rural Colombia." In Conflict
            and Violence in Latin American Politics, Francisco Moreno and
            Barbara Mitrani (eds.), pp. 310–325. New York: Thomas Y. Crowell
            Company.

Whitten, Norman E., Jr., and Dorothea S. Whitten
    1972   "Social Strategies and Social Relationships." *Annual Review of Anthropology* 1:247–270.
Whitten, Norman E., Jr., and Dorothea S. Whitten
    1972   "Social Strategies and Social Relationships." *Annual Review of Anthropology* 1:247–270.
Wiest, Raymond
    1983   "Male Migration, Machismo, and Conjugal Roles: Implications for Fertility Control in a Mexican Municipio." *Journal of Comparative Family Studies* 14, no. 2 (Summer): 167–181.
Willems, Emilio
    1967   *Followers of the New Faith: Cultural Change and the Rise of Protestantism in Brazil and Chile.* Nashville, Tenn.: Vanderbilt University Press.
Williamson, Robert C.
    1971   "Toward a Theory of Politcal Violence: The Case of Rural Colombia." In *Conflict and Violence in Latin American Politics,* Francisco Moreno and Barbara Mitrani (eds.), pp. 325–338. New York: Thomas Y. Crowell Company.
Wolf, Eric
    1959   *Sons of the Shaking Earth.* Chicago: University of Chicago Press.
Yanagisako, Sylvia
    1979   "Family and Household: The Analysis of Domestic Groups." *Annual Review of Anthropology* 8:161–205.
    1984   "Explicating Residence: A Cultural Analysis of Changing Households among Japanese-Americans." In *Households: Comparative Studies of the Domestic Group,* R. McC. Netting, R. Wilk, and E. Arnould (eds.), pp. 330–352. Berkeley and Los Angeles: University of California Press.
Youssef, Nadia
    1973   "Cultural Ideals, Feminine Behavior and Kinship Control." *Comparative Studies in Society and History* 15, no. 3:326–347.
Zamudio, Lucero
    1982   *La estructura familiar en los sectores populares urbanos.* Bogotá: Cenpafal.

Index

Ceremony   or   Politics

Brazil's   Modern   City

Form   over   function

Brazil's   Modern   City ——— ———
——— Bwiti ————————————

                              Reversal =
                              function
                              over
Bwiti = Function

Braizl = Form   Form

        How   Form(Brazil) Functions (Bwiti

— N. Geographic   Doc

)